C000196987

ASPECTS OF BARNSLEY

Aspects of BARNSLEY

DISCOVERING LOCAL HISTORY

Edited by
Brian Elliott

Wharncliffe Books

First Published in 1993, reprinted 2003 by
Wharncliffe Books
an imprint of
Pen and Sword Books Limited,
47 Church Street, Barnsley,
South Yorkshire. S70 2AS

Copyright © Wharncliffe Books 1993, 2003

For up-to-date information on other titles produced under the
Wharncliffe imprint, please telephone or write to:

> **Wharncliffe Books**
> **FREEPOST**
> **47 Church Street**
> **Barnsley**
> **South Yorkshire S70 2BR**
> **Telephone (24 hours): 01226 - 734555**

ISBN: 1-871647-19-3

All rights reserved. No part of this publication may be
reproduced, stored in a retrieval system, or transmitted, in
any form or by any means, electronic, mechanical,
photocopying, recording or otherwise, without the prior
permission in writing of the publishers.

This book is sold subject to the condition that it shall not,
by way of trade or otherwise, be lent, resold, hired out or
otherwise circulated without the publisher's prior consent in
any form of binding or cover other than that in which it is
published and without a similar condition including this
condition being imposed on the subsequent purchaser.

A CIP catalogue record of this book is available from the
British Library

Cover illustration: *Market Hill, c1890, by Warner Gothard.* Brian Elliott Collection

Printed in the United Kingdom by
CPI UK

CONTENTS

INTRODUCTION

by Brian Elliott

Aspects is the first published collection of independently-penned studies and features relating to the town and surrounding district of Barnsley. It may be the precursor of a series of books giving local writers an opportunity to present their work in the public domain. Wharncliffe Publishing Limited are to be congratulated on their far sighted sponsorship at a time when the enthusiasm for local and family history continues to grow. Archives, record offices and local studies libraries are busy as never before. The Barnsley Local History Fair has become a popular annual event attracting people of all ages. The National Curriculum has rightly assigned local studies as an integral part of every schoolchild's education. Local history as a 'subject' can be a worthwhile leisure pursuit but is now generally acknowledged to be worthy of academic research. The interests of all of us can only combine to increase our enjoyment and understanding of the history of local communities.

This very diverse compendium not only reflects a varied history but also some of the special interests, research methods and personal backgrounds of its authors (for biographical details of contributors see pages 248-253). Annie Storey's evocative account of her childhood memories appears as a consequence of sheer enthusiasm and the desire to share reminiscence with a new and very contrasting generation. Ian Harley focuses on a modern organisation which could easily have been overlooked; but the social and vocational roles of young people deserve our continuing recognition. The local historian as 'house-detective' can be seen with reference to one of the less well-known buildings of Worsbrough while a light-hearted look at one of Barnsley's most famous characters is also explored. In contrast, Ray Hearne's sensitive appraisal of Ebenezer Elliott who lived in Great Houghton towards the end of his life will help more of us to appreciate an underrated poet and social reformer. If the result is entirely parochial the book will have failed, for introspection will only result in a warped view of our town and neighbourhood. Families and communities each have their special characteristics but were, of necessity, interrelated, as were towns and regions; and all set within (at least) a national context. John Goodchild's study of local turnpikes, using surviving documents, rightly places Barnsley in a West Riding and national context. Barnsley has always played a part in the economy of an area which became one of the fastest growing industrial regions of the country, and the world. Harold Taylor's detailed survey of bleachworks is a fine example of the local historian combining on the ground observation with maps, photographs and research. The story of our local linen industry is more understandable due to his efforts. Tanya Schmoller's investigation of paper mills provides us with an 'outsiders' view of an industry on our own doorstep which has received relatively little acknowledgement. Barnsley's industrial pioneers also deserve attention and none can have been more innovative than Dan Rylands, described by Denis Ashurst as the 'Tragic Genius of the Barnsley Glass Industry'. The national press in the nineteenth century reported some of the tremors of social and economic change occurring in the coal mining industry. One of the most bitter and violent disputes, involving the Newton Chambers Company and its employees at Tankersley and Thorncliffe collieries attracted regional and national coverage. Melvyn Jones' sources include diaries, newspapers and census records in his fascinating account of 'The Thorncliffe Riots'.

'Rural Barnsley' has not been ignored in this edition: Sam Sykes' article throws light on the evolution of the village and countryside around Dodworth in a most perceptive case-study; Phyllis Crossland combines her local knowledge with new research when exploring the ancient township of Hunshelf whilst the Bosvilles of Gunthwaite is the subject of Vera Nicholson's interesting contribution.

I would like to thank Toby Buchan and John Bayne for the original idea of *Aspects* and Timothy Hewitt, Director of Wharncliffe Publishing, for his confidence in the project. In practical terms *Aspects* would have been impossible but for the efforts of Roni Wilkinson and Caroline Cox. Although relevant acknowledgements are listed after each contribution special thanks are due to Ruth Vyse and Maurice Hepworth at Barnsley Archives and Local Studies Library. Thanks are obviously due to all the contributors for helping to add to our knowledge and understanding of the Barnsley area. Finally, on a personal note, thanks to my wife and family for their support during a very difficult year.

Anyone interested in making a contribution to *Aspects 2* (subject to commercial viability) should, in the first instance, contact Brian Elliott c/o **Wharncliffe Publishing Ltd, 47 Church Street, Barnsley, S70 2AS,** enclosing a brief description of the proposed work. If suitable, guidelines will then be issued.

CRUCK BARN AT FIELDHEAD
PRIOR TO RENOVATION (Sam Sykes)

1. BARNSLEY BOYS CLUB, 1933-93

by Ian Harley

APRIL 10TH 1933 WAS A RED LETTER DAY for Barnsley. The Mayor, former miners president Herbert Smith, the Chief Constable and the Bishop of Wakefield were just some of the dignitaries waiting outside the Arcadian Hall to greet Lord Harewood as he inspected a parade of ex-servicemen wearing their medals.

After the serving of tea, the gathering heard Lord Harewood describe youth as a town's greatest asset pointing out that "boy was the father of man" and therefore, the proper upbringing of a boy, would secure the man of the future who would be of use to the community. In other words, it would create good citizenship. A short while later, the assembly walked from the Arcadian to nearby Nelson Street, firmly located in

Below: The former Old Eagle Inn in Nelson Street became the first real home of the Boys Club ...thanks to the Barnsley Brewery Co. Ltd. This photograph shows the Peashills premises as they were when officially opened by Lord Harewood in April 1933.

what was colloquially known as 'Peashills', where he unlocked the door of the Barnsley Boys' Club.

In its edition of Saturday April 15, the *Chronicle* devoted three photographs and several columns to the visit, leading its coverage with the following:

> *"To raise the standard of fitness in life intellectually, physically and morally, to stimulate interest for occupational pursuits, to promote clean, healthy recreation and to provide congenial facilities and to create good citizenship. . . . These are the laudable objects behind a Boys' Club which has been established through the instrumentality of the Barnsley League of Social Service and was opened on Monday.*
>
> *"The venture was most auspiciously launched inasmuch as the Earl of Harewood paid a visit to Barnsley to perform the opening ceremony and his distinguished presence in the town coincided with a day of bright sunshine and almost mid-summer warmth."*

The need for a boys club, Coun. R.J. Soper, told those present at the meeting had quickly been established by the Council for Social Service the previous October. The sub-commitee responsible for boys' work had found that — of more than 100 unemployed boys in the town —

Below: Four of the club's very earliest members enjoy a drink, a biscuit and the commpany of a cat. Approaching 15,000 have done similarly since this photograph was taken in the 'canteen' in 1933.

Above: There were no shortage of volunteers to spend a few days at Cayton Bay when the Barnsley Rotary Club invited members to a "Boys Club Camp" in 1933.

only nine were attached to any organisation which provided them with any occupational interest during their leisure hours.

Happily, they decided to do something about it and January 1933 saw twelve boys meet in a single room in St. John's Church School Room in Baker Street.

As word about the club got round, the need to cater for more boys became apparent and the committee of the club secured the lease of the Old Eagle Inn in Nelson Street from Barnsley Brewery Co. Ltd who 'kindly' made themselves responsible for considerable alterations and decoration.

Lord Harewood's official opening of the premises, accompanied by the reading of a message from the Duke of Gloucester, wasn't the only red letter day the fledgling club enjoyed that year. The Prince of Wales (later the Duke of Windsor) included a visit to the club as part of a tour of South Yorkshire. He showed a lot of genuine interest in the club and left after expressing the hope that the work of the club would be allowed to expand and that the necessary funds would be forthcoming, both for the annual upkeep of the premises and for the building of further accommodation on a site adjacent to the club.

Happily, a gymnasium was added to the club in 1934, thanks to the Miners Welfare Committee and the Mayor of Barnsley, Alderman B.R. Carter. That meant that Barnsley's boys in the depression years of the '30s were able to get out of the house into different surroundings and meet with other kids in the same position. Activities at the club included physical training, boxing, athletics, handicrafts, library, lectures, debates, football, cricket, table tennis, art, dramatics, billiards, camping and the running of a savings bank, canteen and the club's own newsletter — *The Harlequin*.

By then, the club was catering to around forty junior boys, aged thirteen-fourteen, and sixty senior boys, aged fourteen-eighteen, more than a quarter of which had not had regular employment since leaving school. They were required to pay a weekly subscription of 2d or 3d of which 1d was allotted to the gymnasium kit fund which provided every physically-fit member with a pair of gym shoes, a vest and a pair of shorts a year.

Most activities were free. For others — such as billiards — there was a small charge. Hot baths were available on a Saturday evening at a penny a time.

The club was still quite young when it had to face the war years. Eric Chamberlain had just been appointed full-time leader made possible by grants from the Pilgrim Trust through the Yorkshire Association and National Association of Boys' Clubs. He soon found his voluntary

Above and Below: Members could both exercise their minds with board games such as draughts and chess in the 'library', or (below) opt for practical pursuits. Shortage of space had meant that the cellar of the Nelson Street premises had been pressed into use as a workshop during the club's early years. A glance at the ceiling reveals how the premises had deteriorated by the time this photograph was taken in 1947. The fact that these members' minds were still focused on the recently-ended war can be seen from the fact these members appear to be working on a tank, a battleship, a rifle and an aeroplane.

Above: The provision of a gymnasium — thanks to the Miners Welfare Committee and the Mayor of Barnsley, Alderman B R Carter — resulted in boxing becoming a popular attraction at the club.

staff dissipating. Thinking it would be in the club's best interest, a decision was made to merge with the boys section of Y.M.C.A. but, after a short while, the partnership was amicably broken.

Like the Windmill, Barnsley Boys' Club can boast that it 'never closed' during the war. The Boys Club Company of the Army Cadet Force was the first to be formed in Barnsley and other members served individually in the Sea Cadets, Air Training Corps and Messenger Service. The club also had its own ARP wardens and fire watchers.

As for old boys, more than 100 served in the armed forces; some were commissioned, others reached warrant and non-commissioned rank and seven gave their lives.

The club itself survived the war years largely due to the devoted leadership of Mr Don 'Pop' Pierrepont — the premises survived mainly because of the war. They had been scheduled for demolition before the outbreak of hostilities but the conflict meant staff facing the added burden of keeping the building together.

In January 1947, the sum of £2,500 was raised locally under the aegis of the Brunswick Appeal. The old Westgate Primitive Methodist Chapel, up for auction at the time, seemed a suitable replacement and the boys were soon staging jumble sales, doing odd jobs for money and collecting pop bottles etc.

Part of the old Nelson Street premises fell down at the end of November in 1947 but, by then, the club was ready to move and to face a £10,000 bill for the cost of purchasing, adapting and equipping the new premises. The Club was struggling for the last £2-3,000 but famous sportsman, Norman Yardley, came to the rescue with a special appeal, aimed largely at the business sector. Adaptation and decoration of the new premises took a long time to complete and it wasn't until November 8th 1950 that they were officially opened by the Rt. Hon. Viscount Hyndley.

The 1950s passed quietly for the club although the Duke of Gloucester was another important visitor on November 24th 1954. As always 'Pop' Pierrepont was there to greet him. His thirty-year involvement with the club lasted right up to his death in the early 1960s when Roy Bellamy was the full-time leader. The year 1967 saw the appointment of Eddie

Below: Gymnastics was as easy as standing on your head for some club members.

Above and Below: The club was an early convert to recycling and, when this waste paper salvage team was photographed in 1951, was handling almost anything that could be resold to make money. Left to right: Tony Hawley, Harry Mullins, Derek Ansell, Frank Herbert, Walter Frost, Fred Oxley, Jack Keen and Jack Winder. The proceeds from recycling were required for further improvements to the former Westgate Primitive Methodist Chapel premises (below) which had been officially opened as the club's new premises by Viscount Hindley the previous November.

Above: The front of the Westgate premises with more recent members ready and willing to carry out further improvement work. They are (left to right): Philip Parr, Roy Whittaker, Paul Greenhoff, Peter Matysiak, Gary Ramskill and Trevor Jessop

North as full-time leader. With the change came a much higher profile with the club undertaking a wide range of fund-raising tasks, often for other causes, and the introduction of girls (initially allowed in on just two nights a week).

Two years later saw Peter Boyle take over as club leader helping the club through a modernisation programme before handing over to Doug Carr. An ex-paratrooper, Brian Chapman, took over in 1974 and soon announced that he was to run from Barnsley in Gloucestershire to Barnsley to raise money for the club. Keith Steele, involved with the club since the age of eleven and formerly a voluntary helper, took up the reins in 1978. Among other things, he was responsible for an increase of outdoor activities such as walking, climbing, abseiling, canoeing, orienteering and camping. The club received help from the entertainer, Frankie Vaughan, when it celebrated its golden anniversary in 1983. A keen supporter of boys' clubs, he made himself a 'tower of

Above: Frankie Vaughan, an enthusiastic worker for Boys Clubs nationally, was a popular visitor to the club during its golden anniversary year of 1983.

strength' by selling kisses in aid of the club after a short show at the Civic Hall.

That money was desperately needed for − just ten days before the club was to officially celebrate its 50th birthday with a visit from the president of the National Association of Boy's Clubs, the Duke of Gloucester − the club announced that mounting debts had forced it to start proceedings winding up its affairs. Happily, Barnsley Council, stepped in with a £10,000 grant which put the club back on a secure financial footing.

The fact that Barnsley Boys Club has survived so many years, both before and since 1983, is largely to due to the hard work of its executive committee, its 'old boys' and its ladies' auxiliary committee.

Each contained some of the town's most prominent people. For example, A.R. Keeping was committee chairman in 1964, secretary was S. Jebson, treasurer G. Harrison and members were: Coun. W.R. Gundry, H. Chappell, V. Dunk, W. Gordon Lees, J. Levi, N.W.B. Moody, I.S. Porter and F. Tock. Officials of the ladies auxiliary at the same time were Mrs J.G.E. Rideal, Mrs O. Porter, Mrs E. Raley and Mrs E. Blackburn.

They were well aware the club was then expecting to be made homeless once again for the planned development of Barnsley's Civic

Above: Participation in sport has been an important part of club life in recent years and former Oakwell favourite Barry Murphy found himself busy when asked to officiate at this 1979 presentation evening.

Centre. While John Rideal House, Churchfield Police Station, the Central Library and Barnsley Magistrates Court have been built since then, the Westgate premises have not only survived — they've gained a grade II listing as a building of architectural or historical significance.

Now, however, it seems the clock has turned a full circle and, like the Nelson Street premises during the 1940s, the Westgate premises are in need of urgent repair.

February 1993 therefore saw the club launch a £40,000 appeal to purchase a new roof.

Chairman, Ian Hunter, said he hoped 40 per cent of the cost would be raised through an appeal to former members to make a minimum donation of £1. The appeal was accompanied by an invitation to all former members — whatever their age — to visit the club, make their donation and see their name is entered in a 'Roof Restoration Register'.

"The club was founded to promote the mental, physical and spiritual well-being of boys, especially those in poor circumstances, by providing facilites for their education and recreation," he said, *"We feel that is a role we are still fulfilling and, hopefully, around 15,000 former members will agree with us."*

Below: Girl members of the Boys Club's Disco Dance team also proved they had winning ways in the 1980s. This team was captured in action at the Mecca Ballroom in 1982.

2. THE BLEACHWORKS OF THE BARNSLEY AREA IN THE NINETEENTH CENTURY AND THEIR INDUSTRIAL ARCHAEOLOGY

by Harold Taylor

A CLOSE LOOK AT BARNSLEY'S COAT OF ARMS reveals two shuttles. They represent a textile industry which once had pride of place in the town's industrial life. It was linen manufacture which was primarily responsible for the town's rapid growth of population in the first half of the nineteenth century, before 'King Coal' took over that role. The removal of the stubborn, brown colouring matter from the linen fibres by bleaching was an essential part of the manufacturing process.

Barnsley's linen industry was in decline long before the end of the nineteenth century, and little now remains on the ground to commemorate an activity which grew from early beginnings in the 1740s and expanded rapidly after the end of the Napoleonic Wars. Although a relatively modern mill building (of the 1950s) still stands at Redbrook, all the nineteenth century examples − several of them clustered in the Townend area, as shown on Map 1, − have been demolished, and the handloom weavers' cottages swept away, leaving the old linen warehouse in St Mary's Place and possibly another in Eastgate as the sole surviving representatives of the former industry. On the outskirts of the town and beyond, however, evidence of the former bleachworks can still be found. At Cudworth there are substantial remains. Elsewhere, as at Greenfoot and Swithen, reservoirs which supplied the essential water offer good clues to past activities. At Hoyle Mill, however, only the merest traces of a former bleachworks can perhaps be discerned with the aid of old Ordnance Survey plans, and the site at Stairfoot is no more than hinted at by the street name 'Bleachcroft Way'. Some locations have been completely transformed. The site of a bleachworks at Monk Bretton now lies beneath the landscaped colliery waste heap, and at Old Mill the redevelopment of the site, first for a paper mill, and subsequently for a supermarket, has removed all traces. Enough remains in the district, however, to demonstrate both the location pattern and the physical sites which were favoured by the founders of the bleachworks.

The aim of this study is not only to record and explain the locations and the growth of former bleachworks in the Barnsley area, but to offer a guide for the exploration of some, at least, of the sites.

In order to appreciate the choice of sites made by the master bleachers, it is necessary to give some account of the techniques used in the bleaching process.

The production of white cloth using linen fibres presented special problems. Removal of the brown colouring matter taxed the ingenuity of those concerned over many years, and it seems that new methods were sometimes discovered by trial and error rather than through an understanding of the chemistry involved — 'more a matter of alchemy than chemistry!'[1]

Basically bleaching involved two processes, steeping the yarn or woven cloth in prepared solutions (Bucking) and spreading it out on grass after washing (Crofting). Before the development of larger scale operations here in the second half of the eighteenth century, cottage weavers had spread out the yarn on grassland areas around their homes and on hedgerows, needing to leave it out for months on end. Clearly there was a strong incentive to reduce the length of time required for crofting by improving the technique of bucking. Bucking had been effected through the use of a variety of materials, some of them natural products such as sour milk and pigeon's dung. In the 1740s the Wilson brothers, William and John, consequently deemed it prudent to bring over experienced men in the trade — Isaac and William Hyde — from Pendle on the other side of the Pennines when they established their bleaching business. One of them was to organise the warehouse in the town and the other to supervise the bleaching ground below Honeywell.

Over the years bleachers in various parts of the country tried new materials. In Barnsley the use of potash and vitriol had been introduced by the 1780s. In the early years of the nineteenth century the Dearman firm, which had a bleach ground at Pinder Oaks, was purchasing 'ashes, or alkaline salts, from London and from Manchester.'[2] Records show that Joseph Beckett, whose bleaching ground was at Greenfoot, was using 40 pounds of potash to 240 pounds of yarn in 1815.[3] Much later, experimentation was still going on. Correspondence between Henry Jackson, owner of the 'Midland Bleachworks' at Cudworth, and a London chemist in 1861 seems to imply that bleaching powder was being made up at the works to their own recipe. This comprised roughly equal proportions of common salt, manganese and sulphuric acid. It is clear too from the correspondence that success depended almost as much on the skill and judgement of the man in charge as on the materials he used. Significantly, the foreman, McGee, was a native of Ulster, a notable linen producing area. He had worked for Jackson at his employer's previous bleachworks at Beevor (Oakwell). It is

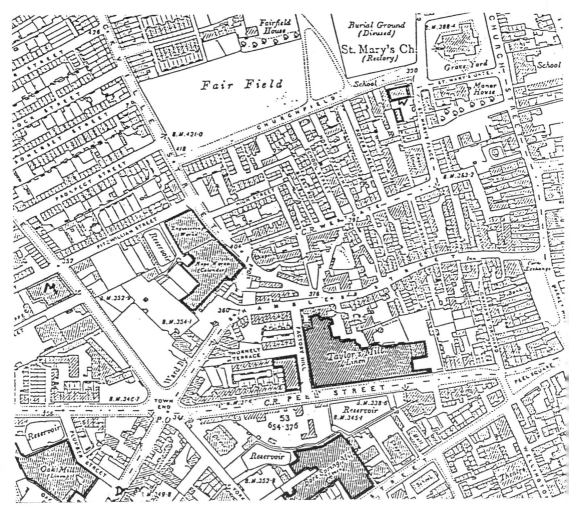

Above: Map 1 O.S. 1904
M = McLintock's Utilitas Works D = Dyeworks W = Warehouse.

interesting that the 'Agreement' signed by McGee and his employer in 1853 required the former not only to 'conduct himself as an honest, true and faithful servant' but to 'keep his master's secrets'. Evidently industrial espionage has a long history![4]

Notwithstanding progress in the chemistry of bleaching, yarn or cloth had to be left out on the bleachcroft for long periods. The large areas shown as 'bleach greens' on the six inch Ordnance Survey maps of around 1850, are impressive. One of the several methods of bleaching described in an encyclopaedia of 1862 required the materials to be crofted for as many as nine times, each for a period of about four days, depending on the weather.[5] While the cloth was out of doors additional labour costs were involved as it had to be watered periodically to remove dust deposits. There was also the danger of theft. It seems that some of the bleachcrofts in Scotland were protected by 'spring guns' and mantraps, and that innocent persons occasionally fell foul of these devices.

Whatever the chemical formula used, however, copious supplies of suitably unpolluted water were absolutely essential for the repeated steeping and washing processes, and this consideration must have played a big part in choice of location. In the Barnsley area good supplies were to be found along the valley of the Dearne and some of its small tributaries, where springs issued from the valley slopes. Here water accumulating in the sandstone aquifers flowed out over underlying shales or clays. By the nineteenth century the Dearne itself had become too polluted to be suitable, and the growth of coal mining, with its polluted drainage, may have rendered other streams unsuitable in course of time. Springs offered adequate supplies if storage reservoirs were constructed, and these became characteristic features of the sites.

There was another locating factor. Out-of-town sites were less likely to be polluted by urban smoke and were consequently kinder to the work of crofting.

Access to coal was important too, both as fuel for heating chemical solutions and, in due course, for steam-raising. However, coal was to

Below: Linen Mill of Thomas Taylor & Sons, Peel Street, c.1900.

CALENDERING MACHINE.

Above: From *Encyclopaedia of Useful Arts* 1862.

be found almost anywhere in this part of the Dearne valley. The advent of canal transport brought additional advantages for some of the old-established sites — notably Greenfoot, Beevor and Old Mill — for the transport of this and other materials. The availability of relatively cheap coal was an advantage too for the 'calendering' processes, carried out either at a bleachworks or by a specialist firm. Steam power was in use by the 1820s in Barnsley to power the calendering machines, which pressed out the creases from the linen after bleaching. The Barnsley weaver-poet, Robert McLintock, was so impressed by the steam-powered machinery in the Union Calender Works at Townend that he felt compelled to set out his thoughts in verse. His poem of 1839 includes the following lines:

> *"Behold its power, from whence did it derive it;*
> *Or how did feeble man at first contrive it?"...*
> *"The active liquid foaming and expanding,*
> *Forcing the wheels, impelling and commanding."* ...
> *"When this strong engine doth its work perform,*
> *Then it resembles a great thunder storm.."*[6]

The considerable premises of the Union Calendering Company are described in the 1848 Rate Valuation List.[7] They comprised '*calender house and machinery, two engines, two engine boiler-houses, turners' shops, carpenters' shops, smithy, dwelling house, warehouse, stable, shed and two reservoirs.'* All this was located on the site of the present Townend Park.

Calendering involved the passing of cloth between pairs of large rollers, as illustrated in the engraving, which dates from mid-nineteenth century. Immediately before this, the linen was passed over the surface of a water cistern, moisture being imparted to the fabric by a circular brush which revolved above the cloth and in contact with it. Pressure between the rollers could be adjusted in order to vary the type of finish. Subsequently starch was applied as the cloth was passed between brass rollers, and drying was achieved by using steam-heated copper rollers. Afterwards the surface of the fabric was beaten in order to impart the desired 'finish'. This latter process, known as 'bettling', also required steam-heating. Clearly, coal and water played a great part in these 'finishing' processes.

Baines' Directory of 1822 lists three calendering firms in the town, all in the Townend area, and six bleaching firms, located a little way outside the town. Some of the bleachworks or bleach grounds were operated by 'Linen Manufacturers', as the trade directories called them, who had warehouses in the town from which they put out work to handloom weavers, many of whom lived in cottages rented from the manufacturer.

Among these industrialists who were active in the latter part of the eighteenth and first half of the nineteenth century, were a number of Quakers. Membership of the Society of Friends played an important part in the promotion of new ventures in the field of linen manufacture centred on Barnsley. Members enjoyed the benefits of mutual trust in their business dealings with each other. Furthermore, their thrift and their determination to use their time effectively gave additional drive to their commercial activities. The minutes of one of the Quarterly Meetings of the local Quakers in 1817 exhorted members to enquire of themselves:

> *"Are they just in their dealings and punctual in fulfilling their engagements, and are they annually advised carefully to inspect the state of their affairs? Are they careful to avoid all vain sports and places of diversion, gaming, all unnecessary frequenting of taverns and other public houses, excess in drinking and other intemperance?"*[8]

Some of the linen manufacturers had diverse commercial interests, such as ownership of coal mines. One of them, Joseph Beckett, was a banker for a time. It was a wise precaution on their part not to depend too heavily on the linen trade, for it was very much subject to depression

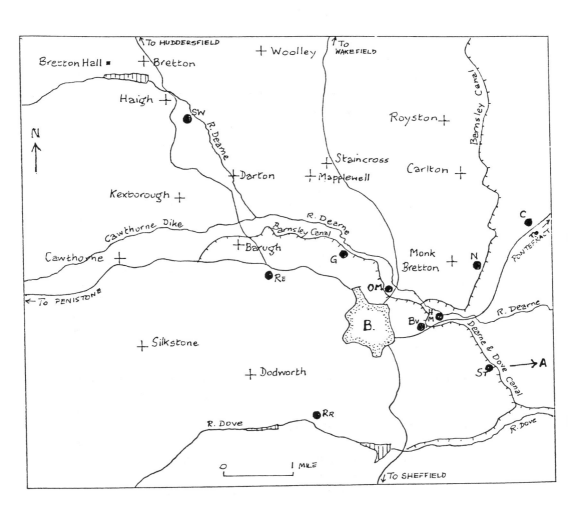

Above: Map 2 Bleachworks in the Barnsley area in mid-19th century.

Key.
B: The built-up area of Barnsley, based on the O.S. 1″ map originally published 1841.
BLEACHWORKS: SW – Swithen; RE – Redbrook; G – Greenfoot; OM – Old Mill
BV – Beevor; HM – Hoyle Mill; N – Newbridge
C – Cudworth; ST – Stairfoot; RR – Rob Royd
A – Ardsley Bleach Croft

from time to time, and to labour disputes throughout its history here.

Paying due regard to the importance of water supply, clean air and accessibility, the exact location of the bleach grounds reflected what may be termed chance factors too. William Wilson was able to set up operations in the middle of the eighteenth century on land owned by his father. Later in the century Joseph Beckett could select a site from amongst the plots of land which he owned, and Samuel Coward, it appears, found a good opportunity to establish his bleachworks around 1818 on a site vacated by a chemical manufacturer.

Barnsley's linen industry and the bleaching activities with it declined seriously in the latter part of the nineteenth century, suffering from competition by Scottish and Irish rivals, injured by a succession of labour disputes in the 1860s and 1870s, and losing its potential male workforce to the expanding coal mining industry. By the end of the century there were still five bleaching grounds at work, at Greenfoot, Old Mill, Redbrook, Cudworth and Swithen, but by 1906 there were only two.[9] Between 1897 and 1913 the number of linen manufacturing firms in Barnsley fell from about seven to three, and in the 1930s there were only two surviving firms. In 1957 the very last company — Hickson, Lloyd and King — closed its mill on the site of an earlier bleachworks at Redbrook, bringing to a close a history of linen manufacture in the Barnsley area extending over more than two hundred years.

In the sections which follow, the bleachworks at Swithen and at Cudworth are treated in greater detail than the rest. There is some justification for this in that both works were distinguished by their relatively large scale of operations. In mid-nineteenth century Swithen was reputed to be 'superior to any in the country'[10], and the main building at Cudworth was 'probably the largest of its kind in England'.[11] Both provide interesting examples of a migration — in which the need to find a cleaner air location may have played a part — from a site near town to one further out. For this reason Hoyle Mill is grouped with Swithen and Beevor with Cudworth in the following accounts. Both works proved to be late survivors of the local bleaching industry, that at Swithen continuing to operate into the 20th century.

The bleachworks which are described in this chapter are located on Map 2.

Hoyle Mill and Swithen

Both Hoyle Mill and Swithen bleachworks were operated by Samuel Coward. He was born in Barnsley in 1776, the son of a wiredrawer, John Coward, but found work himself as a linen weaver, being described as such in the Militia List of 1806.[12] Significantly he had chosen an industry which was growing at the time in Barnsley, rather than his father's trade, which was in decline.

In January 1795 he married Sarah Brearley at St Mary's Church in Barnsley. The page in the parish register which records this marriage makes interesting reading, in that three of the four entries are of men working in the linen trade. One of them, Richard Raywood, would feature later on as a 'Linen Manufacturer' in Baines' Directory of 1822.

By 1818 Coward is described in a property deed as 'bleacher', and by 1820 identified with a bleachworks at Hoyle Mill.[13] His progression from mere 'weaver', as described in 1806, probably owes something to his acceptance into the Society of Friends in February 1806.[14] As mentioned earlier, members enjoyed the benefits of mutual trust in their business dealings with each other, and there were Quakers among the linen manufacturers of Barnsley.

Coward's involvement with the Quakers is recorded in the minutes of the Monthly Meetings between 1806 and 1850, a period which covers the whole of his proprietorship of the works at Hoyle Mill and Swithen. He represented the 'Burton' (Monk Bretton/Barnsley) Friends at Monthly Meetings held variously at Wakefield, Wooldale, High Flatts, Pontefract and Ackworth on many occasions during those years. It is significant that among his co-representatives at meetings in 1812 and 1813 were William Harvey and William Bayldon, as well as members of the Yeardley family, all of them engaged in linen manufacture at Barnsley. Another, John Lister, belonged to the family operating the bleachground at Beevor, close to Hoyle Mill, where Coward would be operating a bleachworks by 1818 or 1820.

Coward's membership of the Quaker community may also explain his paternalistic attitude towards his employees at Hoyle Mill. It was his rule that should any of his workers be absent through sickness or injury, each of the other employees was to pay sixpence a week to help support the absent colleague, a substantial sum then being added from Coward's own pocket.[15]

Documentary evidence connected with Coward's occupancy of premises at Hoyle Mill poses problems concerning the exact location of the works. During the eighteenth century a John Haywood had owned a water-powered corn mill here on the Dearne. A map of 1762 shows the mill astride the river.(Map 3a) In 1806 the mill was rented out to William Thornhill Hodgson, who rebuilt it, with a new goyt, and operated it until 1817, manufacturing a range of chemical products, and experimenting in the production of soda from bleachers' waste. Hodgson moved to Walton, near Wakefield, in or around 1818. Was

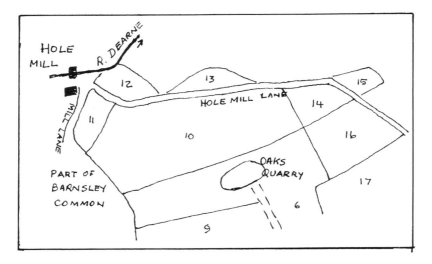

Above: Map 3a Extract from a plan of Ardsley Common, 1762.   *(Sheffield Archives)*

this an opportunity which Sam had been looking for? It may be that he took over the lease at that time.[16]

The Haywood family were also partners in the ownership of a 'mill and dam' at Hoyle Mill, according to the Tithe Award record of 1839, and the document records the existence there of a public house, bleachworks, dam and house.[17] A reservoir is shown on the O.S. 6 inch map of 1854, with a group of buildings closely clustered at its north eastern end. (Map 3b) There was also another cluster between the outfall of the Sough Dike and the Dearne. It is not clear whether there was only one or two bleachworks. Baines in 1822 and Pigot in 1834 list only one in their directories, but this is not conclusive evidence. Whether or not water power was used at a bleachworks here at an early stage is not clear either, though a valuation document of 1817 suggests that the water wheel was not in operation, since it refers to 'the remains of a corn mill'.

The site had the benefit of water supplies from the Sough Dike and its tributary the Measborough Dike, which are seen on Map 3b. The works lay close to the Barnsley-Pontefract Trust Road and not far from the wharf on the Dearne & Dove Canal at Beevor.

After Coward moved to Swithen, in 1826, a bleachworks continued to operate at Hoyle Mill. Pigot's Directory of 1834 lists the firm of Sykes & Jacques & Company here. By 1837 the firm of Jacques & Cooper appears in White's Directory, and Slater lists H.J. Spencer at 'Hoyle Mill Works' in 1848.

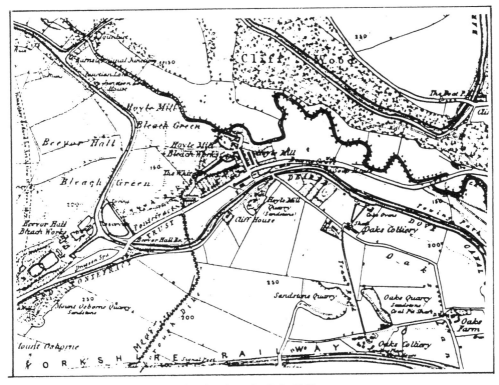

Above: Map 3b Beevor and Hoyle Mill Bleachworks O.S. 1851

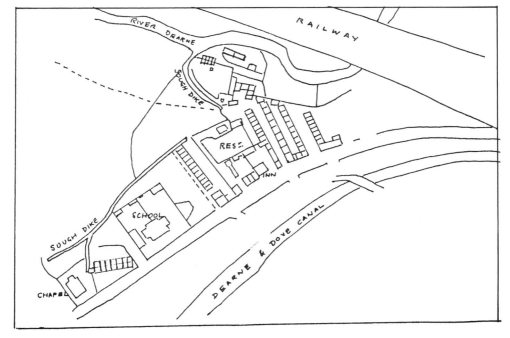

Above: Map 3c Hoyle Mill Bleachworks site 1906.

Surviving evidence on the ground (O.S. Grid Ref:SE 360067)

None of the buildings have survived. All but a remnant of the reservoir had gone by 1906.(Map 3c) However, armed with this map, the qualities of the site can be appreciated through a visit. The outfall of the Sough Dike (emerging from a long culvert) makes it easy to locate the site of the group of buildings which stood between the Dike and the Dearne. A short, curving length of hedgerow and the remains of a stone wall may possibly correspond with features on the map. Landscaping of the "Dearne Valley Park" has no doubt helped to obliterate other ground markings. What can be clearly seen, however, is the considerable gradient along the course of the Dearne upstream from the foot-bridge near the car park. This provided a good 'head' of water for the early corn mill.

Swithen Bleachworks

Samuel Coward began operations at Swithen, several miles further up the Dearne valley, in 1826. From about this time he began to diversify his business interests. In 1829 he bought four cottages on the former 'Warren Common' area of Barnsley, 'with the looms, fixtures and things in or belonging to the (weaving) shops on the premises'.[18] He owned other cottages at Providence Row, in one of the weaving quarters of Barnsley, until 1848.[19] In 1837 he acquired 'The Old Iron Foundry' in Summer Lane, Barnsley, but sold it ten years later.[20] He bought the steam corn mill at Staincross in 1842,[21] and in the same year he was among the proprietors of the newly-formed Barnsley Water Company.[22] His name has also been associated with the Union Calendering Company of Summer Lane.(23)

Coward's new works at Swithen was to grow much bigger than Hoyle Mill. At Hoyle Mill he had employed about twenty workers,[24] but he had fifty-one on his payroll at Swithen in 1851. It has been claimed that at sometime in the nineteenth century the works employed 'not far short of a hundred'.[25] As at Hoyle Mill, the premises were held leasehold, this time from Colonel Beaumont of nearby Bretton Hall.

Although Swithen lacked the advantages of canal transport, it lay alongside the Barnsley and Grange Moor Trust Road. Map 4a shows details of the site in mid-century. The buildings lay on the gentle, lowest slopes of the Dearne valley, while the bleachcroft extended from the Trust Road to the banks of the river, and thus onto the flood plain. Springs — not featured on the map — supplied sufficient water to fill two reservoirs. The opening of the Wakefield-Barnsley railway line,

Above: Reservoir at Swithen, Woolley Colliery beyond 1980's.   *Photo: H. Taylor*

with a station at nearby Haigh, in 1850, may have added another advantage to the site.

It may be that tenancy of the bleachworks was also linked with management of the farm at Upper Swithen, thus offering a broader base for Coward's commercial activities. Possibly he and his family lived in the farmhouse, though there is no documentary or Census evidence to support this until later years. Indeed, an indenture of 1848 refers to 'Samuel Coward of Haigh Hall'.[26] For the later period, however, a map of 1871 (Map 4b) shows that the Swithen holding formed part of a 112 acre farm.[27] Certainly Sam Coward's son — another Samuel — who followed his father in the business, was on good terms with some of the farmers in the area, for in his Will of 1857 he placed his estate 'in trust' to 'two of his friends,' Joshua Jackson and Joseph Walker of

Kexborough, both of them substantial farmers.[28] Jackson worked a 100 acre holding, whilst Walker, living at Kexborough Hall, farmed 363 acres and could employ seven labourers. Sam junior's widow is described as 'Farmer' in the Census of 1861. Sam Coward senior certainly had an interest in agricultural land, for he acquired six farms, totalling 112 acres on the south side of Penistone over the years.[29]

Evidently the business at Swithen prospered, for in 1837 the works was enlarged (at a cost of £927).[30] The original buildings must have been grouped round a yard, for the extensions, which included a 'singeing house' and 'additional drying chambers' were added 'at the east side of the square'. It is perhaps surprising that extensions were carried out at this time, involving as they did, a considerable outlay by the then landlord, Thomas Wentworth Beaumont, who had to face financial problems caused by the extravagances of his parents. During the period between 1831 and 1848 a good deal of estate land was actally sold off to meet expenses. Samuel Coward must have presented a good case!

It is possible to describe the layout and equipment of the Swithen works in considerable detail but only for the situation as it was in the 1890s. A large scale plan and accompanying schedule, dated 1893, are available.[31] Before that the only information about the processes carried out is the scanty evidence in the Census records. In 1861 both the owners and several of the employees describe themselves as 'cotton and linen bleachers', though the terms of a Deed of Covenant dated 1893 stipulated that 'operations were to be confined to the bleaching, printing and dyeing of linen'. Possibly the mention of cotton is a reference to 'Union Cloth', a mixed weave of cotton and linen, an important product of Barnsley mills. However, Spencers at the Hope Works in Barnsley were printing on calico in 1861 and 'manufacturing' cotton fabric in 1871, according to White's Directory. There are no surviving records to reveal what connections Coward had with specific mills in Barnsley or elsewhere.

During the 1890s at least, Swithen carried out a range of finishing processes – bleaching, calendering and bettling. Clearly the efficient distribution of water and of steam through the works premises was of paramount importance. A plan of 1893 (Map 4c) illustrates the grid which supplied these requirements, as well as provision for storage of water and other liquids by means of cisterns of wood or of stone, both inside the buildings and in the yard. Two large cisterns in the yard had 'lead and stone troughs with taps and agitators.'[32]

Power to operate the various machines was derived from a 26 H.P. steam engine, and was transferred through the works by gearing, shafting and pulleys. The buildings were lit by gas, generated on the site in the firm's own retort. Essential ancillary services were available on site — blacksmiths' and joiners' shops, stables and cart sheds, storage space for paint, lime and vitriol. The schedule accompanying the 1893 plan fails to explain, however, what took place in the 'Nancy Room'!

Close to the works buildings there was a residential block containing three dwellings. In 1841 twenty bleachers were living in nearby cottages at Swithen and Haigh. Three lived in Woolley Township and four more in Kexborough. Some or all of the eight bleachers in Darton may also have worked at Swithen. All these places lay within two miles of the bleachworks. A similar pattern obtained in 1861, in which year Cowards employed '51 men and boys'. As the Census of that year only records thirty-six bleachers in Kexborough Township (which included Swithen and Haigh) some of the 'missing' employees may have been among the eighteen males aged between ten and twenty in the Township for whom no occupation is recorded.

There was a wide age-range in the Swithen workforce. The youngest recorded in the successive Censuses was a boy of eleven, whilst in 1881 Joseph Wood, aged eighty-two, and George Sanderson, seventy-nine, still described themselves as 'bleachers'.

Most of the workforce in 1851 — the first census year to state place of birth — had been born locally, but by 1861 the staff included about a dozen who had been born further afield, though all in the West Riding, in Cudworth, Brierley, Royston, Wath and Dewsbury. Few of the employees recorded between 1851 and 1881 were natives of places very far from Yorkshire. In 1861 Thomas Gascoigne, a Sussex man, and, in 1881, Tom Roberts, born in Wiltshire, were notable exceptions. In contrast to handloom weaving in Barnsley, bleaching work at Swithen attracted no Irish. There was a contrast too with the workforce at collieries in the district, such as Woolley Colliery, opened in 1849 about half a mile away from the Swithen works. Typically the mines drew their workers from widely dispersed areas of the country. Woolley provides a notable example, as in 1861 a body of miners was brought in from Bilston in Staffordshire to replace men who were on strike.[33]

Coward's time at Swithen belonged to his mature years. He was already 50 when he moved to the new location At some time between the Census years 1841 and 1851 (he would be seventy-five in the latter year) he retired from Swithen, handing over the management to his son, and settling in Penistone. Now a widower, he lived here with an Elizabeth Brearley, probably a relative of his late wife.[34] Elizabeth may have been a member of the family of Benjamin Brearley, a land-valuer

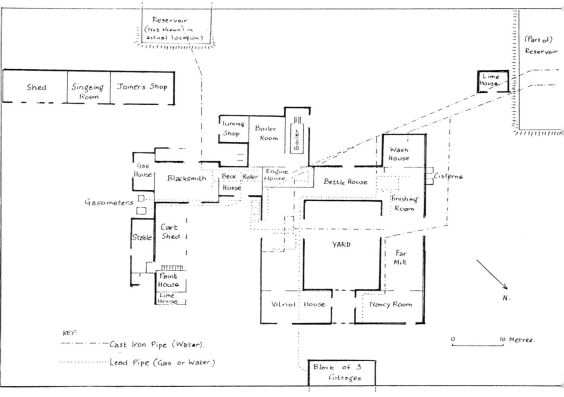

Above: Map 4c Layout of Swithen Bleachworks in the 1890's.

in the town. If so, Samuel may well have used this agent in the course of property deals in farmland and in cottages in the Penistone-Hoyland Swaine area. Samuel died in 1864 at the good age of eighty-four and his grave is to be seen in the Quaker burial ground at Barnsley. The deeds which record his property dealings during the later years of his life describe him as 'Gentleman'. Clearly the humble weaver of 1806 had climbed the social ladder and was now a man of property. His wife, Sarah, had died many years before, in 1844. The local report of her death remarked that she was 'a respected member of the Society of Friends'.

Samuel Coward junior was only in charge of the bleachworks for a relatively short time, for he died in February 1857 after a 'lingering illness' at the age of fifty-seven.[35] Unlike his parents, he never became a Quaker but worshipped at Darton Parish Church. Indeed, it had been his custom to have all his employees go in a body, along with his family and himself, to the church at religious festivals.[36] Two weeks after his burial at Darton a special service was held in the church 'to

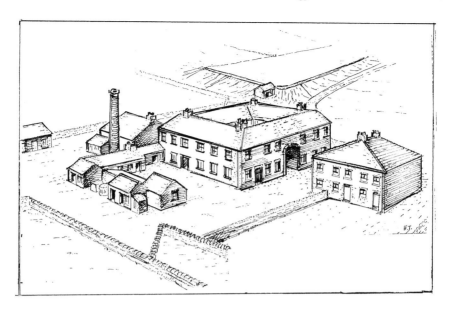

Above: How Swithen Bleachworks might have looked in the 1890's. Sketch based on scale plan and schedule of 1895.

pay tribute of respect to his memory'. He had been 'an ardent supporter of the Protestant cause' through his membership of the 'Sociation (sic) of Loyal Orangemen'. The 'large attendance by members from Barnsley and neighbouring lodges', mentioned in the contemporary report, testifies to the esteem in which he was held in the district.[37]

Sam and his family had lived in considerable comfort at Swithen. The auctioneer's list for the sale of the contents of the house provide detailed evidence.[38] The house itself was commodious, with sitting room, drawing room, dining room and four bedrooms in addition to kitchen and servants' quarters. The reception rooms, with their Brussells carpets, were well furnished, and were graced with china ornaments, potted plants and a number of prints and portraits. The dining room tables and sideboard were of mahogany. The stock of 40 wine glasses, eight decanters and three spirit bottles amply provided for the needs of both family and guests, and in the cellar at the time of the sale , there remained 'eight quarts of whisky and three of rum, along with two and a half dozen of port and sherry.' In the drawing room stood a 'horizontal pianoforte by Collard & Collard' and there was serious reading matter among the 115 volumes on display in the house. These included a three-volume *History of the Reformation* and a *Life of Christ. Coke's Commentary* encompassed six books. A *Life of Wellington* accounted for

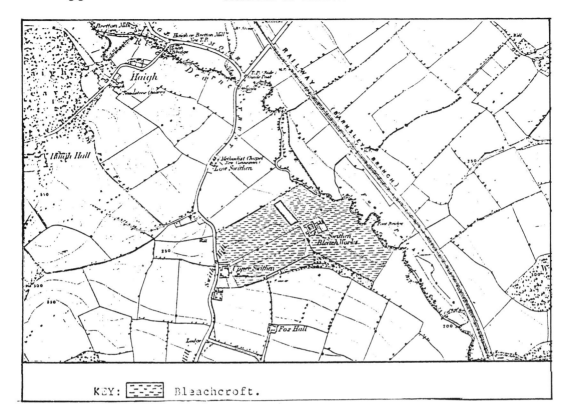

Above: Map 4a The site and situation of Swithen Bleachworks. O.S. 1849-51.

eleven further volumes. Geography was well represented by a thirty-part *Gazeteer of England & Wales* and the eleven books of *Bell's System of Geography.*

After Coward's death, control of the works passed to his daughters, Sarah and Mary, but in 1893 the firm failed. As the rent of £1,050 due to the Beaumont Estate at Martinmas had not been met, a sale was held in the following March to raise funds.[39] The auctioneer's list reveals details of the farm which the family had been running. It was a mixed farm, though the livestock side seems to have operated on a modest scale, unless stock had already been sold. There were four cows in milk, a couple of pigs and eighty head of poultry. On the arable side there were ploughs, chain harrows, a roller and cylinder, a horse-rake and muck-spreader, and a turnip drill. Hay and straw stacks, along with quantities of turnips and swedes, were in the sale.

In November 1894 a twenty-one-year lease of the bleachworks was

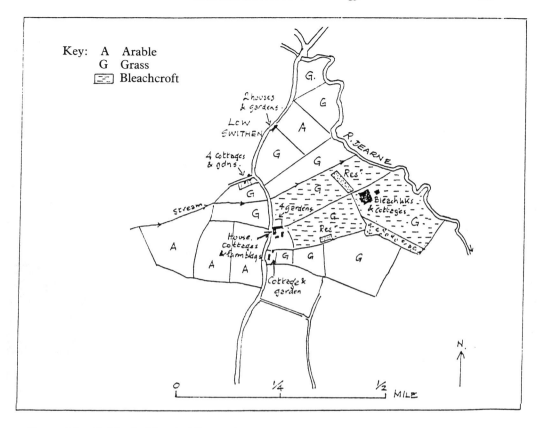

Key: A Arable
      G Grass
      [====] Bleachcroft

Above: Map 4b The Swithen holding on the Beaumont Estate, 1871.

taken up by the firm of Thomas Taylor & Sons, at an annual rent of
£200. This firm, located in Peel Street, Barnsley, operated the biggest
linen factory in the town. Their aim, in acquiring Swithen, was to
effect economies by carrying out the bleaching of their own products
themselves. In the event the firm was able to undertake custom bleaching
too.[40]

Gradually, however, Taylors reduced the scope of their operations
in the Barnsley area, whilst concentrating production in their Ulster
works. By 1922 Swithen had closed.

Surviving evidence on the ground.(O.S. Grid Ref: SE 301115)

The site, which is on private land at Riverside Farm, and occupied by
kennels and caravan storage ground, is approached from the A 637 by
the narrow lane which passes beneath the railway. Only the outlying

buildings of the works have survived. After the works closed, stone was removed for building work elsewhere on the Bretton Hall estate. The cottage block has been replaced by a recently-built house. The larger of the two reservoirs is still there (available for anglers) with the little lime house, and spring water can still be seen entering the reservoir on its western side.

Beevor (Oakwell) and the Midland Bleachworks (Cudworth)

Bleaching of linen was being carried out here in a small way in the eighteenth century by John Lupton, a member of a Quaker family, and a 'custom weaver', who had looms here.[41] Water supplies were available both from springs and from the Sough Dike, which flowed through the site. Subsequently William Jackson and James Lister, both of them relatives of Lupton, bought the business and bleached linen as well as cotton yarns and pieces for over twenty-five years until William's son, Henry, a Barnsley solicitor, took over the management around 1832.

The works had been operating on a large scale, judging from production figures quoted by Rowland Jackson in his *History of the Town & Township of Barnsley* for the period 1814-1838. The completion of the Dearne & Dove Canal in 1804 greatly enhanced the value of the site, a loading wharf being available adjacent to the works. A map of 1822, (Map 5a) which used the features of the 1779 Enclosure Award map as a base, shows the bleachworks buildings which had appeared since then, along with the Canal and another improvement in communications, the Barnsley-Pontefract Trust Road. The later map of 1854 (Map 3b) shows the extensive bleach green, straddling the canal.

Although the Beevor Hall estate, including the residence, was sold to George Jackson, a miller, in 1852, Henry Jackson stayed on a little longer as tenant of the bleachworks. By this time, however, problems had arisen due to atmospheric pollution caused by the mill chimneys, the foundries and the domestic smoke of Barnsley. Rowland Jackson, writing in 1858, remarks that 'in consequence of the prevalence of smoke and dirt caused by the rapid increase of the town, the place (Beevor) no longer serves for bleachworks.'[42]

It may well have been this problem which prompted Jackson to purchase land at Cudworth as early as 1842. His new, and larger works, was completed there in the 1850s.

The date of final abandonment of the Beevor site is not clear. Burland records that Jackson entertained his workmen — seventy in all — to dinner at the Royal Oak Hotel on New Year's Day, 1856. (In the evening 'the females employed by the company were regaled at tea'!) We are not told, however, whether this occasion marked the running down of the Beevor works or was no more than an annual custom.

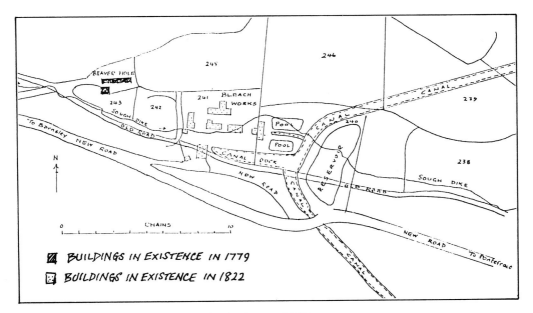

Above: Map 5a Beevor Bleachworks. Garforth map of 1822.

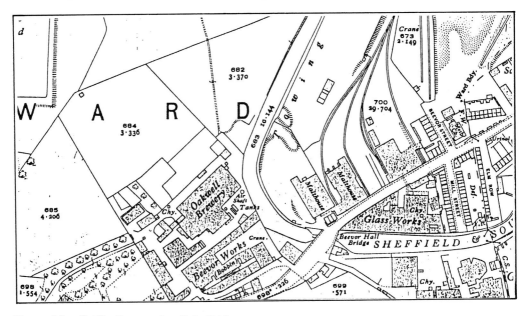

Above: Map 5b The Beevor site. O.S. 1932

Surviving features on the ground. (O.S. Grid Ref: SE 360067)

The bed of the former canal can be seen under the bridge which carries the A 628. With the aid of the old maps the line of the canal, contouring its way in a quite spectacular fashion, can be picked out, and the location of the former canal dock discerned. No part of the bleachworks buildings seems to have survived, unless one or two of the smaller ones have been incorporated into the old premises of the brewery.

Map 5b shows the site as it was in 1932. The Barnsley Brewery was established here in 1888. In the years prior to this, certainly from 1881, Beevor had been the base for the firm of Paul & Guy Senior, whose activities embraced not only malting and brewing but farming and the manufacture of bricks and tiles. The tall, stone building of the old brewery is clearly seen from the A 628. In 1922 Beevor Hall became the brewery offices. The hall can be seen from the main road, and the Sough Dike flows in a culvert beneath the bridge at the entrance to the Hall driveway. Brewing ceased in the 1970s, after the Barnsley firm had been taken over by the John Smith organisation. This firm too has subsequently abandoned the site. The bobbin factory which enjoyed a canal dockside location, was established in 1852 by Wilson & Co. The scene of dereliction in the early 1990s belies the former vitality of this site, and its long succession of industrial activities over more than two centuries.

The Midland Bleachworks at Cudworth

The advantages of this site, further from the sooty atmosphere of Barnsley in mid-nineteenth century, have already been pointed out, though the railway, only a stone's-throw away, cannot have been a kind neighbour in this respect! There is no doubt, however, about the availability of water here. A reliable spring supplied a reservoir on the valley floor of the Cudworth Dike. (Map 5c) From this, water could be pumped to a higher reservoir on the valley slope, above the main buildings of the works, and fed by gravity to the bleaching plant. Some idea of the volume of water required here can be gained from the contemporary description of the pump, which was capable of lifting 7,000 gallons an hour. A further idea of the importance of water in this bleachworks is given by the description of the pipework in the building contractor's specification. There were 276 yards of cast iron water piping, 164 yards of cast iron steam piping, and 38 yards of lead piping.

Considerable detail of the equipment installed has survived in the company records.[43] The construction work was awarded to the firm

Above: Reservoir and surviving buildings of the Midland Bleachworks from viewpoint 1 (See Map 5c). *Photo: H. Taylor*

of Richard Inns of the 'Old Foundry' in Summer Lane, Barnsley. This firm of engineers and millwrights manufactured steam engines and boilers and also produced castings in iron and in brass. An invoice dated 1855 carries the information that the firm was now paying increased attention to the millwright department, 'as applicable to Calenders, Bleachworks, Cotton and Linen Mills.' Estimates supplied by the firm in 1854 and 1855 specified a '30 H.P. multi-tubular boiler' to feed the steam engine, and indicate that the Cudworth works was to undertake the full range of finishing processes. There was to be a 'Dutch Calenderer', with a steam-heated iron cylinder and two drying machines, one with seven cylinders and the other with nine, all of them of 22 inch diameter. There were to be two 'beetling' (bettling) machines and two starching machines, as well as equipment for damping and stretching fabrics. Stiffening machines, rub-boards, squeezers and a singeing frame were among other items listed. Gearing and shafting was to be of cast or wrought iron, these being the days before mass production techniques made available the superior material, steel.

The main building, completed in 1855, was evidently of unusually large dimensions for the period, requiring particular skill in the design of the roof span. Burland claimed that it was 'probably the largest of its kind in England, presenting a novel appearance'. Designed by a Barnsley architect, Hindle, it had an interior measuring 120 by 100 feet. The roof, reported Burland, was 'on the principle of the laminated arch, consisting of five main ribs or arches, each of 100 feet clear span.' The height from floor to ridge was 40 feet, and each of the main ribs was calculated to support 3 tons 14 cwts. 'An immense room was thus formed, without a pillar to interrupt the working.' The roof was half glazed in order to admit plenty of light into this wide building. A feature of the works, visible still from a large area round about, was the thirty yard-high chimney stack.

A valuation list of 1881 fills in further details of the layout of the works. The warehouses and calender houses were of stone, with blue slate roofs. There were blacksmiths' and joiners' shops of brick, as well as a range of open sheds. A separate 'singeing house' was constructed and there was a range of stone-built offices, work peoples' mess room, store and stables. A 'neat, stone-built Elizabethan house' had been built for the foreman, and at the entrance to the site was a 'neat, Elizabethan entrance lodge.' Evidently Jackson and his architect had more than mere utility in mind when designing the Midland Bleachworks.

Jackson celebrated the opening of the works on 27 April, 1855, though it would appear that some of the equipment had still to be installed. To mark the occasion a supper was provided at the Star Inn, Cudworth, at which 74 persons sat down, mainly men who had built the works.[44]

As mentioned earlier, Henry Jackson brought his foreman from the Beevor Works. It is most interesting to find that this man, McGee, though doubtless a very experienced bleacher, was nevertheless illiterate, for he appended his 'mark', rather than a signature to the agreement with his employer in 1853. Evidently McGee was well-valued by Henry Jackson. He was to enjoy occupation of the 'Elizabethan' house and its garden rent-free, and to have free coals, as well as his wage of £2-5-0 a week.

The Midland Bleachworks lacked the advantage of canal transport near at hand, but the railway of 1836, which bounded the site on the west side, may have played a useful role, Cudworth Station (originally 'Barnsley Station') not being far away. However, the rail link into Barnsley was not added until 1870.

Henry Jackson's business activities embraced the manufacture of linen cloth, though not on this site, as well as bleaching, both for himself and for other customers, some of them in Ireland. Until 1862 the firm

Above: chimney stack (1854) at Midland Bleachworks from viewpoint 2. *Photo: H. Taylor*

(Jackson & Hodgetts) operated a warehouse at Barnsley in Church Street, supplying customers in USA, as well as in France, Scotland and Ulster.[45]

Jackson and his family moved out from Barnsley around 1857 to live at the Rectory House in Ardsley. He had become a well-respected member of the Barnsley community, and his household reflected his status, with its governess and nurse to care for the children, its two housemaids and cook. A few years after his move, Jackson was appointed a magistrate, and by 1863 he was a member of the Barnsley Board of Guardians. He died in 1867 but the firm, continuing in his name, is listed in directories of 1881 and 1897. By 1904, however, the works was no longer in use.

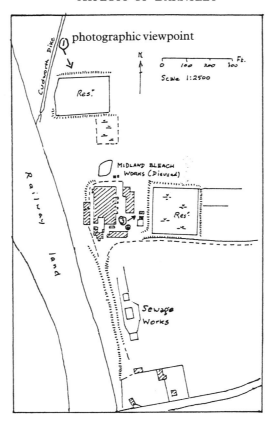

Above: Map 5c Midland Bleachworks, 1904.

Surviving evidence on the ground (O.S. Grid Ref:SE 382089)

The site is well marked by the tall, stone-built chimney stack of 1854, a 'listed' structure. Access to this privately-owned land is only by permission of the occupier of Bleachcroft Farm. Comparison with map 5c will show that, some of the smaller buildings still stand, the larger structure having been demolished. These are of sandstone with blue slate roofs. Windows have been blocked with either stone or brickwork. A gabled house near the entrance appears to date from the nineteenth century.

Two reservoirs, one on the valley floor, the other held against the valley slope by earthen embankments, can be seen, though the latter is silted up and colonised with marsh vegetation. Stone revetments will be seen on one side of the upper reservoir. The photographs illustrate important features of the site, the camera viewpoints being indicated on the map.

Greenfoot Bleachworks at Wilthorpe

The works at Greenfoot was established by Joseph Beckett in the latter part of the eighteenth century. Beckett has been styled 'The Father of the Barnsley Linen Trade',[46] not because he founded the industry (though he was a relative of the Wilson family which did) but because he did so much to concentrate it in the district.

Described as 'a man of extraordinary energy and enterprise',[47] he was a partner in a banking business as well as a 'linen manufacturer', owning weavers' cottages in the town, some of them in Beckett Square (long since demolished) near the present Jumble Lane railway crossing. He was a magistrate for many years and, for a time, Deputy Lieutenant for the West Riding. He died in February 1840 at the grand old age of 88.

By 1789 Beckett was trading as grocer and linen manufacturer, with a warehouse in Church Street. He also owned plots of land outside the town at Greenfoot. Several small buildings are shown there on the Enclosure Award map of 1779, but it is not possible to say whether his bleaching work was being carried out there or on land acquired in the 1780s.[48] However, Garforth's map of 1822 (Map 6a), which uses the 1779 map as a base, shows the group of buildings which Beckett

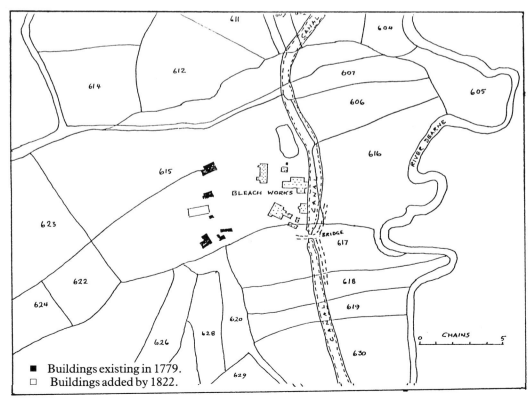

■ Buildings existing in 1779.
□ Buildings added by 1822.

Above: Map 6a Greenfoot on Garforths map of 1822. *(Barnsley Archives)*

had built since the earlier year. Perhaps they post-date the canal (of 1801),as two of them lie on the canal bank itself.

Possibly the Dearne itself supplied water in the early period, though water was evidently a problem at times, as John Staniforth Beckett was purchasing supplies from a mine owner in 1836.[49] At some stage one of the Becketts built the two linked reservoirs on the slope above the works, the upper one, 'Tinker's Pond', drawing its water from a spring.

The buildings were added to after 1822, as can be seen on Maps 6c and 6d, but a point of interest is the positioning of the largest of them on the very bank of the canal. Unfortunately there are no records of the use to which Beckett may have put the canal.

Map 6c also shows the very extensive bleaching green, and its much smaller successor is seen on the 1904 map, Map 6d.

Supplies of coal fuel can hardly have been a problem. At various times in the nineteenth century relatively shallow workings tapped the Barnsley Seam. Among the larger enterprises were Gawber Colliery, located about a quarter of a mile to the west (in mid-century) and later,the Willow Bank colliery, close by on the east side.

By 1837 the Greenfoot works had been taken over by the firm of Sykes & McClatchy, but in 1848 Slater's Directory lists the operator as Matthew Sykes. The Rate Valuation list of that year shows the works to be of considerable proportions at that time, with 'bleachworks, washpits, engine, machinery, engine house, warehouses, stables, cottages and sheds.' Like Joseph Beckett, Sykes also owned cottages with loomshops in the town.

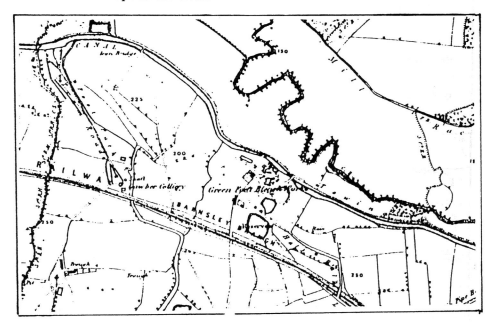

Above: Map 6b Greenfoot – O.S. 1854

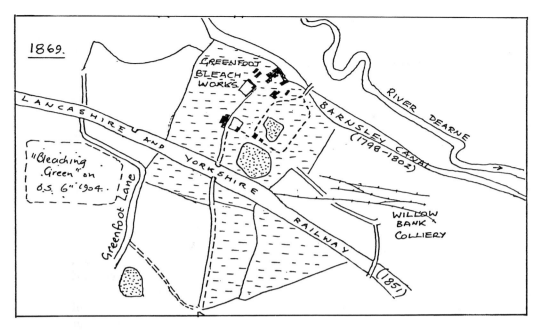

Above: Map 6c Greenfoot in 1869.   (*Barnsley Local Studies Library*)

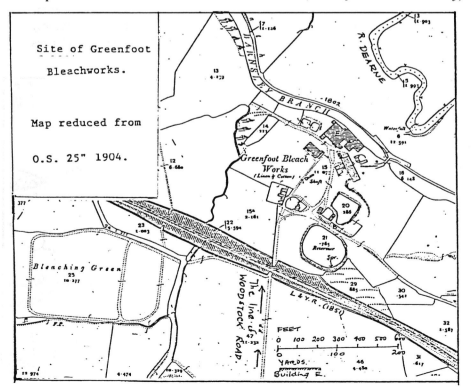

Above: Map 6d Greenfoot. O.S. 1904.

The 1861 Census shows Sykes living at Greenfoot as 'bleacher and farmer', the combination seen also at Swithen. After his death in 1863, his son — another Matthew — soon forsook bleaching work to become landlord of the Vine Tavern in Pitt Street.

White's Directory of 1871 lists Greenfoot under new management again. The new tenants, the firm of Craik & Son, had been working the Old Mill bleachworks, no more than a mile or so further along the canal, since (at least) 1852.

Robert Craik had important interests in coal mining too. In 1861 he opened the East Gawber Hall Colliery (working the Barnsley Seam) at New Lodge, about a half a mile away from Greenfoot across the Dearne Valley, and also operated the pit at Silkstone Fall.

Craik has been described as 'in every sense of the word, a self-made man, the sole architect of his fortune.'[50] In the 1830s he and a partner had set up a linen manufacturing business, his ventures into coal mining coming later, from the 1850s. His enterprise, like that of Joseph Beckett, Henry Jackson and Samuel Coward, illustrates the key role played by personalities in the development of the linen industry in this area.

By 1902 Greenfoot was being operated by Jackson & Co., whose other works at Cudworth have already been described.

Surviving evidence on the ground (O.S. Grid REf: SE 339081)

The Greenfoot site is approached from Woodstock Road, continuing under the railway bridge. A more interesting approach is along the canal towpath from Old Mill or from Smithies Lane.It is all private land, but much of what is to be seen can be viewed from one or other of the public footpaths which cross the site.

All the buildings have been demolished, but with the aid of the map of 1904 (Map 6d) the layout of the former works can be discerned. Most obvious are the two ponds. The stonework retaining these and the stone-lined outlet from the lower pond can be seen. Stone revetments along the canal bank, marking the previous location of the largest building, are best seen from the north bank of the canal. (This stretch of canal was cleaned out and the bridge rebuilt to a new design during the 1980s.) A low brick tower beyond the Dearne to the north east locates the former East Gawber Hall Colliery.

Some disconnected remnants of the foundations of former bleachworks buildings can be seen. Some lines of stone blocks appear to have formed conduits for water and other liquids, having grooves for the insertion of sluice gates. The smaller bleachcroft of 1904 is now the site of Wilthorpe School.

Old Mill Bleachworks

This site was developed by William Wilson in the middle years of the eighteenth century on land made available to him by his father. The land appears on the 1779 Enclosure Award map as Plots 652 and 653.

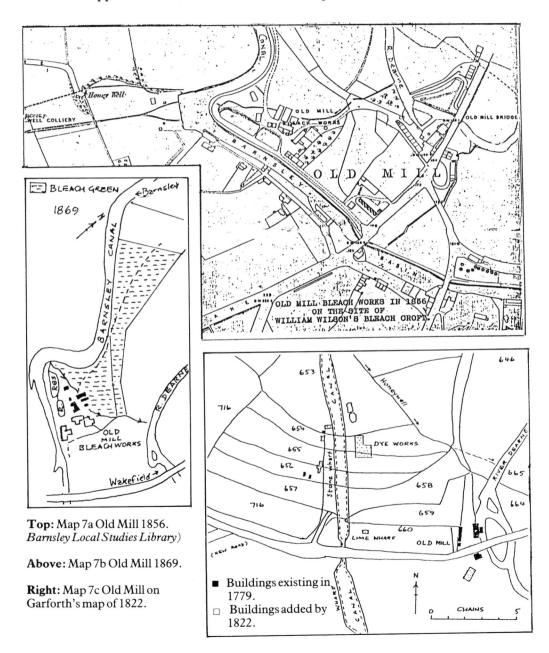

Top: Map 7a Old Mill 1856.
Barnsley Local Studies Library)

Above: Map 7b Old Mill 1869.

Right: Map 7c Old Mill on Garforth's map of 1822.

■ Buildings existing in 1779.
☐ Buildings added by 1822.

In this early period the Dearne itself may have provided suitable water, but there was a stream, flowing from the Honey Well along the north eastern side of the site. The location, a little way out of town, afforded relatively clean air. In 1801 the canal was constructed, virtually bisecting the bleaching ground.

Baines' Directory of 1822 lists Wilson Croft under the name of James Wilson, bleacher of both linen and cotton. Garforth's map of 1822 (Map 7c) shows no more than one small building on the original site (Plot 653) but has a "Dyeworks" east of the canal. The Rate Books of 1848 show a Thomas Wilson as owner of a Dyehouse here. By about 1840 the bleaching works at Old Mill was in the hands of Robert Craik, who had the lease of 'sundry buildings, washpits, engine and engine house', as well as barn and stables. The map of 1856 (Map7a) shows the layout with two small reservoirs, apparently fed by the Honey Well stream and a map of 1869 (Map7b) shows the bleachgreen.

Although Robert died in 1868, a directory of 1871 still lists Old Mill under the name of Craik Brothers. By 1890 the Dearne Paper Mill had occupied part of the site. This works, subsequently known as The Star Paper Mill, closed in 1981, and the site has since been redeveloped by the Asda supermarket firm.

Surviving evidence on the ground (O.S. Grid REf:SE 349071)

The only feature which has survived from the former industrial geography is the line of the canal bed – now dry. The mooring rings are still to be seen in the old canal wall in the carpark of the B & Q Store.

Redbrook Bleachworks (O.S. Grid Ref:SE 321078)

John Pickering, linen manufacturer, and partner in the firm of Pickering & Jenkinson, with a warehouse and calender works in town, held the lease of a bleachworks here from about 1790 to 1810.[51] The site, well out of town, had a good water supply from the brook.

During the nineteenth century, if not earlier, water was collected in a series of ponds along the brook and its small tributary. (Maps 8a and b). The bleachcroft was located in two fields now occupied by the Clayfields Council Estate.[52] By 1871 the firm of Canter, Whaley & Co was weaving linen here as well as bleaching, and between 1888 and 1912 this firm, now called 'Canter & Co.,' also carried out dyeing work.

After a number of changes in ownership, the premises were occupied by Richardson,Tee & Ryecroft & Co., who moved here from their Borespring Works in Pitt Street, Barnsley, in 1929. A 1929 plan of

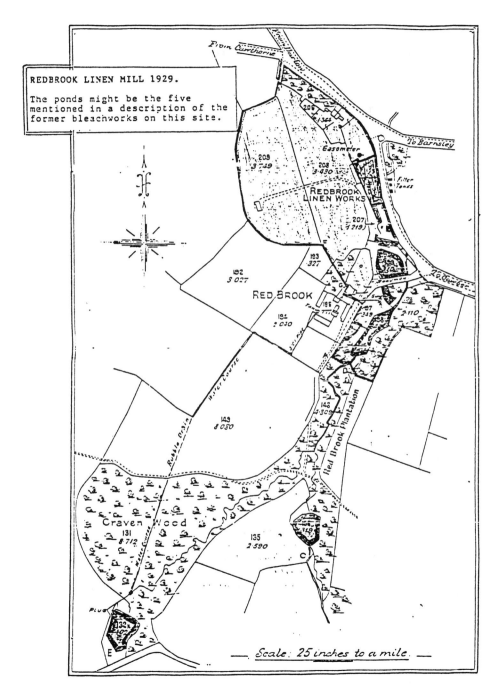

Above: Map 8a Redbrook 1929, reduced from a 25″ plan.

Redbrook Mill shows no provision for bleaching work here at this time. In 1937 the works was taken over by the firm of Hickson, LLoyd & King, which rebuilt the main part of the premises around 1950. Textile manufacture ceased in 1957, the buildings then being put to new uses.

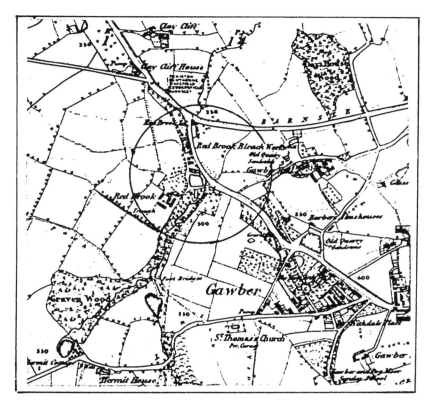

Above: Map 8b Redbrook. O.S. 1854

Newbridge Bleachworks, Monk Bretton (O.S. grid Ref: SE 370077)

Only out-dated O.S. maps witness to the past existence of this enterprise, as the entire site now lies beneath the spoil heap material of the former Monk Bretton Colliery, material which has been redistributed under reclamation and landscaping schemes. The O.S. 6 inch map of 1854 (Map 9a) shows something of the layout of the works, and a few buildings were still standing in 1904.(Map 9b) The location alongside the Barnsley Canal is a notable feature, and it is interesting to trace the former course of this canal from Junction Lock (9357068) in the field.

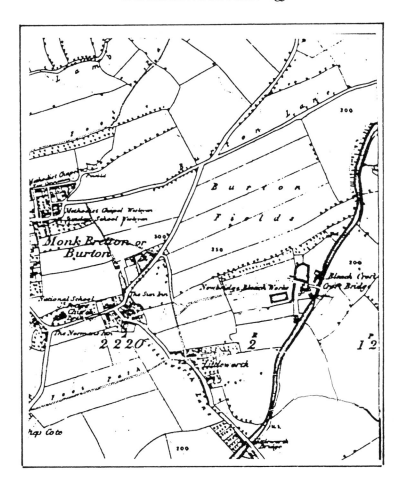

Above: Map 9a Newbridge Bleachworks. O.S. 1854

The Newbridge works appears in Baines' Directory of 1822 with the proprietor, Richard Day. Like Robert Craik, Day too was a coal owner, and is listed as such in White's Directory of 1838. He died at some time before 1852, but work continued at Newbridge under his name until at least 1876, if the evidence of a trade directory may be accepted. At that time, and again in 1872, Thomas Pepper, a native of Ardsley, was manager, living at the works site. Several employees lived there too, an arrangement found also at Swithen.

Probably Newbridge handled both yarn and cloth, for the Census of 1851 lists workers in both processes. Six of the bleachers at that time lived in Castle Row, Monk Bretton, a row which has disappeared, along with the numerous weavers' cottages in the village. Possibly these workers were employed at Old Mill, however, since it is not far away.

The 1881 Census records — very unusually — two women bleachworkers in the Township, one a 'washer and bleachworker' and the other a 'bleacher's maker-up'! Some of the bleachers had other sources of income, however they contrived to fit in their shifts at the works. In 1861 Richard Broad of Church Lane kept a grocer's shop. Robert Hawcroft at Littleworth Hill was a grocer too, and Thomas White a publican.

Directories of 1877 and 1879 do not list Newbridge, though the Census records three bleachworkers at Littleworth in 1881.

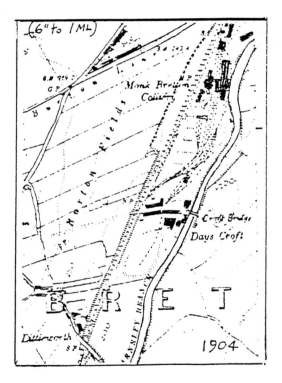

Above: Map 9b Newbridge. O.S. 1904

Rob Royd Bleachworks, Gilroyd, Dodworth

Rob Royd works appears on the O.S. 6 inch map of 1854. (Map10). The site was close to the Dodworth Dike, and probably drew water from it. Surprisingly, no storage reservoir appears on the map. The extensive bleach greens seen on the 1854 map would benefit from the

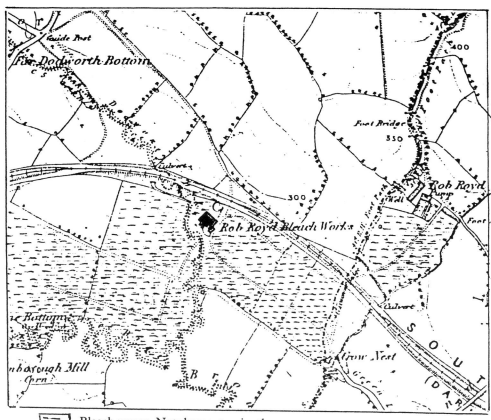

[---] Bleach greens. Note how extensive they are.

Above: Map 10 Rob Royd Bleachworks. O.S. 1854

clean air of this location, well outside town, and on many occasions upwind of it.

The property was leased by the firm of H.J. & J. Spencer of Hope Works, Sackville Street. This town mill, which occupied a dominating position overlooking Townend, until its demolition (as the Barnsley Canister Works) in 1992, was operated by a most enterprising company. The firm won an outstanding reputation for its pioneer work in printing on fabrics by a technique new to the town. Spencers carried out a wider range of operations than other Barnsley linen firms, from the spinning of cotton, probably for 'union cloth', a mixed weave of linen and cotton, through weaving to bleaching, dyeing and printing.

By 1904 the bleachworks at Rob Royd had been replaced by a colliery. This was operated by the Strafford Colliery Company, in tandem with the Strafford Silkstone pit, about half a mile to the west. In the post World War Two era it served as a pumping station for Dodworth Colliery before eventual closure.

Surviving features on the ground (O.S. Grid Ref: SE 330044)

Approached by way of Hound Hill Lane and Green Lane, the site, which is owned by British Coal, is marked by the low,wooded mound of the colliery spoil heap. The former pit shaft has a concrete capping. The M1 Motorway, which skirts the site, makes it difficult to comprehend the former layout, especially its relationship with the Dodworth Dike.

Stairfoot Bleach and Dye Works (O.S. Grid Ref: SE 373055)

Pigot's Directory of 1834 lists Joseph Raywood, bleacher, at Stairfoot. This may have been the works shown on the O.S. 6 inch map of 1854 (Map 11a). The Census of 1851 records the occupant as Edward Parker, a native of Houghton in County Durham. At the time he had twenty employees on his payroll, and was running a 110 acre farm in addition, thus offering an interesting comparison with the Cowards at Swithen. By the 1870s another new occupant, William Sykes, was in charge. Apparently the works is not listed in directories after 1877, but the buildings, grouped round a yard, were still there in 1906.(Map 11b)

The only reminder of the works now appears to be the street name 'Bleachcroft Way', but the dry bed of the Dearne & Dove Canal, passing beneath this road, offers a reminder of other bleachworks located on or close to canals in the Barnsley area.

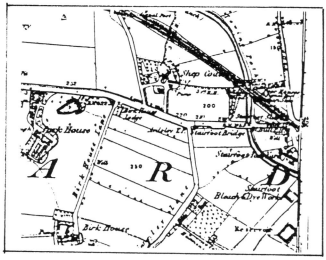

Above: Map 11a Stairfoot Bleach & Dye Works. O.S. 1854

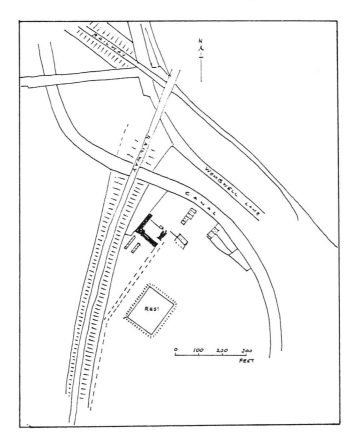

Above: Map 11b Surviving buildings of Stairfoot Bleach & Dye Works. O.S. 1906

Postscript

The wholesale closure of collieries in the Barnsley area in very recent times has laid a fresh layer of archaeological features on the land. Since the linen industry here belonged to an earlier period, any evidence that it has left on the ground is fainter. No less than with the collieries, however, what can be seen is significant, because it too represents a story of industrial growth and decline, of individual enterprise and of a very great deal of human toil. For the interested observer the old linen industry, with its bleachworks, has left a good many clues to the past lying in the local landscape.

Notes and References

Abbreviations used:

BLSL: Barnsley Local Studies Library

BA: Barnsley Archives

LBC: Lawrence Batley Centre at Bretton College (Archives of the former Bretton Hall Estate)

WRRD: West Riding Registry of Deeds (Wakefield)

JGC: John Goodchild Collection, Wakefield

1. *The Wilson Family of Barnsley 1706-1840*, W.G.England. Typescript BLSL.I am indebted to this source for information on early bleaching techniques.
2. John Goodchild: *Golden Threads* p.255.(Wakefield Historical Publications)
3. *ibid*, p.259.
4. JGC, Henry Jackson papers.
5. Tomlinson: *Encyclopaedia of Useful Arts & Manufactures*, Vol 1. 1862.
6. *The Union Callender*; Miscellaneous Poems by Robert McLintock 1839 BLSL.
7. 1848 Rate Valuation Books. BA.
8. JGC.
9. John Goodchild, *op cit* p.267.
10. Dearnley, *History of the Ancient Parish of Darton*, M.S. p. 104. BLSL.
11. Burland, *Miscellaneous Writings* (Microfilm) BLSL.
12. Militia List 1806. JGC & Sheffield Archives.
13. WRRD GU 86 96 and HG 71 77.
14. Minutes of Monthly Meetings; Archives of Society of Friends, Ackworth School.
15. Burland, *Op cit*
16. John Hislop: (unpublished) *Notes on the History of Hoyle Mill* 1985, and JGC.
17. I am grateful to Tom Umpleby for bringing this information to my attention.
18. WRRD KQ 289 214
19. WRRD QD 261 273
20. WRRD MR 68 51
21. WRRD 433 374
22. WRRD OH 423 374
23. Index of Barnsley Censuses and Directories: E.G. Tasker.
24. Burland, *Op cit*
25. Goodchild, *Op cit* p.104
26. WRRD QD 261 273.
27. JGC.
28. Census for Kexborough Township 1861 and 1881.
29. Dransfield, *History of Penistone* p.129.
30. LBC Ref C3 B15 3.
31. and 32. LBC.
33. Dearnley, *Op cit* pp 88-9.

34. Census for Penistone, 1851.
35. Burland, *Op cit*
36. Dearnley, *Op cit* p.104.
37. Burland, *Op cit*
38. BA Lancaster Sale Books Ref. L1 V 43.
39. *ibid*, A 94 131 3.
40. Goodchild, *Op cit* p.264.
41. *ibid*, p.250.
42. Rowland Jackson, *History of the Town & Township of Barnsley*, BLSL.
43. JGC
44. Burland, *Op cit*
45. Goodchild, *Op cit* p.262.
46. England, *Op cit*
47. Wilkinson, *Worthies of Barnsley*, BLSL.
48. Goodchild, *Op cit* p.251.
49. *ibid*, p.259.
50. Obituary in *Barnsley Chronicle*, 12.9.1886.
51. Goodchild, *Op cit* p.252.
52. Batty & Bradbury, *Gawber in Times Past*, 1988, p.33.

Acknowledgements

I gratefully acknowledge the assistance given to me by the staff at the West Yorkshire Archives, the Archives at Ackworth School and at Bretton College. Staff at the Archives and the Local Studies Library in Barnsley have been particularly helpful in locating relevant sources of information for me. I thank Jill Harrison and Tom Umpleby for drawing my attention to particular sources. Robin Masters and the firm of Bury & Walkers kindly made available materials relating to Redbrook.

I thank John Goodchild for making available documents from his Collection at Wakefield, and for giving me the benefit of his expertise in local history in response to my enquiries on a number of matters.

I thank the editors of *Old West Riding* for permission to use material from my article published in their 1992 edition.

Finally I thank Brian Elliott for his editorial advice during the preparation of this chapter.

3. THE PAPER MILLS OF BARNSLEY AND DISTRICT

by Tanya Schmoller

PAPER-MAKING WAS INTRODUCED INTO the south of England from the Continent just over five hundred years ago — at about the time that Columbus accidentally discovered America. The first recorded mill was started by John Tate in the 1490s just outside Hertford, but perhaps due to competition from imported papers and a shortage of rags, it was almost a hundred years before the industry was established on a more permanent basis. The authority on early paper mills, A.H. Shorter, in his *Paper Making in the British Isles* (David & Charles, Newton Abbot, 1971), tells us that of the forty-one paper mills which existed between 1601 and 1650, twenty-three were within thirty miles of London, with other mills thinly dispersed around the country, the furthest north in England being Old Byland in the North Riding of Yorkshire, though no mills are recorded in the county before 1600. There is no further information about this mill, and I believe the earliest reference to paper-making in Yorkshire occurs in Tickhill in about 1611.

In the Barnsley area the earliest record is of the papermaker at Monk Bretton in 1666/7.

Below: Papermaking Machinery (Rivelin Mill, Sheffield).
Workman operating rollers for finishing paper.

Above: Steam-heated drying cylinders on the main paper making machine.

Below: A 'Hollander' beater.

Most of the mills in the area produced brown paper for wrapping purposes, using among other raw materials old ropes discarded by heavy industries such as collieries, which were treated by washing in benzine and boiling for a couple of days. They were then put in the fresh air and turned as if they were hay. After reboiling and beating, chemicals were added — this information I have from someone who worked for Marsdens in Sheffield who also owned the Barnsley mills. The early mills obviously produced paper made by hand, but the later ones used steam power and large machinery.

Barnsley mills

There were two paper mills in Barnsley, the Old Mill (later known as Dearne Paper Works, No 178) and the Smithies Valley mill (No 466), under a mile to the north of the former, both on the River Dearne.

The Old Mill site is recorded as a flax mill from 1823 to 1847, and according to Wilkinson,[1] writing in the 1880s, 'was of late years converted into a paper mill — now belonging to Barnsley Corporation'. Unfortunately the 1851 census is not very legible, but it seems that the Old Mill was occupied by linen weavers.

William Watson is the papermaker at the Old Mill from 1857 to 1862. The 1861 Census reveals that Watson, who did not live at the Old Mill, employed eight men and nine girls. His son, Wright, aged seventeen at the time, was born in Yearsley. A Paper-Mills directory of 1860 records the production of small hands and grocery papers. A tombstone in St Mary's churchyard is inscribed 'In memory of James Wright Watson, papermaker of this town, late of Horsforth, who died 13 June 1858 aged 50', presumably William's brother. William himself

died in 1862, aged forty-three. By 1861 the Old Mill is the address given by Samuel Partington, aged sixty-one, with Jabez Partington, aged twenty-eight, as manager; Samuel comes from Brestage, Lancs, Jabex his son from Preston, and his children were born in Bury. The Watsons and Partingtons must have overlapped here for a short period. Living with the Partingtons was George Holloway, aged nineteen, from Bolton.

From 1863 to 1867 George Toothill carried on the business, the owner of the building being Mr Russell, and at the end of that year Charles Marsden & Sons (of Rivelin Paper Mills, Sheffield) purchased the mill, which had been destroyed by fire in September 1867, the damage estimated at £4000. The *Independent* of 3 September 1867 reports that the works had been very extensive, making brown paper and generally working day and night. The building destroyed was of four storeys: the flames illuminated the whole country round. The fire was even reported in *The Times*.

As the *Barnsley Chronicle* of 16 September, 1893 tells us in Thomas Marsden's obituary (he was the son of Charles Marsden, and ran the mill):

> *the place was then a scene of desolation, but under the direction mainly of the deceased the waste places were restored, and order was speedily evolved out of chaos. The buildings which had been destroyed were restored in a form better adapted to meet modern requirements, and since then extensive additions have from time to time been made until the works may now be said to be almost new.*

This site, on the River Dearne, was later called the Lower Mill and in the 1890s was extended by building the so-called 'top-side buildings' by the Aire and Calder Navigation Canal.

The obituary also tells us that in 1869, after the Ingbirchworth Waterworks were opened, Thomas Marsden negotiated a fourteen-year lease at £75 a year on their old premises at Smithies, and carried on this business, which gave employment to a large number of hands, both male and female, entirely separately from the firm of Charles Marsden & Sons, who soon afterwards bought the Calder Grove Mills near Wakefield and Alders Mill, Tamworth:

> *The works are now among the largest of the kind in the kingdom. The firm have seven paper mills, with eleven machines in all, engaged in the manufacture of cutlery papers, browns, grocers', news, small hand and glazed casings, &c., the weekly production being over 300 tons.*

The 1881 Barnsley census notes that Thomas Marsden was employing 600 to 700 workmen, which seems on the high side.

Mr Alderman Marsden JP rates many column-inches of obituary notice from which we also learn that he was not even a Yorkshireman, but came of a Roman Catholic family in Derbyshire. His grandfather and namesake taught in the village school at Hathersage. He was born in 1831, received most of his education from his grandfather, and was later brought up by his father Charles, a farmer, who taught him agriculture:

> *Young Thomas could plough and sow, reap and mow, thatch, shear sheep, doctor cattle, and in his own mind guess the weight of beasts for sale or purchase. . .Finding, however, that farming was not a lucrative callling, nor likely to be, Mr Charles Marsden in 1847 took a hand paper mill up the river Rivelin, near Sheffield, where two uncles of his — Matthew and John Ibbotson — had worked, and it was there that young Thomas learnt the whole art and mystery of paper making.*
>
> *He used to be at work with the men at five o' clock in the morning, and mastered every department of the trade — the sorting of rags or ropes, the various stages of manufacturing the paper, finishing it, tying it up, and selling it.*

Thomas Marsden married the daughter of the vicar of Stannington when he was twenty-two, and had no children. His estate was worth £57,000.

There is very scanty information for the early years of the Barnsley mills as records relating to the pre-1930 period have disappeared. A large part of the earliest material was probably destroyed when the mill caught fire in 1913. The estimated damage then was £50,000, and the mill seems to have been plagued by fire. In 1902 G Walton, labourer at the Paper Mill, was committed for trial for incendiarism and sentenced to five years' penal servitude.

A Papermakers' Directory of 1876 lists Dearne Mill as having machines of 72 inches and 100 inches, producing cartridges, fine glazed casings and manilla. In 1884 small hands and best browns are added, while the Smithies works, with two machines of 72 inches and 90 inches, produced shops, white and coloured, royal hands, mill wrappers, &c, later expanded to pink, purple, blue and white shops, and titlers. In 1894 Dearne Mills had three machines, one of 56 inches and two of 80 inches, and 'news' is added to their production. In 1903 Dearne adds super-calendered printings and Smithies starch papers:

> *The Barnsley mill was a typical English mill set in a valley, with a chimney not nearly as high as the summits of the surrounding hills. The mill drew its water. . .from the adjacent Dearne. . .and its fuel*

came from the nearby coal-fields. From the point of view of transport the enterprise was very conveniently situated, as the canal which passed right by the mill stretched as far as Goole, near Hull, and so the mill had its own barge harbour as well as water connection with the sea.

A 1902 Barnsley directory lists George Henry Lingard at the Smithies Paper Works. In 1924, after a meeting of creditors and a petition for winding up at the end of 1923, as reported in *The Times*, the mills passed into the hands of the Dearne Paper Works, which had been established especially for this purpose. Most of the shareholders were Oxford undergraduates, who regarded the mill mainly as a kind of experiment; as they could not raise the purchase price of the mill, it remained in the hands of Marsden's creditors. In 1925 a new entrepeneur appeared on the scene when Charles Diamond founded Yorkshire Paper Mills Ltd, but the shares did not sell well and the management was not sufficiently competent.[2]

The *Eckington Woodhouse & Stavely Express* of 11 July, 1925 reports the acquisition for £64,500, and the valuation of the mills at £223,000, adding that the turnover is £400,000 annually. At the beginning of December it printed a long piece about the possibility of producing artificial silk, but this does not seem to have improved the fortunes of the mill as Star Paper Ltd purchased it in 1931. In 1980 they employed 350 people. A newspaper cutting of the time states that the turnover in 1979 was over £49 million and the production 110,986 tonnes. Profits after depreciation were just over £1 million, while capital expenditure for the year was over £3 million, with emphasis on the modernization of their papermaking facilities at Blackburn and Barnsley mills. However, the outlook for 1980 was less promising, but over the next few years the Company planned to spend over £13 million on a modernization and expansion programme.

Eighteen months later, on 14 August, 1981, the *Barnsley Chronicle* reports the closure of the mill, a month ahead of schedule, 'at the end of the night shift for the 250 remaining workers at the mill'.

The 'mill' here is the Dearne mill, while the 'mills' mentioned in 1924 would seem to include Smithies. However, it is not clear when the latter closed down. It is not mentioned un the 1912 Barnsley directory, and 1932 6-inch O S map shows it as 'disused'.

A Paper-Mills directory of 1852 mentions 'Mill No 48 Thomas Hartley, Putting, Barnsley', but this seems to have been a shortlived enterprise, and not actually in Barnsley, but in Denby Dale, some 11 miles to the west. Information from General Excise Letters records this mill, in the Leeds Collection, in 1830, but by 1834 it has 'left off'.

In 1834 Hartley, described as insolvent, is fined £25 for 'removing Paper with intent to evade the Duty'.[3]

Lewden Paper Mill, Worsbrough Dale

Lewden Mill lay on the River Dove about three miles south-east of Barnsley and is recorded as a paper mill on the 1855 O S six-inch map. It is shown on a Fairbank map of 1792,[4] standing on land belonging to F Edmunds, who holds other plots of land together with John Rhodes.

The name Rhodes, Rodes or Roades is associated with the mill throughout, the earliest reference being to Edward Roades of Monk Bretton, whose will was proved in January 1666/7.[5] In it Edward makes bequests to his sons Jonathan and Francis.

According to Joseph Wilkinson[6] 'the family of Rhodes seems to have been long connected with Worsbrough. One family of that name having been manufacturers of paper in the township for nearly 200 years'. This would take us back to 1672, and may be an exaggeration as a water corn mill called Lewden Mill is recorded in 1690.[7] I can find no records of this paper mill before 1792, other than the names of papermakers.

The Parish Register records that Jonathan Rhodes was buried in 1714, John Rhodes became a father in the same year, Thomas in the 1730s and Jonathan in the 1780s. One John died in 1804 aged 56, while another became a father in 1814, perhaps the same John that appears in the 1806 Staincross Wapentake militia records for Worsbrough as being aged thirty-five, with five children.[8] One Jonathan died in 1790 aged seventy. A Josep [sic], of Highstone, is recorded in 1740. All are papermakers.

Shorter mentions a Thomas Rayner, papermaker, of Wombwell, which is close to Worsbrough Dale, who acted as a surety in 1786 at Pontefract Sessions, but I have found no references to him, nor to James Nutty of Worsbrough, for whom John Rhodes was a surety at the Sheffield Sessions in 1794.[9]

An 1837 Papermakers' Directory allots mill No 167 to John Rhodes. The same entry appears in 1853, while between 1860 and 1867 it is George Rhodes who is producing loom cards and engine boards. An 1822 local directory lists John, and one of 1823 John and George Rhodes, card-paper makers. The 1851 census makes John fifty and George forty, which shows that these two names were passed from father to son or uncle to nephew. This last John died in 1858, aged sixty-two, which does not quite tally.

A Worsbrough valuation of 1840 informs us that the mill was owned by one Martin, and occupied by John Rhodes. The name Martin crops up in relation to nearby Thurlstone. The 1852 British Parliamentary Papers record one beating engine at work.

An even earlier reference is in the 1816 Excise Office list, while the mill is mentioned in General Excise Letters up to 1841 (John and George Rhodes). White's Directory of 1871-2 records Charlotte Rhodes, papermaker, but after that date there is no further reference to the trade, though the mill still appears on the 1907 O S map. In the 1871 census Charlotte, a widow aged forty-one, is described as a farmer of fourteen acres, with no mention of papermaking; she was the wife of George and they had a daughter in 1865. Papermaking may have ceased after George's death in 1868.

It is thought that the clean water supply to the mill from the River Dove would have been lost when the Blacker Brook became contaminated by Barrow Colliery. The Mayor of Barnsley expressed concern about water pollution at a function in 1875.[10]

Monk Bretton Mill

Monk Bretton or Burton Smithies is an area immediately to the north-west of Barnsley, and I am dealing with it separately from Barnsley because the paper mill was in operation at a much earlier date.

Shorter mentions the will of Edward Roades of Monk Bretton[11] which was proved in January 1666/7. In his will Edward Roades bequeaths to his eldest son Jonathon all *'that time and term of years yet to [run] of one paper mill which I have lately taken of John Wood at the Smithies. . .and the said Jonathan to have all the cottons, moulds and other things belonging to the said paper mill'*. There is also a bequest to 'Francis Roade my son'. The witness to the will was a well-known Barnsley attorney, so Edward must have been of some status.[12] The Wood family, whose present head is Lord Halifax, had extensive connections with Monk Bretton since at least the middle of the sixteenth century. George Wood purchased Smithies of the Crown in 1625.[13]

One of the Earl of Halifax papers relating to this area mentions George Wood and a 'Fullinge Milne' in 1613, but alas not a paper mill.[14] George and his brother John are the sons of Robert Wood, and the John Wood named in connection with the paper mill must be of a later generation. An inventory of George Wood of 1693/4, who describes himself as a yeoman, lists 'bundles of paper' to a value of one pound. He occupied a substantial eight-roomed property with a large brewhouse and mill.[15] In 1705, when John Wood occupied the site, a corn mill and paper mill are mentioned in a deed.[16]

The Parish Records, curiously, mention the trade of papermaker at a time when few other trades are mentioned, and record that John

Rhodes of Burton Smithies, paper miller, had a son, Thomas, in 1726, and a daughter three years later, when he is described as a papermaker. A Thomas Rhodes baptized a child in 1746/7 in the Old Church in Sheffield. Leader mentions a Francis Rodes of Burton Smithies in 1762. In 1768 a son and namesake of John Wood is baptized, also of Burton Smithies. All these are described as papermakers. The will, dated 1772, of a woman living in the area includes a legacy to her great-nephew, 'son of Joseph Wood of Ecclesfield, paper maker'. Two marriages of papermakers are recorded: that of Solomon Froy in 1755, in the presence of John Rhodes, and that of James Haigh in 1767.

Towards the end of the eighteenth century it seems that some members of the Roades or Rhodes family commenced or continued papermaking at Lewden Mill in Worsbrough Dale.

Thurlstone Paper Mill

This paper mill is referred to as Moorhollows or Moorhall, and is now the site of the Ecklands Bridge Umbrella Works, on the upper reaches of the River Don, about a mile to the west of Thurlstone. Greenwood's 1817 map of Yorkshire shows Paper House; Old Paper Mill and Paper House are shown on the 1854 six-inch O S map, and some of the mill buildings are still in place.

The *London Gazette* records that a Thomas Martin, papermaker, late of Thurlstone, was in Rothwell Gaol, Pontefract, as a prisoner for debt in 1748. This is surprising as he dedicated a sumptuous gravestone in Penistone churchyard to his son Robert and his wife Mary, who died aged fifty-four in 1759. A local history confirms that he had been in

business as a papermaker in 1755,[17] and nearly a century later one Martin is recorded as owning Lewden paper mill. Thomas Martin is recorded at Wood Mill, and a William Martin at Westwoodside, both in the Leeds Collection in the 1816 Excise List.

A Sun Fire Insurance policy (No 265148) at the end of 1768 tells us that Thomas Harriman and Ann Garton of Brightside, papermakers, insured their property for £500, made up as follows:

Household goods in dwelling house & Paper mill & offices £40
on her wearing apparel £10
on their utensils £260
on their utensils & stock in the dry house £20
Mr Harriman's household goods in his house only called Moorhall near Pennystone £40
his wearing apparel £10
on their utensils & stock in barn adjoining £20
on their papermill only separate timber & tiled £60
two drying houses adjoining each other separate from the mill, thatched £40

Do we scent a romance here? However, Ann Garton married James Creswick in 1770 and remained at Brightside Mill. Indeed, in August of that year there is an advertisement in the *General Evening Post*[18] concerning the reversion of a lease of twenty-one years, fifteen of which are unexpired, of a convenient Paper Mill at Thurlstone consisting of *1 engine, 1 vat, 3 iron presses and a large copper. The engine will employ two vats continuously. Also 26 acres of land. The mill will be employed till let. Late tenant laid out £200 on mill & land. Workmen and every necessary will be upon the place. A constant supply of rags may be had at the old accustomed places, as there is a settled correspondence. Also, if required, every needful instruction will be given of the trade. Inquiries to Ann Garton, at Brightside, nr Sheffield'.* Shorter adds that there was every convenience for making, sizing and finishing paper, and that therefore white paper was made.

The register of the Foundling Hospital at Ackworth records that on 7 August 1769, two apprentices, Nicholas Dart, aged about 12, and John Cheshunt, about 16, were indentured to Thomas Harriman of Moorhallis. It does not mention papermaking.

The 1803 list of papermakers mentions George Brown as a maker in the area, though this mill is not specified. The 1806 Staincross Wapentake Militia records for Thurlstone[19] show him to have been a volunteer, aged twenty-six, with no children. A Thomas Brown, aged twenty-seven, with one child, is also recorded as 'serving by substitute'. In 1810 one Jonathan Woodhouse, who died in 1886 aged ninety, was apprenticed to the firm. A Fairbank field book of 1812 mentions the owners appear to be the executors of Jno Hall.[20] The Parish Register mentions the baptism of Brown's children from 1814 onwards.

George Brown is alloted No 166 in the 1816 Excise List (at Moorhall house) and is recorded until 1835, when he has 'left off'. A Fairbank note of 1824,[21] headed 'Hall of the Ickles, Geo Brown tenant on the place', remarks that there is a shortage of water in the dry seasons, and that Brown will subscribe for two shares if the reservoirs are made above his work. He invoices paper supplied to the Silkstone Colliery in 1834.[22]

George Swinden, who is recorded as a papermaker living at the Paper Mill in 1815, is listed as a farmer in 1840.

In 1860 Paper House Estate in Thurlstone is advertised for sale[23] with a water fall of eighteen feet, weir and goit from river to dam adjoining Paper Mill. The building is described as having been formerly occupied as a paper mill, adding that four springs of spring water could be conveyed to it. The tenant is Jonathan Swinden.

George Brown & Son appear in local directories of 1822 and 1834, and in a papermakers' directory of 1837.

Notes and references

1. Joseph Wilkinson, *Worthies, Families & Celebrities of Barnsley & District* (London & Derby, Bemrose, n.d. [early 1880s].

2. J Ahvenainen, *The History of Star Paper 1875-1960* (1976), Barnsley Archives reference B676.2.

3. *Fourteenth Report of the Commissioners of Inquiry into the Excise Establishment* — information from Robin Clarke.

    Additional references: *Barnsley Chronicle* 30 April 1976, 5 June 1981, 14 August 1981, 22 November 1985, etc.

4. FB 75, p 41.

5. Probate document of Edward Roades, Doncaster D Jan 1666/7, from the Brothwick Institute of Historical Research, University of York.

6. J Wilkinson, *History of Worsbrough*, 1872

7. VWM 369

8. John Goodchild Loan Collection, Wakefield Libraries

9. *Leeds Intelligencer*, 11 April 1786 and 15 September 1794

10. B A Moore, 'The Industries of Worsbrough, A Survey of their Growth and Change between 1850 & 1974' (Barnsley Local Studies Library B 338).

    Additional reference: FB 74.

11. Probate document of Edward Roades, Doncaster D, Jan 1666/7, Borthwick Institute of Historical Research, University of York.

12. Information from Brian Elliott.

13. Joseph Wilkinson, *Worthies, Families & Celebrities of Barnsley & District* (Bemrose, [?1883]), see p 35.
14. LD 3.
15. Courtesy of Brian Elliott.
16. West Yorkshire Archives, Wakefield, A 47 26.
17. *A Further History of Penistone*, Barnsley Local History Library 942.74S.
18. Burney Collection 568b (British Library).
19. John Goodchild Loan Collection, Wakefield Libraries.
20. FB 127, p 28; Parker Collection 909/73.
21. MB 548, p 28.
22. CR 137A (101).
23. Sp S sale 6 August 1860

Acknowledgement

The bulk of this article is taken from my book *Sheffield Papermakers* (1992). I am grateful to the publishers, Allenholm Press of Wylam, Northumberland, for permission to reproduce part of the original text.

CHAS. MARSDEN & SONS,

PAPER MANUFACTURERS,

RIVELIN PAPER MILLS,

SHEFFIELD,

ALSO AT

BARNSLEY AND WAKEFIELD,

Beg to call the attention of

MANUFACTURERS OF CUTLERY and

BRIGHT STEEL GOODS to their

PURE ROPE PAPERS,

made specially for the SHEFFIELD

TRADES.

A large stock of GLAZED AND UNGLAZED ROPE PAPERS always on hand, suitable for CUTLERY, EDGE TOOLS, SAWS, FILES, ELECTRO-PLATE, and for every description of HARDWARE.

94

4. BARNSLEY IN THE TURNPIKE ERA

by John Goodchild

THE WHOLE TOPOGRAPHY OF THE BARNSLEY AREA was to be radically altered in the eighteenth and — particularly — in the nineteenth centuries, by the construction of entirely new lines of road, and the patterns of subsequent housing and transport services, and even of industrial development, have been, in part governed by these same route developments into our own day. In Barnsley itself, Huddersfield Road, Eldon Street, Pontefract Road, Upper Sheffield Road, Peel Street and Dodworth Road were entirely new roads, built as virgin routes during this period, while out in the surrounding countryside, new long stretches of our present main roads were built.

From 1741,[1] the imposition of tolls on older routes was followed by the improvement of these old roads by the obviation of more of their bends and steeper hills, and ultimately by the building of entirely new routes such as the new road from the bottom of Market Hill to Dodworth, or the even more ambitious new road from Redbrook via Cawthorne to Shepley Lane Head, itself part of a system of new roads which linked Barnsley and Wakefield with Saddleworth and Manchester from the 1820s. These turnpike or toll-financed roads linked market town with market town, and market town area with hinterland but that they passed through rural villages was a matter of chance only.[2] Increasingly, however, and especially in the nineteenth century, they came to serve recognisable private gain as well as public good, in that they were in part promoted to improve the private estates through or near to which they passed, by providing them with easier and hence cheaper transport.[3] The toll road system, developing an ever more complex web of routes as time advanced, had always served trade and industry in these ways too, while they came also to serve as feeders to the new canals, the motorway-equivalents of the period, opened locally to Barnsley from Wakefield in 1799 (and on to Cawthorne in c 1802) and from Swinton in 1804. The growing coal industry was able to take advantage of better roads — better in regard to surface, to gradients and to directness — while out to the west of Barnsley, the opening-up for grassland of huge areas of moorland, relied from the early nineteenth century on the canal and road system for the provision of the essential agricultural lime.[4]

Inter-town carrying services were increased; coaching services were more numerous and more speedy; the important Barnsley Market was more easy of access; town shopkeepers, tradesmen and professional men could be more conveniently reached from the surrounding countryside; the village carrier was better accommodated; inns served more travellers – and there were more of both inns and travellers. The improved old roads and the new ones contributed to a generally booming economy and a marked growth of population, but they had to be paid for.

The system of financing road repair, maintenance and later improvement by charging the road user with tolls, had been introduced on a section of the Great North Road in Hertfordshire in 1663; it had proved equitable in removing the burden of repair from those who lived in a township crossed by a main road which was used very largely by travellers from elsewhere, and it had proved financially viable. The system spread, each section of road requiring its own Act of Parliament to allow of the imposition of tolls on the king's highway, and each requiring their powers to be renewed at intervals. The toll-road system reached the West Riding quite late, in 1735, with the authorisation of toll-collection on the mountain road from Rochdale to Halifax and Elland, but in 1741 were passed a spate of Acts which were to turnpike a network of roads in the West Riding including the stretch of the Great North Road between Doncaster (but not Bawtry) to

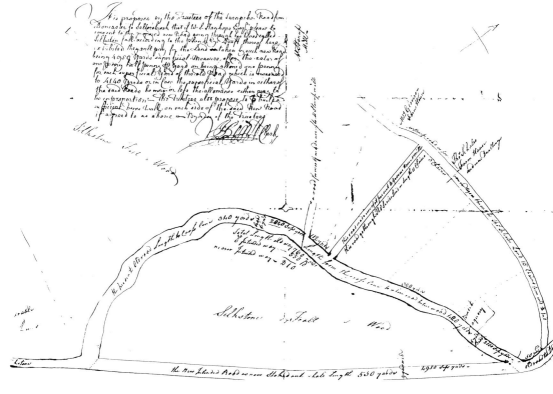

Above: Proposals to alter the line of the turnpike in Silkstone Fall in 1778.

Boroughbridge under two bodies of trustees, and the roads branching east to Tadcaster (for York), Weeland and Selby, and west to Leeds, Bradford and Halifax, to Pontefract and thence Wakefield, to Wakefield from Red House and on to Halifax, and from just north of Doncaster via Barnsley and Penistone to Saltersbrook.[5] At both Halifax and Saltersbrook, the new turnpikes met roads already turnpiked: the road from Manchester to Saltersbrook had been turnpiked under an Act of 1735. The first turnpike into Barnsley was followed by the turnpiking during a further spate of such enactments in a period of further prosperity in the later 1750s, by the Wakefield and Sheffield Act of 1758 and the Barnsley and Grange Moor Act of 1759, the latter concerning the Barnsley to Huddersfield road which connected at Grange Moor with the Wakefield to Austerlands road (and hence on to Huddersfield and Manchester), also authorised in 1759. From 1759 indeed Barnsley was surrounded by toll gates through which only foot passengers could pass free: the gates are shown clearly on Thomas Jefferys' map of Yorkshire, surveyed in 1767-70.

There was a lull in turnpiking roads locally from 1759 until the 1820s, when in a period of national and local boom, for the first time locally entirely new roads were constructed, with the building of new toll roads to Cudworth Bridge (and on to Pontefract), a scheme proposed in 1818 but not then implemented, and the new road via Cawthorne to Shepley Lane Head near Huddersfield, itself part of a new Barnsley and Wakefield to Saddleworth and Manchester road system. Other new roads were proposed, but not built — there was a suggested Dewsbury and Darton scheme — and at this same time major route improvements were made on the Doncaster & Saltersbrook,[6] the Wakefield & Sheffield, the Barnsley & Grange Moor roads — the older Barnsley turnpikes. Indeed, from this decade of the 1820s these older turnpikes were to not only continue the old, piecemeal obviation of hills and bends on their routes, but to build major new sections of highway. As an example, the Wakefield & Sheffield turnpike (now part of the A61) was to ease the hilly entry into the town from the north via Old Mill Lane by the construction of Eldon Street, and from the south the approach over Mount Vernon was eased by the building of a great cutting somewhat to the east of the old line. As it happened, the latter improvement was caught up in the financial difficulties caused to turnpikes by the opening of the new railway route between the West Riding, the Midlands and London, in 1840, and it was not until 1853 that a further special Act of Parliament[7] was obtained to complete and open the new line of road through from Worsbrough Bridge to Mount Vernon Road end, originally authorised by an Act of 1836.

Doncaster and *Salter's-Brook Turnpike.*
TOLLS TO BE LETT.

NOTICE is hereby given, That the next Meeting of the Truftees of and for this Road, is appointed to be at the Houfe of Mrs. Eliz. Roper, the Sign of the White-Bear, in Barnfley, on Wednefday the 28th Day of April, 1784, for the Purpofe of electing new Truftees in the Room of fuch as are dead or removed, or refufe to act; and alfo of letting the Tolls arifing at the feveral Toll-Gates upon the faid Turnpike-Road at SCAUSBY, HARPER-STABLES, ARDSLEY, KERESFORTH-HILL, and BOARDHILL, by Auction, to the beft Bidder, between the Hours of Two and Six in the Afternoon, in the Manner directed in the Act paffed in the 13th Year of the Reign of his prefent Majefty King George the Third, for regulating the Turnpike-Roads; which Tolls were lett for, and produced the laft Year, the feveral Sums following, that is to fay,

SCAUSBY,	£. 38	KERESFORTH-HILL,	£. 90
HARPER-STABLES,	78	BOARD-HILL,	74
ARDSLEY,	218		

above all expences of collecting the fame, and will be put up at the refpective Sums abovementioned, only, as the Toll-Bar in Harper-Stables, which is a Ticket-Bar to both Scaufby and Ardfley, has been difcontinued a Part of the prefent Year, and an Advance of Rent on that Account agreed for, by and with the prefent Farmers of the faid Bars at Scaufby, and Ardfley; the Tolls arifing or liable to be collected at Harper-Stables, will either be put up feparate or jointly, and along with the Tolls arifing at one or both of the faid Toll-Bars at Scaufby and Ardfley, purfuant to Conditions then and there to be produced and fettled.

Whoever happens to be the beft Bidder for, or at all or any of the faid Toll-Gates, or Tolls collected, or liable to be paid and collected at the fame refpectively, muft immediately at the Time and Place aforefaid, pay down as a depofit, in the Hands of the faid Truftees, or their Clerk or Treafurer, one twelfth Part of the Sum for which he fhall be declared the beft Bidder, as the firft Month's Rent in advance, for fuch Tolls fo bid for by him as aforefaid; and alfo give Security with fufficient Sureties, to the Satisfaction of the faid Truftees for the Performance of the Conditions ftipulated, and Payment of the Rent agreed for, and at fuch Times and in fuch Manner as they fhall direct; in Default whereof, the faid Sum fo paid, as the firft Month's Rent, fhall be forfeited, and the Truftees be at Liberty to re-let the fame Tolls, on neglect of fuch Security being given as aforefaid.

BARNSLEY, 23d March, 1784.

Clerk to the faid Truftees.

Above: Tolls to let in 1784.

Yorkshire was to become the most be-turnpiked county in England, and not only did it have the greatest mileage of turnpikes, but in 1838 of the 1,119 independent road-administering turnpike trusts in the country, 118 were in Yorkshire, the next largest number (65) in Lancashire, Sussex had 51, Kent 50, and so forth.[8] The average length of road administered by a trust was 19½ miles, with in the West Riding the Keighley & Kendal the longest and the Wakefield Ings probably the shortest: the roads which centred on or passed through or by Barnsley, ranged in length between some ten and thirty miles.

The documents which illustrate how these Barnsley area roads were promoted, authorised, financed, administered, maintained, improved, used and ultimately disturnpiked, survive in a number of repositories: in no one instance is the documentation complete. In each case what does survive is what each road's lawyer-clerk preserved of his own and his predecessors' road papers, so that for example the present writer's own collection of the papers of Barnsley's first turnpike, the Doncaster & Saltersbrook, is a large one which contains regionally-unique toll books, road surveys and other papers of the eighteenth century, but has no minutes of the road's controlling trustees before the 1830s, and then only in draft form; George Keir (died 1845, aged 73), the able Barnsley lawyer who was its Clerk for many years,[9] retained papers of his own time and of his predecessors, but there are almost none after his clerkship ended and his erstwhile partner took over the office, while for the Barnsley & Grange Moor road, another of George Keir's, only a handful of papers survive at all; for the Barnsley & Pontefract road, very little indeed remains, while for the Barnsley & Shepley Lane Head road there is a set of minute books from 1824 until its end in 1875.[10] So it is from a number of always incomplete collections that this story of the Barnsley main road system derives; at the same time, it must be recollected that the non-turnpike public roads remained the direct responsibility of the individual townships through which they passed – except for those maintained from 1822 by the so-called Barnsley Police Commissioners and later by their successor Barnsley Corporation of 1862, with a subsequently enlarging boundary – until the creation of the new Urban and Rural District Councils under the Act of 1894. There was in fact no regional Highway Board for the Barnsley area under the Acts of 1835 and 1862, although the Board for the Lower Division of Strafforth and Tickhill (which existed from 1863), dealt with the major highways of the townships through which passed the eastern end of the Doncaster & Saltersbrook turnpike; public road administration was by no means wholly in the hands of turnpike trustees.

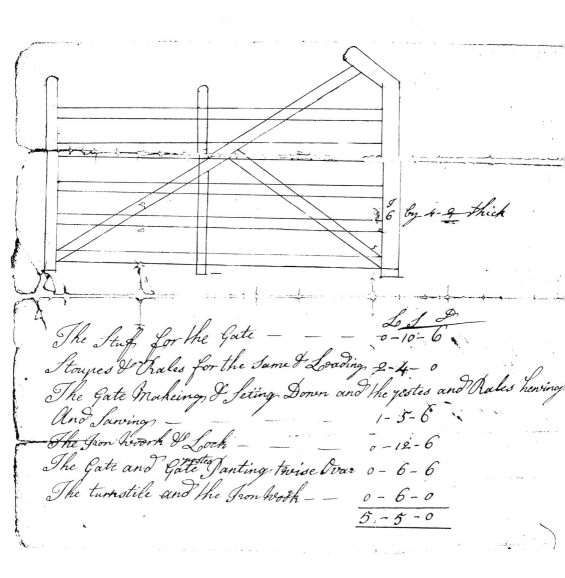

£ s d

The Stuff for the Gate — — — — 0 - 10 - 6

Stoupes & Rales for the Same & Loading 2 - 4 - 0

The Gate Makeing & Seting Down and the pestes and Rales henving
And Sawing — 1 - 5 - 6

The Iron Werork & Lock — — — 0 - 12 - 6

The Gate and Gate posties panting twise Over 0 - 6 - 6

The turnstile and the Iron Work — — 0 - 6 - 0

5 - 5 - 0

Above: An eighteenth century toll gate: Harper Stables Bar.

The creation of an improved highway through the activities of a turnpike trust began necessarily with informal discussions between interested parties who were either personally potential financial beneficiaries, or ratepayers concerned at the cost of current road maintenance, or persons more specifically interested in road betterment as such, often regular travellers. In many cases these interests were combined. The talks which led, for example to the improvement of the Doncaster & Saltersbrook road from 1741 were at an early stage between members of Doncaster Corporation, a body largely composed of tradesmen, and "the people of Barnsley", an unincorporated but busy market town, also dominated by shopkeepers. These talks were initiated in 1734 and at first concerned only the road between the two towns, but Doncaster soon proposed the extension of the improved highway surface which only a turnpike could then bring, up to the Cheshire boundary, to which point Parliament had authorised a toll-financed road from Manchester, with a toll bar at Woodhead where tolls were first collected in 7.1732. The proposals which were ultimately agreed were taken for consideration and support to a meeting of the (then peripatetic) West Riding Quarter Sessions in 1.1735 NS, and a petition to the House of Commons praying for a grant of the necessary toll-taking powers from that court. The petition claimed in standard legal form that the road 'is become so ruinous and out of Repair That Passengers Horses Carts Coaches and Carriages Cannot pass or Travel in the winter and wet seasons without Danger of their Lives', and that only by the imposition of tolls by the authority of Parliament, could the situation be rectified. In the event, the Bill was thrown out by the Commons on a technicality, but it was re-introduced, albeit some years later, when a spate of six turnpiking Bills for roads were approved for the West Riding, and in 1741 the Act was passed, including separate powers for a branch raod from Rotherham to beyond Penistone. The text of the 1741 Act commented upon the convenience of this road for the carriage of goods between the eastern and western seas, and the many heavy vehicles which used them; the Act enpowered a body of 135 named noblemen, gentlemen and clerics — or such of them as qualified themselves — as the responsible trustees for the road.[11]

In essence, this was the process always followed subsequently, although obviously when in the 1820s an entirely new road was to be built, it was the circuitous as well as the decayed state of the current route which was emphasised, and the later Acts also, significantly, included tradesmen, lawyers, doctors in the lists of nominated trustees — a social decline. It is also more easy to trace obvious self-interest in the later road promotions, especially on the part of landowners along the routes proposed.

Borough of Barnsley.

Doncaster Road.

Summary of Traffic taken by George Bell, from July 23rd to July 29th 1891

Date 1891	No. of Foot Passengers	No. of Cabs Wagonettes	No. of Lurries trays &c	No. of Carts	Other Vehicles:
July 23rd	2910	95	106	194	94
" 24th	3310	119	126	183	69
" 25th	2940	109	116	198	152
" 27th	3050	91	112	151	82
" 28th	3170	118	104	159	112
" 29th	3610	124	113	165	85
Total	18,189	656	677	1052	600

Above: A week's traffic in Doncaster Road, Barnsley, in 1891

A couple of books recording the daily traffic through two of the bars on this road survive from the 1760s. At Harper Stables Bar at Goldthorpe, there was overall less traffic passing than the more urban bar at Ardsley, but even at Goldthorpe, Wednesdays, being market day at Barnsley, were busy days.

At Ardsley Bar, most of the road's traffic was local in its origin. Taking the month of 6.1769, of the 1338 single horses passing, only a small part had already passed the Bar at Harper Stables, and of that part, many passed on Wednesdays, when a heavy traffice came to – and from – Barnsley Market. Summer traffic was, interestingly, not necessarily greater than that of winter, and in 12.1769, 1929 horses passed through Ardsley Bar, thirty of them on Christmas Day. A heavy wheeled traffic passed too, largely in vehicles with three or four horses: in 6.1769 this was

Carts with horses				single horses	chaises with		wain with 5 horses	lime carts	chairs
1	2	3	4		2	4			
7	17	321	204	1338	12	4	1	3	6

while the livestock passing was as follows:

beasts	asses	sheep	pigs
32	12	93	267

On one Barnsley Market Day, 7.6.1769, 135 horses and 133 pigs passed through Ardsley Bar, together with twenty three-horsed and twenty-one four-horsed carts.

The Huddersfield Carrier passed through the Bar on eleven occasions in this month, with between three and thirteen horses – presumably in packhorse trains – and the Manchester Carrier nine times, who may have used both a three-horse waggon and packhorses, as on three occasions he paid on one day for both three and eight horses.

There was by the turnpike's earliest days a system wherby passage through multiple numbers of bars was cheapened to a charge less than the aggregate toll for individual gates; there was also provision for the purchase of what would in our own day be described as season tickets.

Constant minor improvements of route were made on the local turnpikes until it was possible by the 1830s for the Doncaster & Saltersbrook trust to describe its road as "the easiest and nearest Line of Communication between Hull, Lincoln, Manchester, and Liverpool",[12] and for the section of road between Wakefield and Barnsley, part of one of the great North to South routes through Britain, to be described in that same decade as "allowed by commercial men, coach proprietors, and in short all that pass on it, to be one of the finest stages betwixt London and Edinburgh".[13]

Major improvements were of course being made by this stage: the new line from the Obelisk to Redbrook was authorised in 1825, the new road to Dodworth was built from 1826 and extended into Barnsley from 1837 as Peel Street, while under powers obtained in 1836, Eldon Street and the new cutting into Worsbrough Dale were being built under contracts made in 1838, and of course entirely new roads were being opened towards Pontefract and to Shepley Lane Head.

It was during this period of major turnpike improvement, that the railways came; huge sums had been raised from Government and/or from individuals for road building, and huge road debts remained to be paid off, as toll incomes sank under railway competition. In 1838, as the first railway to serve Barnsley (the North Midland, with a station named Barnsley opened at Cudworth in 5.1840) was under construction, the Barnsley turnpikes were in this position:

Road	debt		toll income
	mortgage £	total £	
Doncaster & Saltersbrook	4300	4594	1991
Wakefield & Sheffield	14650	19978	4855
Barnsley & Grange Moor	5010	5290	520
Barnsley & Shepley Lane Head		not stated	
Barnsley & Pontefract	7677	8206	632 [14]

Barnsley's first railway station lay at a distance from the town, and it was served by the new Barnsley & Pontefract road; from 1850, however, Barnsley had railways through the town itself, and the turnpikes began to feel the chill wind of local competition: competition for through and long-distance traffic had been experienced already. By 1856 the situation had changed radically from that of 1838:

Road	debt		toll income
	mortgage £	total £	
Doncaster & Saltersbrook	1801	2071	905
Wakefield & Sheffield	11670	12125	2045
Barnsley & Grange Moor	4690	5052	290
Barnsley & Shepley Lane Head	5818	5998	210
Barnsley & Pontefract	4546	4891	583 [15]

In these new circumstances, toll bar leases were less able to calculate likely changes in toll income as both longer and shorter journeys, for both passengers and goods, used rail more frequently. Near towns, of course, as population and industrialisation continued to grow, traffic necessarily increased — some of it indeed to and from the new railway stations. One new road at least, the Dunford District of the Wadsley, Langsett & Sheffield, built under an Act of 1844, actually served a new railway. Under these new situations of increasing railway competition, large-scale toll bar contractors, like the Bowers of Hunslet, took leases of dozens of bars and were able to offset individual losses (made essentially through misjudgement on their part in changing circumstances), through the very size of the business.

The growing railway system meant not only that there was from 1840 a railway route parallel to the Wakefield and Sheffield turnpike, but that from 1845 there was a Sheffield to Manchester line. From 1850 there was a direct line from Barnsley to Wakefield, from 1851 to Doncaster, from 1854 to Sheffield, from 1855 to Penistone (and on to Huddersfield or Manchester), and from 1870 to Cudworth Station. As road toll income dropped, less could be spent on road repairs and more repair money had to come from the township highway rate, while the rates of interest paid to those who had invested themselves or were descended in title from earlier lenders upon mortgage security of the tolls, were lowered. Taking as an example the Barnsley and Shepley Lane Head road, the toll income in 1856 amounted to only some 3½% on the mortgage debt, leaving after interest nothing for repair, administration and redemption of the debt; on the Barnsley & Sheffield and on the Doncaster & Saltersbrook routes in 1856, on the other hand, local traffic remained substantial, so that toll income to mortgage debt was some 17% and 50% respectively. The latter road's substantial investment in improvements and new lines of road had been paid off in considerable part — it was £4300 in 1838, only £1801 in 1856. Some other roads were in an even better situation: the Wakefield and

Austerlands road saw toll income drop form £9924 (the largest in Yorkshire) in 1838 to £6146 in 1856, but the mortgage debt had in that period been reduced from nearly £40,000 to £16,222.[16]

By 1869 the Doncaster & Saltersbrook road still received an annual £975 from toll rents, and its mortgage debt was down to £1601 8 6d: it was able to allow to the townships along its route a total of £535 9 2d towards the cost of its own repair. The trustees of this road memorialised Parliament (via the Home Office) in 4.1869, claiming that to disturnpike their road was inexpedient.[17] But the process of disturnpikement had already begun nationally, and the Barnsley roads were soon to lose their toll bars — the gates going to the (expressed) joy of the local inhabitants. Between 1870 (the Barnsley & Pontefract road) and 1876 (the Wakefield & Sheffield), the turnpike trusts serving Barnsley and its vicinity were wound up; for a period thereafter, the roads became the responsibilty of the townships (or Highway Board districts) through which they passed, until under the powers of the Highways Act of 1878, the West Riding Quarter Sessions, as the County authority, began to adopt sections of main road.

In effect, the turnpike system had collapsed through the weakness of its less able parts; the three weaker Barnsley turnpikes had their counterparts eleswhere, and Mortimer's Road from Penistone had ceased to be worked as a turnpike even in the eighteenth century, as was to happen to some other Yorkshire roads. Even in pre-railway times, in 1838, the Meltham & Wessenden Head road had made only £28 13 5d from its tolls and the Bradford & Thornton only £8 0 1d, while on the other hand a hugely expensive and ambitious road, the Leeds & Whitehall (near Halifax) had a building debt of nearly £82,000 and a toll income which even then only amounted to 4%, while the mountainous Lees & Hebden Bridge road had a construction debt of over £20,000, and a toll income of just over 1% of that sum.[18]

The toll road system had however for some century and a half (the last West Riding road was disturnpiked only in 1890) succeeded in repairing and improving older road routes and building many new ones. Indeed, it established a pattern of highways which is essentially that which we use today. The effects of the turnpike system upon Barnsley is still very clearly to be seen.

NOTES AND REFERENCES

*1 Goodchild John, *West Riding Turnpike Trusts*, A List; Wakefield, 1961, passim. The first West Riding Turnpike Act was passed in 1735

*2 Teesdale H & Co, Map of Yorkshire, corrected in 1827 and 1828

3   eg John Goodchild Collection (hereafter WAG), Minutes and papers of Wakefield & Denby Dale Trust

4   WAG, Barnsley Canal Co MSS

*5   Goodchild John, West Riding Turnpike Trusts, *op cit, passim*

6   *WAG, Doncaster & Saltersbrook Trust MSS*

*7   *WAG, copy of Act*

*8   *House of Commons Papers, Turnpike Trusts, 289,1840, passim*

9   *WAG, George Keir MSS*

10   *West Yorkshire Archives, Barnsley & Shepley Lane Head Trust MSS*

*11   Goodchild John, The Early Years of Doncaster & Saltersbrook Trust, in *South Yorkshire Journal*, part 1 1969, part 2 1970

12   As 6

13   WAG, William Aldam MSS

14   As 8

*15   House of Commons papers, Turnpike Trusts, 1857, passim

16   As 8 and 15

17   As 6

18   As 8

* = copies penes John Goodchild

5. DAN RYLANDS : TRAGIC GENIUS OF THE BARNSLEY GLASS INDUSTRY

by Denis Ashurst

ON THE 11TH SEPTEMBER, 1886, the Hope Glassworks (Figure 1) at Stairfoot, Barnsley, which employed over a thousand men and boys, went on total strike in a dispute over working hours. On Monday, 20th September, Dan Rylands, the owner, sued James Lindley, one of his glass-workers, for the sum of 8s 2d (41p) in the Barnsley Magistrates' Court.[1] Reckoned as Lindley's share of the losses suffered by Rylands during the strike, the amount included:

2s 2d (11p) to fuel costs keeping furnace running

6d (21p) to wages maintaining furnace

71d (3p) to wear and tear on furnace

21d (1p) to management fixed charges

2s 21d (121p) to apprentice wages

2s 6d (121p) loss of production, five gross of bottles

The total actually comes to 8s 21d but the odd 1d appears to have been overlooked.

As a glass bottle-maker this represented an average day's pay for Lindley yet seems a small sum to have caused a major strike at one of the nation's largest bottle works, threaten the loss of hundreds of jobs and put at risk the great advances in bottle production being developed

Below: Figure 1: Hope Glass Works, Stairfoot.

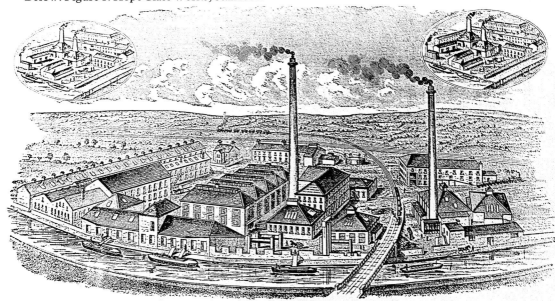

HOPE GLASS WORKS, BARNSLEY.

by Dan Rylands. After a lifetime in the industry he had become one of the most innovative glass manufacturers of the period. The case offers a unique insight into the working conditions in a glassworks at what was, perhaps, the most vibrant period of the industry. It illustrates the dilemma of the owner seeking expansion and the glassworker fighting erosion of his position as a craftsman.

His father Ben Rylands had helped set up the Mexborough Flint Glassworks in 1849 which later became the Don Works. He left there in 1852 with two of the partners, John Tillotson and Joseph Wilkinson, to start a new works at Swinton which became the South Yorkshire Glass Company. In 1867 he left Swinton to Fig.1. Hope Glassworks - Stairfoot, Barnsley build his own works alongside the canal at Stairfoot, near Barnsley, which he called the "Hope Glassworks".[2] His son Dan was seventeen at the time and already well-versed in the business of running a glassworks so that, on the death of his father in 1881, Dan took over the works as an ambitious, but knowledgeable, glass manufacturer.

During the next ten years he was to become the owner of ninety-four British and Foreign patents relating to the glass industry. He was also to have constant problems with the glassworkers, disliking Unions to the extent that he paid members of the Yorkshire Glass Bottle Makers Association one shilling a week less than non-members.

James Lindley had been accepted by the Court as the test case in the dispute amongst the eighty-six who were sued for sums ranging from 6s to 10s (30p to 50p) and embodied the discord which had developed between men and management in the nation's bottle glasshouses. The outcome of the case was to have an effect on labour relations far in excess of the sums involved and be a part of the glassworks owners' collective resolve to destroy the traditional independence of the glassworker in the industry by the aggressive introduction of machinery.

To understand how the situation had reached such a pitch it is necessary to look back two hundred years and examine the development of the role of the man actually working at the furnace and his relationship to the owner who paid for his labour.

Glassmaking was first introduced to South Yorkshire by Sir Robert Mansell who had been permitted by the Earl of Strafford to build a glass furnace making window glass at Wentworth Green in 1631 near his mansion at Wentworth Woodhouse. It was a short-lived venture as the Earl was beheaded on Tower Hill in 1641 for his associations with King Charles I. Francis Bristow, his glassmaker, was imprisoned in 1642 for not paying his dues to Mansell who owned the national rights to make glass.[3]

About 1650, John and Peter Pilmay, descendants of sixteenth century Huegenot immigrant glassmakers, arrived in Silkstone from a Manchester glassworks and built two furnaces near the site of the Silkstone mill. The works prospered, making a wide variety of glass - window, tableware and bottles. After their deaths the business was carried on by John Pilmay's widow Abigail and, after her death, by John Scot, her son from an earlier marriage, until it closed early in the eighteenth century.[4]

All the early glassworks such as Silkstone were small concerns employing two or three glassworkers whose wages were commonly based on the traditional method of paying a third of the value of an agreed quantity of glass produced. Although it seemed a simple enough way to calculate wages, the tradition was already causing problems in the sixteenth century and was soon abandoned as glassworks became larger and more complex.

There were two basic difficulties within any system of payment which could never be resolved; one related to the design of the furnace, the other to the organisation of the men working at the furnace.

Seventeenth century glassworks such as Wentworth and Silkstone were simple structures consisting of a brick dome over a coal-fired hearth. The glass was melted in crucibles (usually referred to as 'pots') of fire-resistant clay, standing beside the hearth. Air was pulled through tunnels under the hearth passing through the coal fire around the pots and out through holes in the brick dome. Molten glass was gathered through these holes on a blowing iron or a gathering rod.

These early furnaces would generally have four crucibles each holding from 100-200kg (2-4 cwt) of glass which had to be worked out immediately it was ready. Unfortunately the precise timing of when the glass was sufficiently fluid and free from bubbles could never be exactly forecast. Depending on the crucible this could take from a few hours to three days. Problems could also arise from the crucible itself - if it cracked, the furnace had to be partly dismantled, the crucible removed and replaced so that the glass founder could start afresh. The glassworkers could do nothing but stay at home until the founder had done his job, then be called to the glasshouse to begin work.

In a small works in a small village as at Silkstone the situation was no doubt frustrating but not insuperable where the owners worked alongside the men in what was a cottage industry. However, a major advance in glass technology in the eighteenth century made large-scale glass production possible and in turn led to a lasting division of capital (management) and labour. It enforced the introduction of a complex payment system yet the old problem of furnace unreliability remained.

The new style glassworks became known as the 'English' glasshouse and can be instantly recognised by its huge brick cone (Figure 2). The actual furnace and the way it operated barely changed - crucibles still stood around the coal-fired hearth under a brick dome through which the glass was gathered, but the whole structure was contained within the brick cone standing to an average height of about 31m (100ft). The glassmen worked in the hot smokey atmosphere within the cone and, by use of the doors around the base, could direct air either into the cone area or through the tunnels to control the heat of the furnace. Of the hundreds that were built in the eighteenth century only four have survived as monuments to this period when British glassmaking was approaching world dominance. South Yorkshire is fortunate to have such a brick cone at Catcliffe, near Rotherham, built in the 1740s, though its internal furnace was demolished in the 1930s and is now concreted over (Figure 3). The cone is protected as an ancient monument by Sheffield Corporation.

Below: Figure 2: Cross-section of a Cone Furnace.

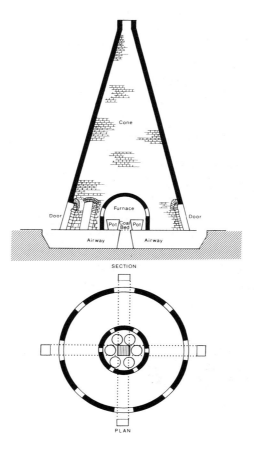

Above: Figure 3: Brick Cone at Catcliffe.

A similar cone had stood at Gawber, near Barnsley, built by William Thorpe of Glass Houghton in 1723. It set the scene for Barnsley's future as a glass-making centre by concentrating on bottle production, mainly wine but also apothecary bottles, achieving national recognition as noted in the Universal British Directory of 1790 which stated, 'A Glass manufactory of black bottles is also carried on near this town [Barnsley] superior to any of the kind elsewhere.' The cone was removed in 1824 when the works closed and nothing remains above ground though archaeological investigation in the 1960s revealed the construction of the actual furnace.[5] The economic demand for works which specialised in bottle production on a large scale originated from a change in the nation's drinking habits in the middle of the seventeenth century. Wines and beers had previously been stored in casks in the cellar then served at table in stone bottles but by the early 1650 s these had been replaced by the new glass bottles. As spa and mineral waters also became widely popular in the eighteenth century, demand for glass bottles grew beyond the capacity of the small cottage industry and the new industry emerged.

The cone glassworks commonly held eight crucibles, though twelve was not unusual, each containing about a ton of glass.

However, the organisation of working the furnace remained unchanged and became formalised into a 'tradition' which glassworkers absolutely refused to modify. The age-old problem with crucibles had never been solved; men turned up for work at 3.0 am on Monday morning with no guarantee that the glass would be ready to work or that it would stay in good condition during the week. If not ready or became unusable, they had to go home and wait to be called, so losing wages. At the time of the 1886 strike, Rylands were operating two shifts of 101 hours, but could vary from 71 to 11 in other works, so giving a period between shifts when the pots could be recharged with fresh raw materials. The week's production ended at 1.0 pm on Saturday to allow for pot changes and repairs over the weekend.

Towards the end of the nineteenth century the coal-fired cone furnace went out of favour as the Siemens tank furnace was generally adopted in glassworks (Figure 4). It aimed to solve the problem by making glass continuously available. Raw materials went in at one end and the molten glass flowed to the other end where the workers could gather through holes in a dome end as before. In solving one problem, the invention created another. The tank had to be continuously heated whether worked or not and, being gas- fired, this greatly increased the capital outlay to the owner who would prefer round-the-clock production. The glassworkers resisted.

From the men's point of view, however, their industrial power to

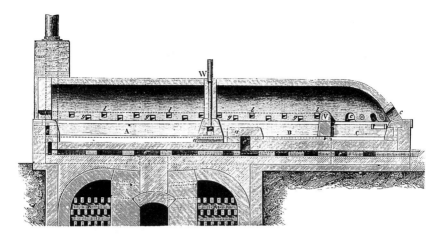

Above: Figure 4: Siemans Tank Furnace.

enforce an acceptable solution was not helped by a serious division between them which emerged in the eighteenth century. Early glassworks such as Silkstone had made all varieties of glass but a division was formulated in a clause of the Act imposing a glass tax in 1745 which prohibited glasshouses that made "ordinary" glass from also making "flint" glass, and vice versa.[6]

The difference lay in the composition of the glass. For "ordinary" glass such as windows, bottles, cheap tableware etc. the ingredients were a simple mix that had been used since the discovery of glass in Western Asia five thousand years ago:- white sand (the brown sand usually found on beaches contains contains too much iron); an alkali such as soda (sodium carbonate) or potash (potassium carbonate) which reduced the melting point of the sand from 1700C to about 1100C within the range of a wood or coal furnace; lime to act as a stabiliser in the finished glass. The proportions could be varied and colouring agents added such as cobalt oxide to make blue glass but the basic composition was always sand/alkali/lime.

In the 1670s George Ravenscroft had developed a new type of glass to emulate the Venetian 'cristallo' for fine tableware and decorative glass. Originally he used crushed flint instead of sand with the alkali and lime but added a percentage of lead oxide (red lead).[7] This produced a heavy sparkling glass, still used today, which could be cut to give highly reflective surfaces and was ideal for chandeliers, decanters, wine glasses etc. To distinguish it from 'ordinary' it was called 'flint' glass and, although sand soon replaced flint as the basic material, the name stuck. It is now usually referred to as 'crystal' or 'lead crystal' but the original name 'flint' still persists and all refer to the same type of lead glass. Again, the proportions could vary from 1% to 50% lead oxide, with or without colouring, but the distinction is always clear between "ordinary" soda/lime glass and "flint" lead glass.

The main effect of this division for the glassworkers was to create an aristocracy amongst them whereby the 'flint' glassworkers saw themselves as superior to the 'ordinary' glassworkers.[8] Their argument was that, for example, a higher level of skill was required to make a delicate three part wine glass in lead crystal than blowing a simple bottle in ordinary glass. They always negotiated higher pay scales and eventually formed their own Union, The Yorkshire Flint Glass Makers Association, failing to help the ordinary bottle makers when disputes arose excepting the major lock-out of 1893 which all the South and West Yorkshire owners joined other than Dobson & Nalls at Barnsley who refused to lock the men out.[9]

The glassworks founded at Worsbrough, near Barnsley, about 1830 by partners Usherwood, Cartwright, Barron and Perkes, which became Wood Brothers' works in 1834 was a 'flint' works. In 1872 it moved to Hoyle Mill in Barnsley and continued in the flint glass tradition, particularly in the production of chemical glassware, until closure in 1981. It achieved high standards of craftsmanship in flint glass but played no part in the early problems besetting the Barnsley bottle glassworks such as Rylands.

No doubt the other main bottle glassworks owners operating in Barnsley at the time of the 1886 dispute (Sutcliffe at Oaks, Redfearns at Old Mill, Dobson & Nalls in Hoyle Mill) took a close interest in the outcome but were not called to give evidence even though their system of payment, which was at the root of Dan Rylands' problem, was identical.

The glassmaker and his team were no longer glass craftsmen in the old sense but regarded more as a human machine able to make a particular product at a certain rate. Wages were calculated in a bottle works according to a formula which had its origins in the cone glassworks when the greater number of crucibles being worked and the drive for increased production enforced a division of labour to create a team, usually called a 'chair' or 'set', in which each member performed a specific task.

The interior of an eighteenth century cone glassorks at Aston, Birmingham, is shown in Figure 5. It is typical of all such works and illustrates the various activities of the members of the 'chairs' working at the holes around the furnace.

Each chair had a hole through which the 'gatherer' removed the

Above: Figure 5: Interior of an eighteenth century glassworks, (Aston, nr Birmingham).

required quantity of glass from the crucible on a blowing iron, a hollow tube about two metres long. A gatherer is seen at the middle hole of the furnace in the etching.

He passed it to the 'blower' who placed the parison of glass into a brass or iron mould, damped with graphite, and blew the bottle shape. Alternatively, for plain bottles, he could blow it free as seen by the blower on the right. It was then passed to the leader of the set, referred to as the 'gaffer' who sat in a special 'gaffer's chair' with wooden arms along which he could roll the blowing iron whilst finishing off the bottle. Empty chairs are seen arranged round the furnace and in the middle a gaffer is finishing a small bottle.

The 'wetter-off' standing by the gaffer is attaching a solid iron rod, the pontil, to the base of the bottle using a small blob of molten glass. The blowing iron would then be removed by adding a drop of cold water to its end and giving it a sharp tap. The gaffer could now finish off the bottle mouth where the blowing iron had been.

When the bottle was finished and the pontil in turn was snapped off, again using a drop of water and a sharp tap, it left a rough mark on the base referred to as a pontil or punty mark. In later works where bottles were made entirely in moulds and handled with tongs, the process left no pontil mark. After the wetter-off had removed the pontil from the finished bottle he passed it to the 'taker-in' (usually a young apprentice as seen in the foreground) who carried the bottle, still too hot to handle, on a rod to the 'Lehr'.[10]

All blowing irons and pontil rods had to be kept hot and the apprentices had to remove waste glass by plunging them into a trough of cold water, seen on the right, then placing them in the furnace mouth to be immediately ready for the gatherer. A number can be seen resting in the spare gathering holes.

Typical standard wages for the week in 1886 were; gaffer 30s [£1.50], blower 28s [£1.40], gatherer 23s [£1.15], wetter-off 9s [45p] and taker-in 8s [40p]. The wetter-off and taker-in were often apprentices. Rylands employed 102 and, although the indenture forced the glassworks owner to find them work, they were often sacked at the end of the apprenticeship to avoid having to pay them full wages.

A day's work was called a journey and the men had to attend for five journeys in a week at hours fixed by the owner between 3.0 am Monday and 1.30 pm Saturday. At an eighteen pot furnace there would be ninety men and boys working around it at any one time plus a number of boys cleaning up. When their journey finished the next set would take over the holes. However, it had long been accepted by men and owners that some articles were more difficult to make than others and, by taking longer, then a 'chair' would make fewer. To overcome this a system had evolved called 'moves' whereby it was agreed beforehand between men and owner how many of a particular article could be made within a certain time. At Rylands the normal journey was 111 hours (including 1 hour for dinner) and it was generally accepted that a set could make 67 dozen 'ordinary' bottles a journey but only 57 dozen 'patent' bottles.

If the set only made one type of bottle then the journey equalled the move but if they had to make different kinds of bottle during a journey then a 'move' was calculated for each type to allow for the different rates of production of each. This was particularly common at a works such as Wood Brothers where a day's journey might consist of short moves making, for example, beakers, decanters and wine glasses. It was less common at a specialist bottle works such as Rylands but one journey could still include a mixed production of 'ordinary' and 'patent' bottles each within an agreed 'move'.

However, calculation of the actual 'take home' pay was further complicated by the fact that a set could, in reality, make more than the agreed number in the available time and any additional bottles were paid to the set at a different rate. This meant that it was not unusual at Rylands for a set to increase their week's earnings by 6s-8s [30p-40p] each and often up to 10s [50p]. It is little wonder that Alec Clark, owner of Beatson Clark at Rotherham, confessed in 1980 that in his early days it took considerable time to calculate his men's wages - 'It became quite involved'.[11]

It must be emphasised that the actual time the men could work at the furnace was fixed by the owner and working longer, that is *overtime*, was not permitted. The additional earnings for producing more than the agreed 'move' was called *overpay* or *overwork*. Clearly this was a constant source of friction built into the system as the men always sought a small number as the standard move to allow more time for overwork, whereas the owner tried to increase it to reduce overwork, this being a higher rate of pay.

From the evidence given to the Court by the glassworkers in the 1886 dispute it was clear they were able, given a good furnace, to make the required 57 dozen 'patent' bottles within seven hours in 1886 leaving three hours for overwork. John James, a bottle maker from Bar House, Hunningley, who had spent 23 years at various glassworks in Lancashire, Gloucestershire and Yorkshire complained that, '... scarcely a week passes but one or two holes of the furnace have bad metal ... they put up a stopper and wait an hour or so ... if it doesn't work they give over for the shift.' John Lindley of Dearne Terrace, Stairfoot, said he '... had the good fortune to work at a very good hole...' and in 1884 he had to make 52 dozen of 'patent' bottles a journey but made 25 dozen a week extra at 5d [2p] a dozen.[12]

Much of the arguement revolved round the question of how many 'patent' bottles could be made, particularly after William Bagley, owner of the Knottingley glassworks, claimed his men could easily produce on average 84 dozen bottles and even up to 97 dozen. Proceedings were disrupted with cries of disgust and disapproval from the Rylands men in the Courtroom. The lawyers for Rylands men complained that this was for 'ordinary' soda water bottles whereas the Rylands glassworkers were producing 'patent' bottles.

They were referring to the so-called 'Codd' bottle which became the foundation of the Rylands fortune and which swept the world in its popularity (Figure 6). Hope Glassworks was the largest producer of "Codds" in Europe and, together with those produced under licence by the other Barnsley glassworks, they were exported in vast quantities to Australia, New Zealand, South Africa, South America and India.[13]

Its inventor was Hiram Codd, a Soda Water Manufacturer in Islington, London. Born in 1838, he registered his first patent (3070) in 1870 for a mineral water bottle which was sealed by a glass marble.[14] The need

Above: Figure 6: Codd mineral water bottle.

for such a seal had been apparent since the mid-eighteenth century when spa mineral and aerated waters became popular. The Gawber works had specialised in spa water bottles particularly for the water from Bad Piermont in Germany, but the only seal available was a wooden stopper wired onto the string rim, a rib of glass applied to the neck. Such a seal could not retain the pressure of aerated waters which would consequently rapidly go flat.

The Codd bottle overcame this by having a glass marble inside the bottle which was forced upwards by the pressure of the gas in the mineral water onto a rubber ring fitted inside the top of the neck. Codd improved the design in a new patent (2212) in 1871 which had a constriction at the base of the bottle neck to prevent the glass ball falling to the bottom of the bottle. However, the ball could still roll into the mouth of the bottle when pouring and Codd patented a further improvement (2621) in 1872 which included grooves on the side of the neck into which the ball fell when forced off its rubber seating and held it when pouring. This became the 'Codd Proper' or 'No.4' as the standard design for all future bottles of this kind though minor improvements continued over the years.

The marble itself was a minor masterpiece. Cast perfectly round in moulds and any rough surfaces filed smooth by hand, they had a slightly higher melting point than the bottle glass. This was to prevent the marble sticking to the soft glass of the bottle when it was dropped in during manufacture and before the final shaping of the mouth. If a marble did stick, the bottle was rejected as 'flown' for which the men received no pay. The marbles had originally been made for Codd in London but from 1895 were supplied by the Manor Flint Works adjacent to Rylands at Stairfoot.

Apart from the enormous advantage of keeping the contents sparkling fresh, it also proved possible to fill the bottle at a vastly improved rate over the old cork and wire method. Although, almost inevitably, Rylands led the field in the development of bottle-filling machinery, others such as Sutcliffe at the Oaks Glassworks were also endeavouring to find a niche in the growing market. A *Barnsley Chronicle* report of 24 July 1875 stated that, 'Mr T.Sutcliffe, owner of the Oaks Glass Works ... has succeeded in inventing a glass stopper which will do away with the necessity for corking and wiring.' It was a variant of the Codd bottle but the main interest at the demonstration was the speed with which another machine developed by Sutcliffe could fill the bottle. He claimed 70-80 dozen bottles an hour which was more than double that achieved by the 'string and cork' method.

Such machines achieved these speeds by filling the bottle upside down so that, when full, the glass marble fell down into the bottle mouth by gravity and the pressure generated by the mineral water held it firm against the rubber ring when the bottle was returned upright.

The Codd bottle had been an instant success when Hiram Codd launched it in 1870 and by 1873 over twenty licences had been granted to bottle manufacturers amongst whom was Ben Rylands at the Hope works, granted in 1874. By 1877 over four hundred licences had been approved when Hiram Codd and Ben Rylands went into partnership to further the invention under the name of 'Rylands & Codd', with Rylands having four-fifths of the investment. When Ben died in 1881, his son Dan bought into a renewal of the partnership but apparently not without some difficulty, perhaps reflected in the change of its name to 'Codd & Rylands'.

Unlike that of his father, the relationship between Dan Rylands and Hiram Codd was always uneasy despite joint patents for improvements in 1882. The partnership dissolved in 1884 with some hint of bitterness which came to the surface in Court action brought by Codd against Dan Rylands for patent infringement of the tool used to make the internal groove for the rubber ring.

Rylands lost the case so he immediately invented and patented an alternative. All Codd's patents had expired by 1886 and many manufacturers brought out variations but by then the Hope Works of Dan Rylands reigned supreme as the largest manufacturer of Codd-type mineral water bottles in the world as his inventiveness kept him ahead of the competition. In the four years after he had bought out Codd at the dissolution in 1884 Dan Rylands had increased production by 66% and more than doubled the size of the works. In 1885 he designed a machine to automatically feed glass to a bottle machine so dispensing with the need for a gatherer; in 1899 he made an automatic bottle making machine which produced six 'ordinary' bottles a minute. His range of invention knew no bounds and, as an owner constantly looking to increased profits, anything which reduced labour costs was to be considered.

This was, perhaps, the true tragedy behind the Court case of 1866 to which we now return. The lawyers acting for the men implied Dan Rylands was trying to reduce their wages and increase his profit, whereas he claimed his actions to be in the men's best interests.

On the morning of Thursday, 9th September, 1886, a tank furnace was found to be cracked and dangerous to work. Dan Rylands and his manager decided it had to be closed down to cool and be repaired. He pinned up a notice to tell the men normally working those holes to transfer to the another furnace where work for both sets of men would be at three shifts of 71 hours instead of two shifts of 101 hours. 'Mr Rylands desire was not to dismiss his hands ... he wished to retain his hands that they should not be scattered over the country ... he wished to find them work and a reasonable opportunity of earning money during the time the furnace was out for repairs.'[15]

He considered this allowed each set or 'chair' to work five journeys of seven working hours, enough to complete the move of 57 dozen

Codd bottles a day with time left to make overpay. The men immediately sought an interview with Rylands when they stated their case - they did not object to only working the seven hours; they did not object to the times they were to commence work; they flatly refused to work three shifts and made it plain their only acceptable solution was for Rylands to sack one third of the men so that the remainder could work normally. Rylands refused to sack anybody and the men were called out on strike by the Union on Saturday 11th September for the case to be brought to Court. Joseph Taylor, bottle-maker from Stairfoot, when asked if it was not better for three shifts to share the work, told the Court, 'No, there would be a living for no one it they worked three shifts ... it would be better for the two-thirds at work.' He was then asked about the other third, "They had better play16 than be at the glass works earning nothing .. It would be better to be at home looking at my wife.'

The Barnsley Magistrates, F.H.Taylor, R.Inns and E.Lancaster delivered their verdict on Monday, 28 September, 1886; 'They were not quite unanimous ... but were agreed on this - Mr Rylands only gave short notice ... It had been agreed they thought that one week's notice should have been given on either side ... as Mr Rylands did not give a clear seven day's notice, they were compelled to dismiss the case.'[17]

The immediate effect on Dan Rylands after losing the case is unknown but three shifts were eventually adopted only to be stopped again by the men's Union in 1890. However, in 1888 he restructured the business and formed it into a Limited Company of which he became Managing Director. He received £136,000 for the property and £66,000 in shares. In 1889 new capital was raised to increase production further by installation of automatic bottle-making machines but an eighteen week strike over wages and growing personal financial difficulties led to him resigning in 1892 at the age of forty-three.

He would seem to have become thoroughly disillusioned with the glass industry and, after his selling out in 1888, had turned to mining speculations. They proved to be disastrous ventures and in 1893 he was declared bankrupt to the extent of £300,000 liabilities and in July made his first suicide attempt when he was found at his home at Shepcote House in Ardsley with his throat cut. Prompt attention by the local doctors saved him but the immense pressures under which he had built up the Hope Works in the ten years after taking over from his father, the constant outpourings of his inventiveness and the disruptive labour problems had taken their toll on his mind. 'He suffered with his head.'[18]

Following a brief period as a colliery agent in Southall he became increasingly eccentric even to the point of confessing to bigamy in 1908 for which there was no evidence. He was admitted to Horton Asylum in Epsom in 1909 and, after discharge in 1910, went to live in Battersea, London, with his sister, a Mrs Wilkinson. Unfortunately she was a manic depressive with an obsession for cleanliness who tried to strangle herself and he agreed to commit her to the Bethlehem Hospital (asylum). On the day in April, 1910, when he was to sign her commital, the hospital staff were unable to enter the house. After breaking in they found Dan Rylands dead in the bathroom after having cut his throat with his razor. He was sixty years old. In declaring his verdict of 'suicide during temporary insanity' the Coroner criticised the situation where two such mentally ill persons had been allowed to live alone together.[19]

He was never to know the fate of his beloved Codd bottle which had brought him fame and fortune but by 1920 it had become clear to bottle manufacturers that, despite all attempts, a machine capable of automatic production of its complex shape would never be possible. Bottles with screw tops and crown corks were relatively simple to make in a totally automatic process capable of previously unimagined rates of production which dispensed with the entire chair of skilled glassworkers. Even the earliest of automatic machines introduced after Ryland's retirement such as the Owen was capable of almost unattended production at 2500 bottles and hour, compared to the hopeful 100 of a 'chair'.

However, the general trading difficulties experienced by the nation's glass industry in the 1920s brought about its virtual collapse. Machinery capable of producing millions of bottles a day compared to the hundreds of the old 'chair' system saturated a market already under serious threat from foreign competition bringing a rapid decline in the national industry.

Of the once great Barnsley industry which had employed thousands and founded its wealth on bottles and jars only one survived, the Old Mill Glassworks. In 1862 the brothers Joshua and Samuel Redfearn had taken over a small works set up by James Wragg in 1861 on the banks of the canal and built it into a major works which moved to Monk Bretton in 1946 after the collapse of its canal link. Although no longer a family firm it thrives today as PLM Redfearn Ltd.[20]

The old Rylands works at Stairfoot was less fortunate. With hindsight, a major error of judgement was made in concentrating its major manufacturing base almost totally on Codd bottle production and when the market suddenly failed in the 1920s the works could not adapt. It tried to expand into engineering and packing-case manufacture but finally closed in 1928. Beatson Clark of Rotherham bought the empty site in 1929 to build a new factory which still preserves the connection of glassmaking and Stairfoot.[21]

The solid achievements of the Barnsley glass industry over three and a half centuries of glassmaking should be seen as an important contribution to the national scene, though still often not fully recognised. Its trials and tribulations, its technical innovations and the prosperity it engendered are too readily forgotten. It is perhaps sad that an insight to the hopes and fears of both men and owners as the local industry grew to its national eminence can now only be gained from such rare glimspes as when Dan Rylands, who ultimately gave his life to the industry, was brought to Court in 1886 because a furnace cracked.

Notes and References

1. "Strike at Mr Dan Rylands works", *Barnsley Chronicle*, 25 September 1886 and 2 October 1886.
2. Ashurst,D., *The History of South Yorkshire Glass*, (1992), Sheffield University, 73/74.
3. Godfrey,E.S., *The Development of English Glassmaking 1560-1640*, (1975) Oxford. Also Sheffield Archives, Straff.MS 21/69 and 20/30.
4. Ashurst,D., "The Silkstone Glasshouses", *Old West Riding*, Vol.12, (1992), 15-19.
5. Ashurst,D., "Excavations at Gawber Glasshouse", *Journal of Post-Medieval Archaeology*, Vol.4 (1970), 92-140
6. Thirteenth Report of the Commissioners of Excise: Inquiry into the Excise Establishment and into the Management and Collection of the Excise Revenue Throughout the United Kingdom – Glass (1835).
7. Charleston,R.J., *English Glass* (1984) Allen & Unwin, 113-115.
8. Detailed review of the growth and effect of the often bitter divisions between 'flint' and 'ordinary' glassworkers throughout the national industry in Matsumura,T, *The Labour Aristocracy Revisited*, (1983) Manchester U.P.
9. Comprehensive survey of the formation of workers' and owners' Unions in Brundage,D., *The Glass Bottle Makers of Yorkshire and the Lock-out of 1893*, unpublished M.A. thesis, Warwick University, (1976).
   I am grateful to Mr.L.Thorp for sight of his private thesis on the "Hand made Bottle Industry of Castleford" which details the formation of the Yorkshire Unions.
10. The "lehr" or "annealing oven" was a secondary furnace in which the glass products were reheated then allowed to cool slowly over many hours. Annealing was a vital part of the glassmaking process to remove stresses built up in the glass whilst it was being worked. Unless annealed it would shatter immediately when used.
11. Clark,A.W., *Through a Glass Clearly*, (1980) Golden Eagle, 25.
12. *Barnsley Chronicle*, 2 October 1886.
13. "Depression in Trade and Industry", *British Parliamentary Commission Report* (1886), 21. Appendix A,74.

14. I am indebted to the comprehensive researches of Olive Talbot
    for details of Patents in this section, published under "The Evolution of Glass Bottles
    for Carbonated Drinks", *Post*
    Medieval Archaeology, Vol.8 (1974), 46-54.
15. *Barnsley Chronicle*, 25 September 1886.
16. See Trudgill,P., *The Dialects of England* for distribution of 'play' meaning 'take time
    away from work'. The bottle-maker, Joseph Taylor would appear to have originated
    either from the north-east or a southern county. It would have been more likely for
    a South Yorkshireman, and Barnsley in particular, to have used 'lake' rather than 'play'.
17. *Barnsley Chronicle*, 2 October 1886.
18. I am grateful to Maurice Hepworth, Local History Librarian, Barnsley Central
    Library, for his invaluable assistance in seeking out this Coroner's report in the
    Barnsley Chronicle, 29 May 1893 and of Note 19.
19. *Barnsley Chronicle*, 16 April 1910.
20. Historical and technical survey of all the 63 glassworks of South Yorkshire, including
    Barnsley, currently published in Ashurst,D., *The History of South Yorkshire Glass*,
    (1992) Sheffield University.
21. Clark,A.W., *Through a Glass Clearly*, (1980) Golden Eagle, 33/34. Mr.Clark provides
    a full history of the Beatson Clark, Rotherham, glassworks up to the mid-1970s
    including the firm's close involvement with the Barnsley industry.

6. "OWD WATTER JOE", BARNSLEY'S ORIGINAL WATER VENDOR [1]

by Brian Elliott

THERE CAN NOT BE TOO MANY QUAKERS WHO, in their own lifetime have had Beer Houses named after them! This was but one manifestation of the claim to fame of one of Barnsley's most remarkable characters: Joseph Broadhead.

Broadhead was born at Thrumpton Hall, Nottinghamshire, in about 1772. His father, Caleb, was a tenant farmer but shortly after Joe's birth moved to Woodsetts, near Anston, about three miles from Worksop. Caleb died when Joe was aged five.

Joe's mother, Ruth, soon remarried and went to live in London. Poor Joe was despatched to live with an aunt near Kirkburton. William and Mary Earnshaw brought the youngster up on a small farm at Shepley Wood End. He acquired a basic education at a dame school and also at a rural academy.

Joseph soon picked up the art of weaving during spells when Esther Roberts, a journey woman employed by his uncle, left her loom. He became a dab hand at throwing the shuttle and boasted to be the best lindsey-woolsey weaver in Shepley.

Eventually Joe entered the service of Mr Emmanual Helam of Hunslet and worked as a footman for about one year. Next stop was Raistrick, Halifax, weaving fancy cloth. It was here that he fell in love with Hannah Lees, the daughter of his employer. They were married in the meeting house near Brighouse. A certificate, dated 10 January, 1798, was presented to the couple as confirmation of their marriage and the whole assembly signed their names to the document.

The Broadheads had a son, Caleb, born towards the end of their first year of marriage and another child was born in 1799 but in the same year Hannah died of dropsy and was interred at the Friends' burial ground.

Joseph came to Barnsley in about 1806 probably attracted with the prospect of work in the developing linen trade. He was first employed in the dual-occupation of farmer-weaver by Mr John Greenwood who was once a book-keeper in the warehouse of the formidable Joseph Beckett, Esquire. Greenwood did well for himself, living in a genteel residence in Church Street. He next found employment with Mr Joseph Lister who had a small farm near Old Mill Wharf and took in 'custom work' which he bleached as well as wove. Again Joe was a farmer-weaver, before the days when weavers were confined for long hours in 'cellar-shops'.

Joe began to get something of a reputation. He had a round selling potatoes to folk in the surrounding villages. One day he met with a friend, 'John Barleycorn', and had a long chat. The horse, one of Mr Lister's favourites, got fed up and galloped in the direction of town throwing spuds in all directions like cannon balls at Trafalgar. Also dispersed was his copper money, much to the delight of local children. "Darby", the horse, headed straight for its own stable but failed to negotiate the garden wall, turning over the cart and its remaining contents.

Mr Lister, his Quaker master, was not very pleased but being a man of peace admonished Joe via some expressive verses from the scriptures and relegated him to hewing wood and drawing water. Joe, enterprising as ever, started a rival 'tatie run' and with some success.

Joseph Broadhead started water vending in Barnsley in about 1816 and soon became a very popular figure in the town. At this time, and indeed for more than twenty-five years, Barnsley folk obtained their water from several wells. There were pumps at Town End, Shaw Lane, Agnes Road as well as the well-known Oak Well and Honey Well. For many this involved a long and tiring trek. For a copper or two Joe would deliver water 'to the door' providing a much sought after service. It was a much appreciated though by no means distinguished occupation but what Joe lacked in status he made up for via a wit and repartee which would have had them rolling in aisles in any towns' music hall.

His appearance alone made passers-by, especially strangers, stop and stare. Joe sported a hat with an unusually wide brim, boots with wooden soles (they could certainly hear his approach) and a huge swallow-tailed coat, laps dangling at his heels. Someone once had the cheek to suggest to our Joe that his coat was too short; he replied that it was long enough until he got another.

An old nag called 'Duke' was his main source of power and a large barrel resting on an old cart contained his store of water. Duke had such a reverent view of Joe that when he occasionally fell off the cart he stood, ignoring the upturned vehicle and waited patiently for his master to recover his senses.

Joe soon became a living legend. Following the Beer Act of 1829 numerous 'Beer Shops' opened in Barnsley. One opened under the sign of "Watter Joe" sited appropriately opposite the town pumps and displayed a striking portrait of the local hero and his water barrel. Underneath could be read the following legend :

Above: "Come drink with 'Watter Joe'" (Beer House Sign).

All you who love a social drop,
Come in and sit you down,
And here you'll find as good a tap,
As any in the town,
The merry host with jest and song,
Will keep you on the go;
Come then and taste this liquor strong —
Come drink with "Watter Joe".

The Beer Shop was owned by another local wag known as 'Old Tom Topping'. Tom, also an enterprising fellow, had a further notice displayed outside his premises:

Here lives T.T.
Sells good ale.
No better can be.

Tom doubled up as a gardener, scavenger and general servant to Mr Speight, draper. Every Sunday morning he was out sweeping the pavement in front of Speight's shop cracking jokes with passers by.

Old Tom soon acquired a new nickname: "Strawman". He had been given the job of protecting Mr Speight's garden which was situated between Foundry Lane and Dodworth Road and had recently been plundered by unidentified thieves. Tom armed himself with a shot-gun and one evening, as darkness approached noticed a shadowy figure in the garden. "Hello" shouted Tom. It did not answer or even move. The call was repeated with the same result, followed by the stern warning, "Begone, or I'll shoot". Still no response so Tom fired his gun at the offender after which there were bellowing shrieks of laughter coming from the summer house. Old Tom had talked to and blasted a scarecrow placed there by Mr Speight's apprentices and much to their great amusement.

Richard Crookes, Esquire was a surgeon who practised for many years in the Barnsley area. The 'Old Doctor' was also a noted local character who enjoyed a joke and even took on the mighty 'Watter Joe'. Joseph was once delivering water to the doc's residence when the following exchange took place:

"Joe thy water is very dear" (Doctor).
"Soa tha methink" (waterman), *"but it be a deal dearer when tha's med it into physic".*

On another occasion the doctor was attending the solemn funeral of a deceased patient and who should be passing — Yes, 'Watter Joe' and he couldn't resist the opportunity:

"Tha'rt takking sum o' thee bad wark hooam", shouted Joe to the mournful procession. The poor old doctor, in keeping with the occasion was for once both stunned and speechless. However, that was not quite the end of the story. The cunning physician secretly pulled the tap out of Joe's sacred barrel. Water flowed into the streets of Barnsley but Joe proceeded apparently totally oblivious of the event but with 'Old Duke' having an increasingly lighter load.

There were warning shouts to Joe of "Yol loise all yer watter − taps aght" but all apparently to no avail. Joe stoically trudged to Oak Well for a fresh supply. Guess where Joe went the very next day? The doctor found him sitting snugly in his morning surgery. Joe managed to claim compensation from the doctor for his grievous loss!

Water vendors loudly proclaimed their presence in many a town and no doubt carried out their services with a smile and a joke but there was only one Yorkshire town called Barnsley and certainly only one waterman called Joseph Broadhead. By the early 1800s Joe's fame rivalled that of any national figure, including Nelson and his 'victories' over uncertain odds even eclipsed a certain hero of Waterloo. His abilities were such that he received the ultimate accolade from Barnsley folk: "He had an answer to everybody".

A mail coach once ran between Leeds and Barnsley, stopping at the Lord Nelson Inn, Shambles Street. One afternoon the important vehicle, when leaving the hostelry was slightly delayed by old Joe's watercart. "Go-ahead, old boy," shouted the postman, "this is the King's carriage, and can't be stopped". "Weel, weel," replied the waterman, "ha hooap his majesty al hev a little bit a patience wi' me, as ha hev him partly to keep".

Joe, despite his Quaker background, was not averse to spending both his time and wages in the town hostelries. On emerging he was occasionally challenged with well-meaning advice. One kind person was brave enough to reprimand him for his habits. "Joseph", says he, "if thee does not correct thy tippling propensities, thee will not have a rag to thy back. "Friend", replied the exhilarated waterman, "tha shouldn't say what tha doesn't mean".

"If thee knows my thoughts better than I know them myself", rejoined the well-wisher, "what does thee think I do mean?"

"Tha means", replies Joe, "That ha shall hev nowt but rags to me back". Old Joe wandered on leaving his officious friend meditating on the futility of giving advice to the famous.

Old Joe's bacchanalian interests often reduced him to a penurious state and prudence was not one of his strong points. He was frequently in financial difficulties. Yet he was always able to gain help from friends. Frequent appeals to their benevolence had the desired effect. On one occasion he found himself without a horse so had to lug the water barrel around himself. Not to be outdone he soon employed the use of a wheelbarrow and diversified into collecting manure and delivering coals.

Joe varied his employment by visiting Mount Osborne Colliery for a barrow full of coals, for which he paid one penny, and which he sold again for two-pence halfpenny. Quite a good profit margin but it also took account of labour.

One anecdote concerning Joe relates to the occasion when he was 'put behind the door' by way of penance by the Barnsley Friends because of his love of drink. One busy-body accosted him and endeavoured to make fun of his recent plight. "What, Joe, hav heard at Quakers hev turned tha aght, what's it all abaght like?" "Nobbut weshing me kneck like" came the laconic reply. "Ny, mun", said the inquisitor, "they cudn't turn tha aght for that like, cos cleanliness is next to godliness". "Eh, but tha knows", replied Joseph, "ha weshed it inside like".

During the last few years of his life Broadhead resided in a small apartment in Beckett's Square, paying rent of nine pence per week. He had removed there from even more spartan accommodation: a stable. Apart from the few coppers he earned from carting water he also received two shillings and sixpence a week from the parish. Friends continued to help the likeable character with gifts of food and clothes.

Joe passed away on Tuesday 28th December, 1852, aged eighty, and was interred in the Friends' burial ground, Huddersfield Road, Barnsley. It was reported that many respectable folk attended his funeral.

NOTES AND REFERENCES

[1]   This item is based on an article by the writer which appeared in the *Barnsley Chronicle* in the series 'Barnsley Folks of Yore', 1987. Other sources include 'The life of Joseph Broadhead' by John Hugh Burland in the *Barnsley Chronicle* 16.8.1902; also see *Barnsley Chronicle*, 2.5.1896, 16.5.1896 and 3.4.1897

7. A KINGSTONE CHILDHOOD REMEMBERED[1]

by Annie Storey

CHILDHOOD MEMORIES, WERE THEY THE happiest time of your life? they were for me. Nostalgic memories of a bygone Kingstone, a little village nestling by Locke Park in Barnsley. If you go today to look at Kingstone, you will see neat council houses with their own little patch of garden, and flats where my dear late uncle, Ned Barrett spent his last days in one of them. He, along with other Kingstoners made the transition of old to new, quietly and effectively.

To look at the place now is to see a completely different environment to the one that I used to live in. The old terrace houses were completely demolished in the late fifties, apart from a few leading down to Gilroyd. I will try to describe it. The main road, Keresforth Hill, went straight through the middle of the village leading from St Edwards church, down and through to Gilroyd. There was Back Sykes Street and Sykes

Below: Three good pals in Kingstone 'backs', Lorraine Halligan, Frank Barrett (my brother) and Doreen Rayner, c. 1949. This shows well our play area.

Above: Back Denton Row showing the front of the terrace.   *Barnsley Archives*

Above: View across Keresforth Hill Road from my grandma's front door. The gap to the left leads to houses in 'Cut Throat Yard' – real name Court No. 1. *(Barnsley Archives)*

Street itself branching off on one side and down to Raley Street. On the other side this led to the backs, or 'piece' as we called it where all the children played. On the other side of the 'piece' was another long row of houses named Back Denton Row. I was born at number thirteen, but when I was a few months old my mother, Frances Barrett, and my dad, Frank, moved to seventy-six Keresforth Hill Road so our front door led onto the pavement of the main road and our back door led into a yard and thereon to my beloved 'piece'.

Were the summers really long and hot, and the winters bitingly cold and crisp, or is it my imagination running riot? The long, hot, balmy days when we packed rose petals into bottles of cold water, and made scent. We'd wait for the petals to turn brown because that was a sure sign that it was working and we could be drenched in heavenly perfume. What could be nicer than a bread and jam picnic, surrounded by buzzing wasps.

Nearly all the grass had disappeared in between the two rows of houses. This was natural considering that nearly every child in Kingstone ran amok over it. We played at cricket, (even the girls) nipsy, marbles, kick-can, dobby, allevio, and tigs. The poor old soil suffered another giant setback every year when we had the bonfire on November the fifth. Even that was a fresh adventure, not content with the excitement of the night before with all the kids rushing around screaming, "It's lit, it's lit", we would go looking for dead bangers and Roman candles the next morning. If my grandchildren went looking for these things

Above: Back of Kingstone Club – which was next door to grandma's house; me with my dad and my brother.

now, I'm sure I would snap "What do you want those things for"? Our long suffering mothers had to put up with spent fireworks clutched in our grubby, sticky, charcoal'd fingers. They were treasure indeed.

Anyway I divert, for the moment I will concentrate on the houses themselves. Community spirit was very much alive then. Gossip went off behind closed curtains, and the kids loved it if there was a row between the mothers. This was entertainment with a first class seat. On the whole though, it was a warm hearted community, and if anyone needed help, most people pitched in did their best for their neighbour, any warring factions forgotten.

The houses were mainly two up and two down. The majority of them red brick, but a few built of grey stone. There were no inside toilets of course, at least, not the houses that I used to go in. Our toilet was in the backyard. It was called a Ducket, it wasn't a water toilet like my gran's, who lived further up the row, apparently a bucket overturned in ours. It was like a big black pit. I didn't like it, but it was something you got used to.

As for the bathroom, that was our kitchen of course. We had a tin bath stuck in front of the fire every Saturday night. I think I was pretty good at scrubbing backs. My mother used to kneel in front of the bath on bath night, and I used to wash hers. When my dad came home from the pit before they had showers installed, he used to stand at the stone kitchen sink in his pit trousers and hand me a wet flannel. I used to stand on a stool and work a good lather up on his back and keep rinsing it off. I can still see the dirty grey lather getting cleaner with each soaping. I used to draw patterns in it and my dad used to go mad saying "Stop tickling and get on with it". I think my artistic aspirations were coming to the forefront.

In my mind's eye I can still see the old blacklead fireplace, not strictly my mother's domain. I used to clean it as well, till it gleamed and gleamed. The 'pit' cupboard was at the side in the alcove. It was called the 'pit' cupboard because thats where my dad kept his work clothes and boots and a belt with his 'snap tin', a knife and a grey stone sharpener on it. He used to wet the stone and run the blade of his knife up and down on it until honed to a perfect sharpness. Sticks for the fire were also kept in this cupboard, and a mousetrap; occasionally we got mice.

On the other side of the fireplace was the setpot. A brick-built boiler with a fire underneath for the washing of our clothes. On washdays my mother would remove the gas ring which was resting on top of the lino which in turn rested on a wooden board which slatted into place above the boiler. She would light the fire underneath the boiler after having filled it with water. She would then boil some of the clothes in

Above: A Kingstone crowd on Blackpool Pier, Auntie Annie (Barrett) front row; with my mother third from left back row.

Reckitt's washing powder. These would then be transferred to the tub where she rubbed the garments with a brush on the scrubbing board. These were always rinsed with a bag of Dolly Blue and then put through the mangle. Quite a tedious business, nothing like today's modern miss. I did help with the aid of a peggystick. A wooden structure like a milkmaids stool with a long handle projecting from it. My gran had a posser to do hers with. Whereas you twisted mother's from side to side, gran's posser went up and down and the water poured from the little holes around the edge of it. Both methods got the clothes clean.

Of the two rooms downstairs, one was always kept for the best. There was a little bit of carpet in the best room and lino and clipping rugs in the kitchen. We spent all our time in the kitchen-cum-living-room. We washed, ate, cooked meals and spent our leisure time there. No couch potatoes in our house, straight backed chairs around the kitchen table and a low chair with wooden arms on it by the fire. My dad used to sit in this chair when he came home from the pit. Mother would not let him sit in it though until he had washed and changed. I remember once, my Auntie Annie, my dad's sister, had climbed onto the arm of the chair to reach the top cupboard above the pit cupboard. I don't know what she wanted, but she slipped and her foot crashed into my pot doll that I had left lying in the chair. One of the legs was smashed (not Auntie Annie's, I hasten to add,) and I let out such a wail. I was far more concerned about my broken doll and not my lovely aunt. She did pay for another leg for it later on, it wasn't the right shade or size but it sufficed and I was happy again. My Aunt Annie was a very happy person. I always remember her singing and dancing around the house. She had cornflower blue eyes, blonde hair, and a very infectious grin. I loved her dearly. If you look at one of the houses near Kingstone opposite the church at the top of Park Road, you will see there are two stone globes on either side of one of the gates. I remember my aunt pretending to try and tug them off every time we passed them. She'd say, "Well we'd have a game of football if I could get one of these off". She died in childbirth when she was twentynine and I was five, so her memory must have made a big impression on me, I never forgot her.

There were a few shops in Kingstone. At the top of Sykes Street there was a paper shop, it changed hands a few times though. Opposite this shop across the main Keresforth Hill Road were two shops straddling either side of a street that led up to Back Denton Row. Mrs Dunne lived in one and Mr and Mrs Sergeant in the other. The latter was an off licence. They had pumps on the counter. My grandma used to send me for a pint of draught Guinness most lunch times. Mrs Dunne's shop wasn't her main abode. She had one of the more modern semi-detached homes right at the end of Kingstone. Every morning she would walk to the shop with a dog. It was rather large with curly cream coloured hair and brown spots. Mrs Dunne sold hot black eye peas for a penny a bag. I used to love those and Uncle Joe's Mint Balls. She also sold liquorice root. You could either get plain black liquorice in sweet form, like long black shoelaces, or you could have the actual root, which you could suck and suck all day long until all the flavour had disappeared and you were left with long yellow soggy strands of tasteless root. Other delights were Aniseed Balls, Yorkshire Mixtures, Old Fashioned Humbugs, Black Imps, Gob Stoppers, sweet lollies on a stick, jelly babies, dolly mixtures, Highland toffee, pink spearmint toffee, and a host of other sweets. Sometimes we'd buy a 'pennorth' of lemonade crystals and dip our fingers in. These were all after the war though when rationing had ceased. One of the cheaper delights

Above: 'Look out Tiller Girls here I come', I pose for the camera in the middle of the 'piece' on the backs of Keresforth Hill Road.

was dipping a stick of rhubarb in sugar, or my gran would mix cocoa and sugar together and I would dip my finger in that.

There was another shop further up Keresforth Hill Road, it was Wollerton's. My mother purchased most of our staple foods from there. I used to watch Mr Wollerton pouring sugar into dark blue bags, and patting slabs of butter which he'd cut a bit off or add a bit on. "That enough Mrs Barrett or would you like a bit more?"

One of the strange things I think about is all the dieting that goes off today, and yet my dad would take bread and dripping to the pit, sometimes cheese and butter sandwiches and never got fat. I suppose it was hard work down the mines, that would help. If my mother ran short of money before payday she'd say to me, "Go to Wollertons and say you want something on tick, but whisper it, because you never know who's in". Above Wollertons were two more shops on either side of Back Sykes Street. One was up some steps, it was a tiny newsagent, the other one was Strawbridge's the butcher's. My mother for some reason or other used to have Hyslops down Racecommon Road. I used to journey there for our meat, and then I would have to go to Strawbridge's for Mrs Armstrong who lived in the end house of Back Denton Row. She would give me a penny for this errand every Saturday. She would always say, 'Say that you want that 'theer' for Mrs Armstrong''. I was always given a round parcel of something wrapped in a newspaper. I'd tuck it under my arm and take it to Armstrong's. One of my friends once asked me what it was. I said, "Well it's meat", she persisted, "What kind"? Being a child I'd never thought about that. Anyhow curiosity got the better of me and I pulled away at some of the newspaper until I'd made a hole in it. All I saw was a row of grinning teeth. I threw it in the air with a loud shriek, "I've been carrying a dead head under me arm". The upshot of course that it was a sheep's head that Mrs Armstrong had been boiling and that was the end of me asking for that 'theer'.

On either side of the street separating Dunnes shop and Sergeants were the ends of the terrace rows. On the high walls were large enamel tins advertising products of the day such as Ty Phoo Tea, Creamola, Burdalls Gravy Salt, Pears Soap, etc,. We had a game whereby we would stand in the middle of this street which led off from the main road and aim rubber balls at the letters on these tins. You started at the beginning and once you'd hit the first letter you'd carry on to the second and so and so forth until all the letters had gone. Unfortunately the occupant of the shop, Mrs Dunne, would come out shouting, "Right you little sods, you can just stop that". We would wait until she'd gone in and turn round and start on Sergeants on the opposite side, until they would come out and stop us. It was great fun for us but upon reflection it must have been awful for the residents with the bang, bang upon the tins. They were kindly people though. I remember going into Dunnes the first day that she sold sliced bread. A rubber band was fixed around the slices to keep it all in place. We must have been very fit in those days. I and my friends spent a lot of time standing on our heads against the shop walls, with our frocks tucked into our knicker legs. Anyone who could do the crab ie. walking your legs down the wall was extremely revered.

A lot of the boys spent most of their time on the floor directing marbles into the 'podge'.

Another shop opposite us was really just a terrace house but Mr and Mrs Benfell sold fruit and vegetables from it. There would be crates stacked up inside their living room, and Mr Benfell, a large man, would sit by the fire in a high backed chair puffing his pipe until someone came into the shop. We used to buy ropes from him for a penny, or if it was extra long without knots, tuppence. I suppose these came off the lorries which brought the produce. We had great games with these ropes. When we played at skipping, nearly all the street would join in. You had to ask permission of course, depending on who had bought the rope and if you were in their good books. One of our favourite chants was:

"On the mountain stands a lady,
Who she is I do not know,
All she wants is gold and silver,
All she wants is a nice young man,
So come in my very best friend, my very best friend, my very best friend,
So come in my very best friend while I go out to play".

Great days!

Our house was next door to the Working Men's Club. Years before, apparently, three terrace houses had been demolished and the club built in their place. A fourth terrace was occupied by the steward and his family. Their living quarters led directly into the club. The downstairs had a snooker table in it, and upstairs had another snooker table. Whenever there were wedding receptions or the Christmas party or something special, both rooms would be in use. Every year I used to tap-dance on a board laid across one ot the tables. Anyone with any talent was encouraged to have a go. With hindsight, I'm quite sure that most of the kids were bored stiff with my entertainment but out of politeness and with nudges from the parents, I usually received a decent clap. My dad was a great one for getting the entertainment going. With us living next door to the club, when he was in full singing voice the sound would filter through the bedroom wall where my brother and myself were sleeping. There was also the sound of Mr Whiles playing his banjo, usually the George Formby numbers. I was responsible for my brother and lying there in the darkness it was quite comforting, listening to all the club noises.

The yearly trip to the seaside was a unique event. Everyone would congregate outside the club and wait for the coaches coming over the hill. We would be literally choking with excitement. My father was on the committee so my brother and myself would always finish up on the same bus as he. Everybody would sing for most of the way. "Slow boat to China", "April showers", "Beautiful dreamer", "Ten green bottles", "One man went to mow", and lots more. What a difference between the songs of yesteryear and today. We were given half a crown spending money, what riches!

The first glimpse of the sea was magical and mystical. My money burning a hole in my pocket, didn't take too long to go. Priority would be a new bucket and spade for the beach, or a brightly coloured ball.

Above: On the front at Cleethorpes with our name labels pinned to our coats — the annual club trip, summer 1949. Myself, Shirley Hunt, and 'ar kid'.

Sometimes I bought an 'American' comic. To have one of these gave you great bargaining power. 'Batman', and 'Plastic Man', were worth two 'Dandies' or 'Beanos'. We used to have the 'Mickey Mouse' comic delivered to our house each week, which to my mind was quite a soppy paper, strictly for babies. My mother wouldn't give in on this one. I used to swap it as fast as I could. I was always an avid reader. Even the sauce bottle on the table recieved my undivided attention. We also had the 'Weekly News' delivered and if my mother caught me reading 'Dandy McLean', the detective, or the love story bit, the paper would be snatched out of my hands with declarations of hell fire striking me down dead.

Once I let myself down badly with the comic swapping. One dark night when my parents were in the club, I set off across the 'piece' to Halligans, who lived opposite us. I would be about ten, and my brother about four. I carried him with the comics in my hand also. I was having to struggle against the wind, everything was flapping away, and in the pitch darkness I dropped my little brother. He cut his hand badly, and the doctor had to come and clean it up. I was in disgrace over this. So much for the quest for the written word! Another time I dropped him again. I tripped up coming from Locke Park down the path by Jacksons field. He had been sitting on my shoulders and he went rolling down and down like a rubber ball. He collected a scar above his eye from

Above: Good old Locke Park, just round the corner, where the band played on Sundays during the summer. *(Photo courtesy of Brian Elliott)*

this one. He has his own business these days, panel beating, so he did survive in the end, despite my tender, loving, care!

I used to love going to Locke Park on Sundays and listening to the Band. It made the whole place come alive somehow. We would go and play on the 'swagger', the 'bobbies helmet', the slide, and in the sandpit. There was also a round hut with a run around it where they used to keep rabbits. Another delight was going up Locke Park Tower. The public were allowed free access then. It was a wonderful view of Barnsley and the surrounding districts once you had toiled up the spiral staircase and reached the top balcony.

Another favourite walk of ours was walking down to the 'Yellow Waters'. There were flagstones nearly all the way down. The walk itself started from Keresforth Hall Road, opposite the park. It would pass many a pleasant hour on, following the stream and feeding the ducks and the geese from the nearby farm.

Another path, opposite the cricket field in the park, led down between the allotments and Jackson's field. This is another place entirely covered by council houses now. We loved to play in the sweet-smelling hay at harvest time, rolling in it and throwing it all over. Other times we'd make daisy chains and test everybody under the chin with a buttercup to see if they liked butter. Anyone with a yellow glow there swore they liked it even if they detested it. Beyond the field were the woods. Usually we would go in there to pick bluebells, one of the nicest flowers around I think.

Speaking of colours, I remember my first day at Racecommon Road

Infants school. Brian Raynes, the brother of Jackie Raynes, who sells nylons on Barnsley market, took charge of me. He assured my mother that he would dry any ensuing tears. Not being the crying type, I loved my first day and my first memory. After marching around the hall in crocodile fashion to the tune of 'The Teddy Bears Picnic', I was taken along to the classroom. I did realise later that this particular tune was alternated by 'Soldiers of the King', a very rousing piece which I suppose was meant to give us a good start to the day. Upon reaching the classroom, we were presented with sticky backed paper to cut shapes out of. I can still remember the glory of those lovely colours. Squares of red, blue, green and gold paper. I kept thinking "Is this really for me?"

Unfortunately, I was off school a long time with ill health. I had scarlet fever, followed by adenoids and tonsils being taken out, followed by impetigo. Have you ever, repeat ever, had the indignity of going to school with a broad band of purple dye plastered around your lips. I think it was permaganate of potash. The Black and White Minstrels had nothing on me. My only saving grace was that the nit nurse didn't find anything. The junior school for most Kingstone children was Agnes Roads, an excellent school. A lot of the time my best friend and myself were sent out to the corridors for misdemeanours, mainly harsh coughing, which ensured at least one missed lesson. We would pass time running the cold water taps in the middle of winter and submerging our hands to see who could stand it the longest. My friend's name was Pauline Beverly, she lived down Sykes Street, and incidentally we are still best friends to this day.

The sawmill was behind Pauline's house. Fanny Crackles and her husband ran it. We always thought that Mrs Crackles was a bit eccentric. She had lots of cats which she seemed to dote on. We would venture to the mill when she wasn't around and beg squares of wood that Mr Crackles had thrown away. They were ideal for hopscotch. The other alternative was to fill an empty shoe polish tin with grit, plenty of that around Kingstone.

One of the pleasures of this bygone ers was the Whit Walk. Getting new clothes once a year was an occasion to be remembered. Everything brand spanking new, down to shoes, socks and hanky. What a thrill! Going round friends and relations and showing them off and being treated to a few coppers, sixpence if you were lucky.

V.E. day was a very good parade day. There were street parties down the main road and surrounding streets. Lots of people were in fancy dress, and we all marched right into town. My gran was dressed in a white sailor suit and she had stitched tiny flags of all the different nations around the hat. We walked to the Princess cinema and the

Pavilion at Townend at the bottom of Racecommon Road. I can remember the night that the Pavilion cinema burned down (September, 1950). Originally it was built as a roller skating rink. The night it burned to the ground, you could see the sparks shooting into the glowing sky from our house. It was a sad loss. The Princess, or Prinny, as we called it, was a must on a Saturday morning. On the bill would be Roy Rogers, Hoppalong Cassidy, The Lone Ranger, Rin-Tin-Tin and Lassie, all hot favourites. One of the most frequent memories was the audience of youngsters all screaming, "Behind yer, He's behind yer". Good value for threepence or sixpence, depending on whether you could afford the stalls or the 'gods'.

Regarding entertainment, I would hotfoot it home after school to tune into 'Dick Barton', special agent. I would hope and pray that I didn't have to run to the shop for anything whilst this was on. I would place my ear next to the large wooden wireless and listen to the exploits of Dick and his assistant Snowy. Another favourite was the Francis Durbridge series, 'Paul Temple'.

Another walk that I used to enjoy was walking to Dark Lane past Jackson's farm. The only thing that was a bit scary was passing the large wooden gates that had a black bull behind them. It was never a danger of course, but we were always a bit scared that it might escape. On the way we would pass the White House. This was a tiny one up and one down cottage that stood on its own. Mr George Roome lived there by himself. He was a quiet old man, I don't think I ever saw him without his flat cap off. He had a big white moustache and was always

Above: Upper Sykes Street — when this slope got a covering of snow it was great for sledging.
Barnsley Archives

Above: The Locke Park Hotel which used to stand on the corner opposite St Edward's Church.

Barnsley Archives

smoking a pipe. If you asked him a question, he would puff away quietly, perhaps take out his fob watch on it's gold chain, and then decide to answer. He grew a few vegetables and had a few chickens and seemed to be a very contented man. Sometimes in the summer he would squat in the shade of the trailer which held Ashcroft's fairground equipment on the 'piece'. His house no longer exists now, I should think he was the last person to live in it.

Wintertime in Kingstone provided a lot of pleasure. To wake up one morning, look through the window, and see a beautiful white landscape was enough to send shrieks of delight through the house. Sledging would take place down Back Sykes Street where it was quite steep. There were one or two winters when the snow was so deep, it was shovelled into piles about six feet high on either side of Keresforth Hill Road. Sometimes I used to wear clogs with irons on them, and I used to walk in the snow with them and it would collect on the soles and get higher and higher as if I were walking on stilts. Another winter pastime was making rugs. Sacking was stretched across a wooden frame, and clippings were pushed into holes with a brodder. This was a piece of metal with a point on one end and a hook on the other. The clippings came from old coats. A lady named Mrs Baldwin, who lived in between Sykes Street and Raley Street, used to make large rugs and sell them. She would think up very nice patterns for the villagers who purchased her wares.

Christmas and the New Year were good times. My dad used to take me round at midnight letting the New Year in. We would go up the road as far as the old Bush Inn, cross over to the Locke Park Hotel and

Above: Grandma Barrett, a well-known Kingstone character and Auntie Clara Hudson.

down the other side. Everyone would make us welcome with mince pies, or some treat left over from Christmas. I suppose winter would be bad for the miners though, when the knocker-upper came around with his long pole tapping on the windows in the middle of the night. With very little transport they must have been freezing cold before they even went down the mine.

One of the things I took for granted in those days was the passage of people through my gran's house. I have already mentioned that our house was on one side of Kingstone club, well my gran's was next door but two on the other side. Also, next to her was Jordans the bookies, so if anyone wanted to place a bet, or visit someone on Back Denton Row, they would use my gran's as a short cut. Walking straight through her house was easier than going around the end of the long row of terrace houses.

My grandma was a very well known character. She was born in Wigan, Lancashire, June 2nd 1886. She came to Barnsley with four small children and acquired a fifth when Grandad was home on leave in the first World War. She did lots of things to earn a living. She took in washing, went out cleaning, and had a succession of lodgers. This helped to pay the bills. She also allowed card playing in her home at the weekend. I can still remember the smoke-laden kitchen and the pile of money on the table. It used to get packed. The curtains would be drawn, the lights on, and we kids had to look out for the 'bobby'. Card playing for gain was illegal in those day, or at least you had to have

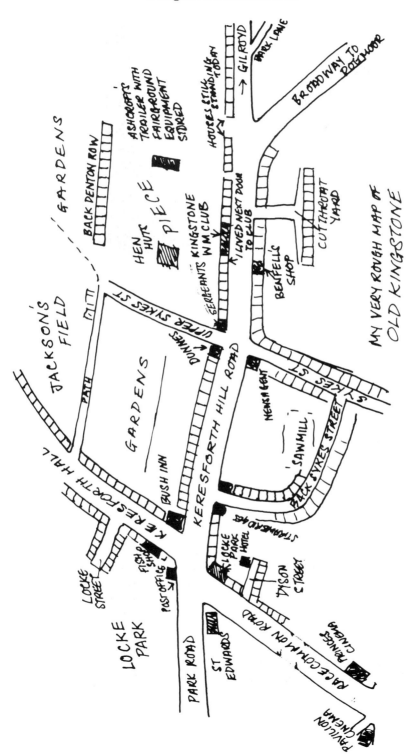

a licence. One man who did come around though in the afternoon was the 'Hokey Pokey' man. He sold bars of ice cream for tuppence.

Another time we were lookouts for the police was when my dad and other Kingstone and Dodworth men would go to the 'Bull Fields' on Broadway for the 'tossing' school. This was the area now occupied by Kingstone school and the surrounding fields. Throwing coins in the air and betting on whether they landed heads or tails. We children would pass our time throwing stones into the marshy pond. It was a dark place, overhung by big trees. Not a place I would like to venture on my own. The men would quickly disperse though if there were any sign of police.

I remember looking at my grandma's face about three weeks before she died on July 8th 1956. I was standing in her kitchen, and she was sitting on a kitchen chair. As she looked up at me to speak, I had the strangest feeling that she hadn't got long to live. I noticed the brilliant blue of her eyes shining through the lens of her spectacles. The sun's rays were hitting my back and bathing my gran in a golden light. She had a beautiful pink and white complexion even at the age of seventy. The soft peach-like down showed up on her cheeks, in sharp contrast to the iron grey hair cut straight and even and held back with numerous hair grips. She gave me a quizzical look and held her gnarled hand up to her eyes to shield them from the sun. I just looked at her and determined to keep this moment in time forever. She had a face full of character, had my gran. Her nose was slightly crooked, she had long thin features, a thin body, and was quite tall. Coming from Lancashire, she always wore a shawl and a pair of black clogs. The shawl would envelope her thin shoulders and hang down on the working smock that she always wore. These were wraparound aprons, very popular with the women of that erea. They usually had a tiny print flower on a dark background. Her stockings would be of thick lisle and she would wear garters just above the knee. She loved good plain food. Every Saturday she would boil up mussels from Barnsley fish market. I would stand over the pan and watch them all open up in the steaming heat. When cutting them out of their shell my biggest thrill was trying to find a pearl. I did gather several seed pearls which I put in a matchbox with some cotton wool.

Everyone called my grandma 'Nan'. Besides her husband being killed in the war, she had a little girl who died through fire. I was told that Bessie had been dancing on the kitchen table and her shawl fell on the gas mantle and onto her. The second tragedy was Tom, he was killed in the pit when he was fourteen, and the last of course was Annie who died in childbirth. This left her with two children, my Uncle Ned and my dad. During the second World War, she took in three evacuees, along with lots of Barnsley people. They were Peter, Ronnie and Norman Hardwick from Romford. Originally, they were upset at living in Kingstone, their own home was a modern semi-detached and it took some time to get used to the old terrace houses. By the time they left though, they were very upset at leaving, they had grown to love Kingstone.

When the planes were flying over Barnsley we would sometimes shelter on cellar steps in our house, or go into the air-raid shelter on the 'piece'. The shelter was very cold and draughty, and we didn't half look funny in our gas masks. Our cellar was not very suitable because in bad weather it would be half full with inky black water, the colour of course coming from the coal. I remember one night when a 'screamer' bomb passed over Kingstone, my Auntie Clara my gran's pal, flung herself on the back door where all the coats were hanging. With arms outflung she screamed, "My God, my God, we're all goners". I found it all rather mystifying and just thought, "What's up with her?" My gran always had a cat, and she would treat them like dogs. She would feed them raw liver and one cat in particular was very fierce. He used to guard gran's chair and I didn't dare stroke him. He was pitch black all over, we called him the appropriate name of Blackie. He would follow her everywhere and obey her commands. He would scratch her all up her arms and almost every day she would have torn up bits of newspaper stuck there to stop the blood, she didn't believe in elastoplasts. This cat walked out the day she died and was never seen again.

To all intents and purposes my gran presented a rough and ready face to the world, but I have seen her when they played 'The Beguine, the Beguine', (Aunt Annie's favourite tune,) and I have seen the tears fall down her face. In actual fact she was the kindest and most loving woman I have ever had the good fortune to meet.

Sunday was a ritualistic day. My day would consist of various things, the most significant being that I had to attend church or Sunday school at St Edwards. It was a very nice church inside particularly at Harvest Festival, or at Christmas. They always put a pantomime on in the church hall, it was great fun. Sometimes, I would go to the chapel on Keresforth Hall Road, opposite the park. The hymns and services were of a less conventional type than the church. Occasionally, Mr Riding, the organiser, would give lantern shows in the evening. These would very often be stories of the 'Crusades', and other Biblical stories. We would have a little sing-song afterwards to round off an enjoyable evening.

Above: St Edward's Church pantomime – a breathtaking performance of Cinderella – or so it seemed . . . I'm the fairy in the centre.

My mother would bake every Sunday without fail. Even if the weather was blistering hot outside the fire would be blazing away in order to get the oven hot. Cakes and bread would be made ready for our consumption the following week. My dad would love to take her 'oven-bottomers' down the pit. I think that it was definitely a labour of love on my mother's part. Occasionally, a lady on Back Denton Row, her name was Mrs Hirst, used to make and sell toffee apples. Sometimes it would be just toffee, but either way it was very tasty. I think of her whenever I make them for my own family.

By the way, a girl jumped on my back once when we were playing together. I collapsed to the ground and my knee burst open. I had twelve stitches inserted at Barnsley Becket Hospital. Fifty years on, I still have some Kingstone 'muck' in my knee. I told you I couldn't bear to be parted, didn't I?

Above: Happy Kingstone memories – Beryl, me, my best friend Pauline, and 'ar Frank'.

Notes and References

In writing this material I must thank my friend Pauline Clarke (nee Beverley) for helping me with some of my memories, and indeed for helping to create them too. I would also like to thank Barnsley Archives for their help in providing photographic material. Thank you to all Kingstoner's for creating my happy memories.

Above: Demolition of the upper part of Keresforth Hill Road in the late 1950s. Strawbridge the butchers is on one side of Back Sykes Street with the newsagent up the steps on the other side; Woollerton's is just below the newsagents. *Barnsley Archives*

Below: Top of Upper Sykes Street. You can see the top of the chapel on Keresforth Hall Road. *Barnsley Archives*

KINGSTONE
by Mrs Pauline Clarke

Of happy places mentioned, one springs into mind,
A place of love and laughter, of people who were kind.
Days filled with joy, and gaily spent, happy as a lark,
Playing on the Bull Fields, and down a lane called Dark.
Picnics in a hollow, by a trundling stream,
Oh sweet memories, of which I often dream.
My place sits upon the edge of town, perched upon its throne,
A delightful little village, known as old Kingstone.
Everyone knew everyone, most people were related,
Our joys and tribulations, to one and all belated.
Idyllic days of summer, spent playing in Locke Park,
A glorious place for young and old, of which we all felt part.
We too had characters in Kingstone, as many places do,
Dear old Mrs Crackles, was one I recall, do you?
There are many tales of Fanny, we Kingstoners can say,
But kindness to God's creatures, was her special way.
Spreading bread crumbs for the birds, as she trundled into town,
Her house was filled with pussies, which made some people frown.
Perhaps we laughed behind her back, never to her face,
To have her tell our mam and dad, would put us in disgrace.
We had wondrous parties too, filling all the streets,
Tables swaying in the middle, all with tempting eats.
Where did it all come from, times weren't all that good,
But Kingstoners could come up trumps, when they needed to.
There was old Ginny Morris, dressed up for the procession,
Her knickers made from a Union Jack, showing to the heaven.
Then poor old Olive, who could not leave the house,
Her home a haven, where everyone could grouse.
There were days of podging marbles, spinning whip and top,
Skipping to our hearts content, with ropes from Benfell's shop.
Todays kids scream with laughter, and clearly think it funny,
When you recall playing shop, with broken pots for money.
Perhaps there is a lesson, in memories of the past,
The glorious days of summer, were never meant to last.
I wonder if there are others like a 'body sen',
Who sit and reminisce, of the days we lived in then.

I know within my heart, the place that I call home,
Is a little village on a hill, known as old Kingstone!

Above: Back Denton Row from the back. Part of Keresforth Hill Road showing across the 'piece' (the backs).   *Barnsley Archives*

8. MARROW, A BIOGRAPHY OF A WORSBROUGH HOUSE

by Brian Elliott

WALK DOWN THE RIGHT-HAND SIDE OF Vernon Road from
Ward Green towards Worsbrough Bridge and about 250 metres before
the junction with Haverlands Lane are gateposts guarding the driveway
leading to a house on a site of more than local interest. Today modern
properties align this side of the road but within living memory, Marrow
House's principal neighbours consisted of two farms: Wigfield, on
Haverlands, and Ward Green near the top of the hill.

The Finlay family moved into Marrow House in 1980, having begun
a major rebuilding and enlargement programme five years earlier. Allan,
a well-known local businessman with Scottish ancestry, and his
Barnsley-born wife, Joan, have created a modern country home with a
period atmosphere. The main house, is now linked by means of an
extensive range of accommodation and service rooms to form an
integrated whole but which could, if required, easily divide into separate
units. The owners' concern to re-create traditional craftsmanship is
reflected structurally in the extensive use of local stone and re-used
masonry from old mansions in Sheffield and Rotherham, whilst
internally the installation of fireplaces from Middlewood Hall (Darfield)
and an imaginative adaptation of fittings from Barnsley's redundant
St George's Church are but two further examples of their aim.

Below: Marrow House in c.1880

Age and Evolution

Although the site may have been 'continuously occupied' since the Elizabethan era the fabric of the house is substantially of the Regency period and style, reflecting a major re-build in the nineteenth-century, probably during the early years of the Field tenancy, and significant modifications by the Finlays. However, two-light mullioned windows in all gables and interesting roof timbers may be remnants of an earlier structure. Remains of multiple-light mullions were still visible to the first floor of the north end of the house as recently as c.1975, later replaced by 'Regency' windows. A datestone of 1662, formerly part of the courtyard stable block that faced the north end of the house, has been re-inserted into the masonry of the new range though its provenance is uncertain.

Architecture

The house is basically a double-depth structure of two storeys and roof-space, giving an M-shaped profile to the end elevations. Coal-measure sandstone masonry is arranged in regular courses. The stone-slated roof is steeply pitched with kneelers at the angles. The

Below: Front and end elevation in 1977. *(BMBC)*

front has three-bays with vertical sash windows. Bay windows (Victorian?) to the ground floor of the south end elevation. Until recently interesting moulding could be seen framing the central doorway, the only decorative feature on a plain but purposeful facade. Stone out buildings almost abutting the north end of the house, used in the nineteenth-century as lodgings, carriage house, stables etc were replaced by the modern units referred to above.

The Setting

The walled grounds extend to two acres and include a summer house and modern garage blocks. The attractive lawned front garden has several magnificent mature trees complementing shrubs and bedding. The extensive rear garden commands panoramic views of the pleasant countryside to the west and south, including Wentworth Castle and Worsbrough Country Park. The single-storey summer house has been recently extended, the original half, known as 'Garden Cottage', having an interesting original doorway with a lintel datestone of 1704 inscribed under the initials 'I M', probably referring to a John Marrow.

Family History

1. The Turners

On a warm summer evening in the 1740s a middle-aged man raised what he could of his corsetted four-foot-six inch body and gazed thoughtfully towards the Thames across a small lawned garden, the vista enhanced by the cascading branches of a willow tree, the first to be seen in England.[1] He had every right to feel contentment from the peace and solitude of a villa garden of his own creation — the "glory of my little kingdom", as he called it. Across the Twickenham road lay his larger ornamental plot and connecting both was a unique underground grotto where he loved to sit, work and entertain. For him to work was to write and to entertain was to engage in philosophical discourse with the leading literary figures of the day. His name was Alexander Pope.

Pope, who never married, shared much of his life with his parents and must have been well aware of their Yorkshire origins. He had a deep affection for his mother, Edith, who lived to the great age of 93. After her death he erected an obelisk in his garden to her memory and inscribed it with

> *"Ah! Editha!*
> *Best of mothers,*
> *Most affectionate of women,*
> *Farewell!"*

Above: Edith Pope (nee Turner).

Edith Pope (nee Turner) was born in Marrow House, or Gods Croft, as it may have been known then, baptised in St Mary's chapel, Worsbrough on 18 June, 1642.[2]

About twenty years earlier William Turner, aged twenty-four, grandson of an official of the Council fo the North, married Thomasine Newton of Kilburn in Huntington parish church, near York. The Turners, a well-to-do Catholic family, temporarily left their York estates, moving to Worsbrough Dale in about 1641, following a short stay at Birthwaite Hall in Darton parish, probably at the request of the Burdets with whom there may have been family connections. William may have assisted in administering the Burdet's affairs which were in a state of uncertainty when a heir of only one and a half years old had inherited, their estate having been otherwise subject to the influence of the Rockleys of Worsbrough.

The Turners only remained in Worsbrough for a few years prior to returning to their York estates but succeeded in bringing four new children to the font of St Mary's. The last to be baptised, Jane, in 1645, was in fact their eleventh, and a further six were to be recorded in York registers.

Edith remained a spinster until about 1686 when she married widower

Above: Alexander Pope (1688-1744) by William Hoare.

Alexander Pope, also in his mid-forties. Pope had 'amassed a handsome fortune' from the London drapery trade, enabling the couple to retire to Binfield, Windsor Forest, and escape from persecution. A son, named after his father, was born in 1688 but the sickly child caught a spinal infection, possibly tubercular, causing permanent disability and chronic ill-health. It soon became clear, however, that Alexander junior's mental capacities were far from being impaired. By his teens he was showing poetic and satirical talent of astonishing maturity. Actual publication began in 1709 with the *Pastorals*, followed by *Essay on Criticism* (1711) and probably his greatest achievement: *The Rape of the Lock* (1712). Pope's translation from the Greek of Homer's *Iliad* (1715-20) and later *The Odyssey* (1725-26) enabled him to move his parents first to Chiswick and then to a rented villa in Twickenham. Interestingly, one of his neighbours and sometime friend was Mary Wortley Montagu (Lady Bute) who had spent the early part of her married life in a South Yorkshire 'villa', Wharncliffe Lodge, amidst Wharncliffe Chase; and no doubt would have described to a Pope a prospect or view virtually unequalled in Europe.

Pope died in 1744, aged fifty-six and was buried near his parents in Twickenham Church.

Ebenezer Elliott, the Corn Law Rhymer and 'Poet of the Poor', who died at Great Houghton in 1849 and lies in Darfield churchyard, was proud of Pope's maternal connection with our area, referring to Edith's birth-place at what he called 'Marrow Thorn'.

2. The Marrows

John Marrow and his wife, Anne (nee Hobson) are believed to have settled in Worsbrough Dale from Doncaster in about 1671.[3] Two family memorials survive inside St Mary's church. On the floor leading to the entrance of the lady chapel lies a gravestone with a latin inscription in memory of 'Jacobi [James] Marrow', gentleman who died on 25 November, 1690. An interesting stone oval tablet can be seen on the chapel wall commemorating the death of John Marrow, gentleman, on 7 December, 1701 aged fifty-six and his wife, Anne, who died twenty-six years later 'in the 72nd Year of her Age'. John Marrow's last will and testament survives, made just sixteen days before his decease and provides us with our first detailed picture of the family.[4] We know, for example, that he had recently 'bought a farm at Kendall Greene', its future causing him concern. Describing himself as 'infirm', he wanted the property, occupied by John Slater, to go to his daughter, Elizabeth and not to Roger Marrow, his son and heir who had been promised it by 'Mrs Beard', widow of the former owner, who had 'no power att all'

Above: Marrow family memorial plaque, St Mary's Church, Worsbrough.

to do so. Roger, subject to various conditions, got 'money due upon a mortgage' from land in Bradfield and the rest of the goods and chattels, his father explaining that 'no more' could be given because of having to pay debts of more than £500 contracted by the late Robert Beard of Kendal Green Farm and an agreement to pay Mrs Beard £10 annually for the remainder of her life. Elizabeth, his daughter, also received a bed, a silver tankard and two spoons whilst Anne, his wife, had the benefit of the 'Red bed' and 'all my plate Rings Linen and other goods which were hers before'; and 'one silver Salvar a Silver Sugar Box and a little Silver cann'. Another son, John, was only to receive ten shillings because of lands which he would inherit via his parents' marriage settlement. A third son, Thomas, 'may have and enjoy his Mare Red Cow and Black Calfe without trouble' but no other provision seems to have been made. Among minor bequests was the sum of forty shillings 'for the poore of Worsbrough' and twenty shillings each (for mourning rings) to two of the townships leading citizens: Henry Edmonds, Esquire and 'Mr Carrington'. The Carringtons, of 'The Yews', Worsbrough Dale, were a well-known family of attorneys. A Leeds branch of the Marrow family also seem to have had members in the legal profession. A Roger Marrow of Leeds was a cloth-merchant, dying there in 1732. In his will John Marrow makes little reference to the house in which he was actually living but he may have been a tenant of the Edmunds' estate.

The probate inventory of John Marrow, gentleman, probably the son referred to above, was taken in 1717.[5] Although the document does not relate to the present house it does provide us with detailed information about an earlier building and its contents. The four appraisers started by valuing the deceased's 'purse and apparrell' or ready cash and clothes, worth £5 and proceeded to list the contents of the kitchen which contained:

> *'One range [fireplace] one Grate fire Shovell & Tongs & a pair of End Irons & the rest of the Iron things belonging the firestead, £1., a Jack & Two Iron potts a brass Skellett [saucepan] 3 brass Candlesticks & a warming pan, £1., for Pewter, 2,10s., Two Tinn dripping pans, 1s.6d., one table 3 Chairs & 2 Stools & a bench, 15s.'*

Next door was the 'Hall', a term not commonly found in local inventories. In medieval houses, the hall, at the centre of the building, was open right to the roof, with a fire on a hearth in the middle, smoke finding its way through openings at the end of the ridge. Such houses were generally modernised by the insertion of a floor with a staircase. In this example it was a term used to describe the main living room or 'house' as it was more usually known in our area. By the side of the hall-range was a 'still' for distilling liquor and the room was furnished with 'a long table 2 little a Couch Chaire [sofa] & ii Chaires & 6 buffets [stools]'. The presence of 'a clock and Case, £1., bookes & pictures & mapps, £3' suggests that the occupier had refined tases.

The appraisers then entered the parlour. In most of our local houses this was used as a bed sitting room and John Marrow's house was no exception. It had a bed, worth £2 (often the most valuable piece of furniture in a room), a chest of drawers, a 'close stool' or night commode, and 'Seeing Glass with dressing box a little table with Carpett & a little stand & 12 Chaires'.

A fourth ground floor room, described as the 'office' may have been used for work or storage since it only contained two 'line wheels' for spinning flax during the process of making linen. Upstairs, the 'Chamber over the Office', was furnished as a bedroom, but contained a somewhat surprising item: 'a fish Nett, 4s.'. The two rooms above the hall and parlour were used mainly for the storage of dry goods such as malt and cereals. The heated chamber over the kitchen, with a bed worth £2.10s., a chest of drawers, desk, trunk, close stool and three chairs' was the best bedroom and probably housed the bulk of the household linen which, along with 'plate' was valued separately.

Moving out of doors, the appraisers stopped at the 'Garden House' which contained 'one little range, 2s., a table a Lang Setle [long high-backed bench, usually with arms] & three Chaires a watering pan & a pair of shears, £1.' and probably refers to the outbuilding still to be seen in the rear grounds of the house, furnished for a farm servant or gardener. Near the main house were the 'Brewhouse', 'Buttery' and 'Laythe' or hay barn.

Like most of his contemporaries John Marrow had some farming interests. Two acres of 'hardcorn' or mixed corn were growing, valued at £1.8s. and his livestock consisted of 'a Cow and a heifer, £3.10s.'; and a pig worth eight shillings. A 'mare & foal, £5.' were also listed.

The total value of John Marrow's goods and chattels amounted to £59.19s.6d., on the face of it making him little better off than neighbouring farmers though his gentry status, property and lifestyle placed him socially way above most ordinary Worsbrough inhabitants.

The Marrow family may have continued to live in Worsbrough Dale during the early Georgian period. In 1731, for example, John Hobson, the Dodworth Green gentleman tanner and diarist, recorded 'Mr Thomas Marrow dead at London' as though he had been visiting the capital, perhaps on business.[6] Elizabeth Marrow, widow, was buried in Worsbrough churchyard in 1745.

3. Regency and Victorian Families

In the 'bottom churchyard' of St Mary's is the gravestone of Francis Wood, son of Thomas and Jemima Wood of Newton House in the parish of Ledsham, 'formerly of Marrow House in this township' who died on 30 August, 1830, aged 22. The inscription also records Jemima's death as 24 October, 1835, aged 47.

Nearby, almost entirely surrounded by a wrought iron fence, lies the distinctive table tomb of persons who were clearly of local importance. The principal epitaph relates to

'JOHN FIELD Esquire
formerly of Low Moor near Bradfield
but late of Marrow House
in this Township
who departed this life
on the 7th day of March 1840
Aged 54 Years
deeply regreted by his
Family and Friends'

A John Field, aged 21, 'steward' or estate manager is listed in a Worsbrough militia list of 1806.[7] A year later, in the Yorkshire election, 'John Field of Marrow House' was one of only thirteen Worsbrough freeholders who recorded their votes at York.

Writing in the 1870s, Joseph Wilkinson in his History of Worsbrough described that 'in more recent years' Marrow House was the residence

Below: Field Family grave, Worsbrough churchyard.

of 'Mr John Field, and afterwards his sisters, who were at one time interested in the coal and iron trade of the district', adding 'The house was partly re-built and improved by Mr Field in the early part of the present century, the original character and style of the building being adhered to'.[8] Field, initially with Messrs Cochrane and Faulds and later with Faulds and the Coopers, managed ironworks at Worsbrough Bridge. He was leasing coal-bearing land from the Edmunds estate in 1831 and had earlier been manager for the Edmunds' Worsbrough collieries.[9] At the 1835 West Riding election John Field 'of Worsbrough' and James Cochrane 'of Marrow House' were among the electors who voted. Field may, therefore, have left Marrow during the 1820s and 1830s, though it is also possible that both the Woods and Cochranes enjoyed joint occupation.

The North side of the above monument records the death of 'ANNE FIELD late of Marrow House' on 4 January, 1844, aged fifty-one whilst the opposite side is dedicated to 'HARRIET FIELD' of Marrow House 'and late of York' who died on 24 March, 1866, aged twenty-eight.

We can now turn to the census enumerators' returns, to give us more information about the Fields' tenancy of Marrow House.[10] In 1841 Miss Harriet Field, 'aged 47' was head of the household, her Rank, Profession or Occupation given as 'Coal Trade'. She was, therefore, not the same person named on the family tomb, unless her age had been inscribed correctly. Harriet lived with her younger sister, Ann, also a spinster, together with two female and one male servant. 'Marrow Cottage', probably the adjacent building, was occupied by iron welder Joseph Wright, his wife, Mary and labourer Benjamin Jubb. Ten years later Miss Harriet Field, 'aged 60', born in Barnsley, remained head and had a visitor, Miss Catherine Sikes, in the house on the night of the census. Hannah Webster, housekeeper, born in Horsforth and Mary Gledhall, cook, a local girl, completed the household of 1851. Labourer Benjamin Jubb, aged fifty and now married, continued to occupy outbuildings as did Charles Neatherwood, labourer, aged twenty-five, with his wife and two infants, together with 'lodger' George Neatherwood, labourer, aged twenty-one.

An 'Inventory & Valuation of The Fixtures and Effects of Miss Harriett Field' taken on 17 November, 1857 by local agents Lancasters provides us with interesting information about the house at the end of the Field occupation.[11] The ground floor consisted principally of Breakfast Room, Drawing Room, Dining Room and Kitchen. There was also a storeroom and cellar. Above were four bedrooms, the last described as being 'over [the] Nursery'. The staircase and passages were also listed, the latter housing a 'water closet'. Outside the main

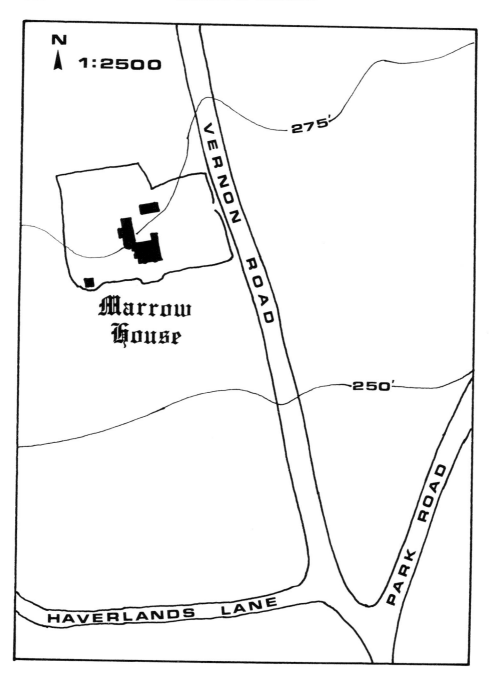

Above: Location of Marrow House

dwelling Benjamin Jubb's 'House' contained an oven and range, brewing pan and staircase. Charles Neatherwood's 'Cottage' had an oven, passage and hearth grate. The document gives an impression of a fairly typical well-to-do Victorian household but the Fields were the last of the 'leisured classes' to enjoy Marrow.

At the 1861 census the house was occupied by Durham-born mining engineer Ralph Rawling Maddison, aged thirty-nine, his wife, Elizabeth, aged thirty-four and seven children ranging from nine months to eleven years. Several other Maddison children died in infancy during the early 1860s. The large family had the benefit of two servants: Mary O'Neill, aged twenty (born in 'North America') and eighteen year old Sarah Siddall who may have accompanied the family from Durham. The cottage was married quarters for a farm labourer. At this time important new mines were being sunk or developed in the Barnsley district but it was also th age of the great disasters – with devastating consequenced for our local communities. Ralph Maddison would have been well aware of the recent tragedy at Lundhill (1857: 189 deaths), Edmunds Main (1862: 59 deaths) and the Oaks Colliery (1866) when 361 men and boys perished in what remains England's worst mining disaster.[12] Engineers or 'Viewers' as they were first known, were often engaged by coalmasters and owners on a consultative basis, especially when they were of some status; in this respect Maddison's Durham coalfield background may have been to his advantage. He appears to have come to Barnsley in 1856 'to take up an appointment at the Royd Collieries' though ultimately may have been employed at Worsbrough Park Colliery.[13] Maddison's mother had Barnsley connections, being a Porter, a family well-known for the early development of coal mining in the town.[14] By the mid-1860s the Maddison household had suffered the loss of its mother and a further child, though two births meant that eight sons and daughters were recorded on the census of 1871. In a trade directory of 1871-72 Ralph Rawling Maddison of "Mara [sic] House" is described as 'colliery manager and underground viewer'. Maternal duties were probably taken over by the two eldest daughters, Elizabeth (aged 21) and Mary (19) with the help of a single resident 'domestic', Stainborough-born Elizabeth Hepworth. The eldest son, Robert Davis Maddison, aged nineteen, worked as an articled clerk and became a notable Barnsley solicitor and Justice of the Peace.[15] Marrow Cottage housed blacksmith Jabus Bennett, his wife, Sarah and three young children. This family originated in Kimberworth, near Rotherham.

Another mining engineer, James Hunter, appears to have succeeded the Maddisons by the late 1870s, being listed in White's trade directory and was resident at the time of the 1881 census. Kelly's directory of

1889 lists a Hugh Higson, 'private citizen' as occupier of Marrow House; also possibly a mining engineer.

4. Edwardian to Present Day Families

(i) Hewitt, c.1900-1906

The Hewitts were tenants at Marrow for a few years during the early 1900s. Joseph Hewitt, born in Barnsley in 1867, was recently described by historian and archivist John Goodchild as 'an excellent example of the self-made man', rising from modest origins to be 'a highly successful solicitor, to be managing director of a considerable number of colliery companies, to head a local colliery owners' association of his own establishment [and], to be a director of a whole range of companies'.[16] Hewitt, a pupil at St Mary's Boys School, gained a Locke Scholarship to Barnsley Grammar, subsequently gaining employment as a junior clerk with one of the town's leading legal practices: Newman & Bond. He qualified as a solicitor in 1893, shortly after his marriage to a daughter of George Guest, the well-known Barnsley grocer, and by 1897 was living at Cavendish Road, off Huddersfield Road. Joseph Hewitt set up his own practice in 1899 and shortly afterwards moved to Marrow with a family that eventually consisted of two sons and four daughters. Earlier, in 1889, Hewitt had become Company Secretary of the Barnsley Chronicle initiating a successful family ownership which of course continues to the present day.

Joseph Hewitt's mining interests concerned Wharncliffe Woodmoor, Woolley & North Gawber, Haigh, Swallow Hill and Darton Main

Below: New range attached to main house (1991)

collieries. The family moved to Ouselthwaite Hall and Sir Joseph was created a Baronet in 1921. He died in 1923.

(ii) **Gregory, 1906-32**

Writing to Allan and Joan Finlay from Brighton in 1981, Maud Gregory, aged 92, described how the house had been empty 'for 2 or 3 months' following the Hewitt tenancy when the owner was Martin Edmunds and the agent a Mr Burroughs, who lived at Wortley. The Gregorys moved to Marrow in 1906 and stayed for twenty-six years. In her letter Maud, the eighth of ten children, was able to remember, remarkably precisely despite a gap of 75 years, the position of a well, subsequently obscured, which was 'very near the tree in front of the little front gate – about 7ft away and (I think) on a line between the tree and side-door of the court-yard'.

(iii) **Recent Residents, 1933-present**

Following the Gregorys' the house was occupied on a caretaker basis by a Mr Gillespie, a woodman from the Edmunds estate and probably other temporary tenants and lodgers until, in the mid-1930s, the property came under the ownership but short residency of Mr Harold Slack.

In 1936 Marrow House became the home of the Winter family, its head being Mr W Winter, the well-known Barnsley solicitor. The Winters remained for almost forty-years, until all the property was purchased by the Finlays in 1975.

Marrow House may not be a building of outstanding architectural interest but its historical associations deserve wider recognition. In the care of Allan and Joan Finlay the property has been given a new lease of life, hopefully to be enjoyed as a family home or homes in future generations.

Notes and References

1. Stevenson S, *Middlesex*, 1972, p.179

2. Wilkinson J, *History of Worsbrough*, c.1880, p.108

3. Wilkinson, *op cit*, p.123

4. Borthwick, 22 Nov 1701, Don.Deanery

5. Borthwick, 15 Feb 1717 (proven Dec 1718), Don.Deanery

6. 'The Journal of Mr John Hobson, late of Dodworth Green', *Surtees Society*,   vol.LXV, 1875, p.303

7. Courtesy of Mr John Goodchild (private collection), Curator at Cusworth Hall,   now Wakefield MDC archivist.

8. Wilkinson, *op cit*, p.123

9. Communication from Mr John Goodchild, Wakefield MD Library HQ, 8 Apr 1991

10. Barnsley Archives (BA), Census Returns (Worsbrough), 1841-81

11. BA, Lancs I & V, Bk 44, 1857

12. For details see Elliott B, *Explosions in Coal-Mines; The Tragedy of the Oaks Colliery*, 1970, (B.Ed dissertation) in Barnsley (Local Studies) Library.

13. Information from Mr A K Clayton, Hoyland Common, 1991; *Transactions of the South Yorkshire Viewers' Association*, vol 1, 1857-8 lists Mr R R Maddison, Worsbro' Park Colliery as an ordinary member; also Ralph Maddison was in charge of works connected with the opening of Wentworth Pit on 24 December 1857 by Messrs Cooper & Co (information courtesy of Mr M Hepworth, BL/LS, 1991)

14. William Porter started his Barnsley Colliery interests in 1790, succeeded by Joseph Porter who resided at Park House, Ardsley. Porter's tramway ran from High Stile Colliery to the canal in Pontefract Road closed in 1841, but was revived thirty years later (information courtesy of Mr John Goodchild)

15. R D Maddison, J.P. born Haltwhistle, Northumberland, 1851, died Barnsley, 1903.

16. Goodchild J, *Coals From Barnsley*, 1986, p.60

Acknowledgements

Thanks to Mr John Hislop, Conservation Officer, Planning Department of Barnsley MBC, and Dr Denis Ashurst. All uncredited photographs by the author.

Below: Present owners: Joan and Allan Finlay.

9. HISTORIC HUNSHELF

by Phyllis Crossland

THE PARISH OF HUNSHELF, SITUATED above the upper Don Valley about three miles south-east of Penistone, is one of Barnsley's more picturesque areas. Still predominantly rural, with splendid views of the surrounding hills, it attracts an increasing number of country-lovers from the town, especially in summer, including rambling groups who enjoy walking the footpaths.

Prior to 1974 when it became incorporated into Barnsley Metropolitan Borough Hunshelf was one of eight townships which formed the extensive parish of Penistone. It formerly comprised all the land contained in the fork between the Greater Don River to the north of the township and the Lesser or Little Don to the south. Since the re-adjustment of boundaries, however, Hunshelf does not extend as far as the Little Don. Its southern boundary is now the ridge of land across the top of Hunshelf Bank. This means that the whole area of Hunshelf Bank which slopes steeply down to the Lesser Don is no longer in Hunshelf Parish but in Stocksbridge under the authority of Sheffield. Hunshelf's other neighbouring parishes include Langsett, Oxspring, Thurgoland and Wortley.

Early History

The name Hunshelf suggests that one of the first settlers on this site was either an individual named Hun or a tribe of that name. The word 'shelf', spelt 'scelf' or 'scylf' in old documents, literally meant shelf or ledge of land, so Hunshelf was the land which 'shelved' or sloped towards the river and which was originally claimed by a person or persons by the name of Hun. Just when this was we cannot exactly know, but it could have been around the seventh century.

We do know that in 1066 A.D. a Saxon called Ailric held three carucates of land in Hunshelf, a carucate being the amount of land which could be cultivated by one plough in a year. In the Domesday Book of 1087, however, the land was recorded as 'waste' as were other wide areas of Yorkshire. We know that, during his conquest of England, William I devastated much of its northern regions as punishment to people who resisted him. There is a recent theory that lands defined as 'waste' in the Domesday record might not necessarily have been totally destroyed but the inhabitants moved elsewhere. Whether or not this was so the situation in Hunshelf might not have been as bad as in some other places. Though Ailric's estates passed to the powerful Norman, Ilbert de Lacy, Ailric was allowed to retain several manors including Hunshelf and Cawthorne, possibly as the nominal owner under Ilbert.

It seems likely that in Norman times a manor lord was placed at Hunshelf whose successors were known as 'de Hunscelf'. The name, with slight variations, appears in several charters of the thirteenth and fourteenth centuries. In 1310 a William de Hunschelf was witness to a grant concerning land in Oxspring, while a document of 1365 reads: *'Eve of the Apostles Peter and Paul, 39 Edward III. Release by John Salforth of Ruthbirchworth to John Hundeschelf of all claims in the lands . . . Salforth had had of the grant of Richard in the vill and territory of Oxspring'.*[1] Another record informs: *'Grant by Simon de Hunself to Thomas Billeclive his brother, for his homage and service, of all his land of Billeclive formerly held by Ralph de Billeclive and three parts of his land of Ricroft, in addition to a yearly rent 18d. Witnesses, William the parson of Penigiston, and William his son, William de Deneby, Robert son of Matthew de Oxspring, John his brother, John de Penigston, Robert de Gunnilthuait, Henry his brother, Henry de Claii.'*[2] Today there are still two old farms, Upper Belleclive and Lower Belleclive in Hunshelf's neighbouring parish of Langsett.

Whatever the transactions were between manor lords at that time, life for the peasants would be mainly a struggle for subsistence. They were bound to their overlord, having to work his land as their own. With crude ox-drawn ploughs and simple tools they toiled to produce oats and rye, their staple crops. Animals were kept, of course, for milk, meat, wool and leather.

During the Middle Ages there were two main settlements of population in Hunshelf, one near Hunshelf Hall in the middle of the township and the other at Snowdenhill, a small hamlet to the west. Snowdenhill is mentioned in several medieval documents with a variety of spelling. Invariably the old words begin with 'Snod' and one theory is that an Anglo-Saxon settler called Snodda gave the place its name, Snoddanhale meaning Snodda's Nook. Another theory is that the names derive from an old Norse word 'snoddin' meaning bare or bald. This does not seem unlikely because in that area today there is a field known as 'Bare Pasture'.

In 1379, according to the Poll Tax returns, there were only nineteen married couples and seven single people over the age of sixteen who were paying the tax.[3] There could have been other inhabitants who were either exempt or evaded the tax, and of course there would be

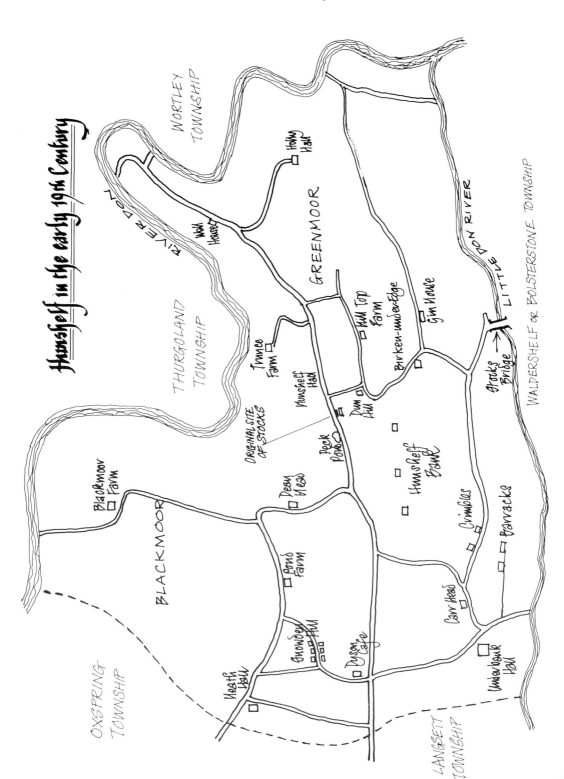

Hunshelf in the early 19th Century

no children whose names were not recorded. Even so, the population is seen to be very sparse. It is interesting to note that no de Hunschelf is recorded here, but a Robertus de Hundechell was in 'Villata de Oxpring' at that date and two others, Willelmus and another Robertus were at 'Roderiham'. Why they moved is a matter for conjecture. Another point of interest is that, whereas a document of 1333 shows a 'William the smith' living in Hunshelf, the 1379 record has no smith.[4] This might have suggested a lapse in arable cultivation but the fact that Johannes Burias is described as a 'thresher' discounts the theory. While most of the inhabitants in Hunshelf paid the lowest tax of fourpence in 1379, there were seven men who paid sixpence because they had a special skill or trade. Besides the thresher these included 'diker, skynner, mason, mawker, souter, and sclaster'.[5]

The ancient stocks which served Hunshelf's early community were sited by the roadside between Hunshelf Hall and Peck Pond, a nearby smallholding. They were only moved in 1937 to Greenmoor village on the occasion of King George VI's coronation. By that time Greenmoor had become the main centre of population in the parish.

Landowners, Freeholders and Tenants

In 1569 the manor of Hunshelf was sold to Francis Wortley by John Byron esq. and Alice his wife. It is likely that John was descended from a Richard de Byron mentioned in 1307 as being granted free-warren by King Edward II 'in all demesne lands including Huddersfield and Hunshelf'. Francis Wortley already held the adjoining lordship of Wortley as his ancestors had done for centuries. The Hunshelf property he acquired in 1569 was described as: *'Manor of Hunshelff and 6 messauges, 6 cottages, and a watermill with lands in Hunshelff, Peynyston, Silkeston, Byrcheworthe, Thurguland, and Snodell, and free fishing in the waters of the same.'*[6]

On Francis Wortley's death in 1583 the manor passed to his son Richard who in turn bequeathed it to his son, another Francis. According to the records in 1604 this boy, then aged twelve, inherited from his father Richard: *'The Manor of Henshelfe with appurtenances in the said Countie and Fower Messuages eight cottages and divers landes tenements and hereditaments etc. etc. in Hunshelfe and Snodell, holden of the said Edward Talbott by the yerelie rent of 2s. 10d. and what other service they know not and are worth by yere above all charges £5.'*[7] Some of the young landowner's other properties were worth considerably more. While Hunshelf was only worth £5, Wortley Manor was worth £21 13s 4d, Newhall £12, and Carleton £14, though Hoylandswaine was only valued at £2!

While the Wortley landowners received rent from their various tenants, there were a number of families in Hunshelf who occupied land and dwellings on a freehold basis. In 1602 Richard Wortley had signed an agreement with the freeholders concerning the commons and wasteland of the manor.[8] This was to the effect that they could be divided — the freeholders to take half the area while he took the remainder, though there is no evidence to show that this was carried out at that time. Perhaps this was because Richard Wortley died in the following year and his successor was only a boy. The freeholders named in that agreement were Francis West, Francis Greaves, John Greaves, Thomas Ellis and John West.

Francis Wortley who inherited the manor in 1604 was created a baronet in 1611 and knighted by James I. He was a staunch Royalist supporter during the Civil War of the 1640s, being a Colonel of Foot for Charles I. His fortunes are reputed to have suffered in consequence and he was actually imprisoned for a time in the Tower of London. In 1665 a rental account was drawn up of lands in Hunshelf owned by Sir Francis at the time of his death.[9] The names of tenants and rent they paid were: *'Nicholas Hobson £11, Thomas Hobson £4 6s 8d, Rafe Parkin £3, Will Dungworth £7, Francis and Jiones Wordsworth 13s 4d, John Dowson 15s 0d, Jo Sampson £2 15s, Rob Roads 1s 8d, Will Skelton £6, John Smith flor mills £5.'* Incidentally, the Rafe Parking mentioned was tenant of Trunce Farm, my present home. He is recorded elsewhere as Ralph Parkin.

More information about Hunshelf's inhabitants of the seventeenth century is given in the West Riding Hearth Tax Returns for 1672.[10] From the number of hearths a man had we can deduce who were likely to have been the more affluent members of the community. It is seen that William Skelton had 7 hearths, George Helliwell 6, Steven West 5, George Walker 4. John Howard, Thomas Lynley and John Priest all had three. Those who had two were Joseph Skelton, William Dunghouse, Jarvice Masson, William Wadsworth, Thomas Armfield, John Sampson, Thomas Hobson, Jonas Broadhead and forge, George Dyson, William Sanderson, William Marsden, and Joseph Morton. The people with only one hearth were Widow Hobson, Jonas Rich, Thomas Crossley, Thomas Dyson, William Bagshawe, Francis Wadsworth, Christopher Sanderson, Thomas Armfield, one — not yet finished, Francis Armitage, Richard Graves, Edmond Stocks, Ralph Parkin, Thomas Armfields, William Sanderson, Edmond Brammah, John Hoyland, Francis South, Executors of Sir Francis Wortley one — empty, John Marsden, Edward Pitt, John Marsden 1 — not yet finished, Mr Smith one — poor, John Senyor one — demoll.

WARRANT.

West=Riding of Yorkshire, } TO WIT. { To the Constable of *Hunshelf* ——— in the said Riding, and to all other Constables in the said Riding.

WHEREAS Information and Complaint upon Oath, have this day been made unto me, one of Her Majesty's Justices of the Peace acting in and for the said Riding, by *Ann Crosland* —— of *Hunshelf* —— in the said Riding, *Married Woman* That *James Crosland* ——— of *Hunshelf* ————— in the said Riding, *Labourer* ——— on the *fourth* ——— day of *August instant* at *Hunshelf* ——— in the said Riding, did unlawfully assault and beat the said Complainant, against the Peace of our Sovereign Lady the Queen, and contrary to the Statute in that case made and provided :— These are therefore, in Her Majesty's Name, to command you forthwith to apprehend the said

——————— *James Crosland* ———————

and bring before me, or some other of Her Majesty's Justices of the Peace acting in and for the said Riding, then and there to answer the said Complaint, and further to do and receive what unto Law doth appertain. And you are hereby also required to give Notice to the said Complainant, then and there to appear and make good h *er* said Complaint. And be you then there to certify what you shall have done in execution hereof. Herein fail not.

Given under my Hand and Seal at Barnsley, in the said Riding, the *sixth* ——— day of *August* ——————— in the year of our Lord One Thousand Eight Hundred and *forty.*

[M.]

[signature]

Above: Warrant for James Crossland, 1840

In 1707 a great dispute arose between the Wortley landowners and two of the Hunshelf freeholders, Richard West and George Walker. During the seventeenth and eighteenth centuries the West family of Underbank Hall and the Walkers of Hunshelf Hall were the most influential freeholders of the township, being accorded the title of 'gentlemen' in documents of their time. The dispute concerned common land. It appeared that the freeholders were claiming right to enclose some of the common waste on Hunshelf Bank under the terms of the old 1602 agreement signed by Richard Wortley. They had in fact already done so and were growing crops when servants of Sidney Wortley arrived on the scene and: *'did breake and Enter and their grass and corne there growing with their Cattle and otherwise Did Tread downe Eate up and consume and 20 Roods of plaintiffs' stone wall there lately erected did cast and throw downe . . . .'*[11]

The line of defence taken by the Wortleys against the indictment was that the 1602 agreement was invalid: 'It's plaine if this a Reall Deed (as wee believe it false) that it passes nothing at most it amounts but to a Covennt.' The Wortleys brought many elderly witnesses to testify they had enjoyed uninterrupted use of the commons for 'time beyond memory'. One witness was Ralph Parkin, their tenant at Trunce Farm. In that year of 1707 Ralph was sixty-two years old but still had twenty years more to live![12]

The plaintiffs Walker and West were supported in the case by the Wests' relative, William Fenton who later succeeded to their estate.

The dispute continued for four years, the Wortleys insisting that: *'This pretended agreement was made above 100 years agoe and noe possession has gone along with it . . . . . It will certainly be difficult for them to mentaine such an agreement which has never been heard of this 100 years.'*[13] Despite the mass of depostions and correspondence connected with the case, the outcome is not clear.

In 1756 the Hunshelf freeholders were involved in another dispute where they took sides with Edward Wortley against Godfrey Bosville who owned the adjoining manor of Oxspring. That argument concerned the boundaries between Snowdenhill in Hunshelf and Roughbirchworth in Oxspring. On its settlement a number of boundary stones were erected with initials E W carved on the Hunshelf side and G B on the Oxspring side. The freeholders named were:- William Fenton of Underbank, George Walker of Hunshelf Hall, John Cockshutt of Huthwaite, Gentlemen: Thomas Pearson of Snodenhill, Joshua Newton of Hunshelf Bank, John Pearson and George Pearson of Rough Birchworth, Yeomen.

The Wortley family continued as chief landowners in Hunshelf for over two centuries more following the 1707 Dispute. The Walkers and Fentons continued to hold their property as 'gentlemen' — the Walker family until 1826 and the Fentons until 1950. When a daughter of the Fentons married a Major de Wend in the nineteenth century the family name became de Wend Fenton.

Farming

In the early years of the eighteenth century John Stocks held a 'messuage, farm or tenement and two small cottages and inclosed land in Hunshelf vix. the three over fields, the three Roe-royds and the four holmes, 36a 3r 17p. Also six acres of pasture on which a cow could range in a common field.' This land occupied by John Stocks was by the Little Don river at the bottom of Hunshelf Bank and consequently the bridge over the river at that point was referred to as Stocks Bridge. In time the whole area of the valley was called by that name which endures today in the thriving steel-town of Stocksbridge.

The open field system of agriculture prevailed in Hunshelf until the end of the eighteenth century when certain freeholders made an agreement to enclose the town fields. What they did has been regarded as not strictly legal but they did it nevertheless. Between 1790 and 1793 the four areas of land named as upper Town Field, Nether Town Field, Naked Man Field and Dasy Field were apportioned to these freeholders. Out of a total area of 129a. 1r. 25p. Miss Margaret Walker received the lion's share of 60 acres 4 perches. Miss Frances Fenton received 21a. 2r. 5p., John Bedford 13a. 3r. 32p., George and Thomas Roebuck 11a. 0r. 3p., Mr Hirst 4a. 3r. 18p., Jonathan Denton 8a. 3r. 0p., and Thomas Pearson 7a. 3r. 0p. Miss Walker was not resident in Hunshelf but at Middlewood Hall in Darfield, another of her family's properties. Her late father George had also chosen to live there after putting Hunshelf Hall on a twenty-one year lease when his father died.

In 1810 the Hunshelf Inclosure Act passed by Parliament allowed enclosure of the common lands.[15] These were divided and allotted three years later on completion of the Award. As a result the Hon. James Archibald Stuart Wortley gained three hundred acres which included the whole of Blackmoor, Greenmoor and Trunce Commons. Misses Betty and Mary Walker received 98 acres and William Fenton 74, fifty of these being Snoddenhill Common. So it was that the most land was allotted to those who already had the most. The poorer folk were the losers because they had little or no land and had also lost their rights to the commons. Fortunately for them, other forms of employment were forthcoming.

During the eighteenth and ninteenth centuries the type of farming in Hunshelf continued to be mixed. Oats and wheat predominated as cereal crops, with barley being grown to a lesser extent, also some peas, beans and turnips. There is a road today named Pea Royd Lane at the bottom of Hunshelf Bank. Potatoes were not grown on a large scale in the area until the beginning of the nineteenth century, though by that time horses were also employed. In an age when modern fertilisers were lacking, manure was all-important. An account of Tillage for 1758 gives the following items:-

Town Field	-	4 Load of Lime upon Grass	£4	16	0
In 6 Acres	-	63 Load of Manure	£4	17	0
		4 Load of Lime	£4	16	0
Summer fallow plowing 4 times			£7	0	0
Pitt Lands	-	Clover Ley plowing 6½ acres	£1	12	6
" "		for 26 Load Manure	£3	5	0
Nether field	one half turnips	34 Load Manure	£4	5	0

We are not told how big the loads were! Somewhat smaller than by today's standards we can imagine, when manure had to be forked manually on and off the cart.

After land was enclosed farming could be done more efficiently. Throughout the country at large the aim was for greater production to meet the needs of a growing population, especially during the Napoleonic War period when imports were restricted. In Hunshelf as elsewhere tenant farmers would have to be efficient in order to pay the large rent increases imposed by their landlords. At Trunce Farm, for example, the acreage was doubled by the addition of common land. In 1804 Thomas Bramall was farming twenty-five acres, while in 1852 his son James had fifty-two for which he was paying the Wortleys a rent of £36, quite a substantial sum considering the extra land was only rough. To make ends meet James had embarked on a new venture — he established himself as a butcher to augment his farming income.

On the bigger farms labourers were engaged. Robert Illingworth who died in 1870, aged 72, worked for Mr Hague at Blackmoor Farm when a young married man. His wages were twelve shillings a week in summer and ten shillings in winter. Boys were paid fourpence to sixpence a day. Single men were often contracted for farmwork at the Martinmas hirings in November when they would undertake to stay in the same employment for a year, living in with the farmers' families. Where there was mutual satisfaction between worker and employer at the year's end, a man could be hired again for another year or more. Otherwise the labourer could offer himself at the next hiring to another farmer.

Introduction of machinery speeded up cultivation of land and harvesting of crops during the nineteenth century but in Hunshelf this happened only gradually. As late as the 1890s corn was cut with scythes. One year two men only were employed in cutting the twelve-acre Town Field by this method. The crop was wheat and the work kept both men busy from Monday morning until Saturday dinner-time. One of the men engaged in this laborious task was George Crossland, father of former Penistone Grammar School teacher, Mr Austin Crossland.

During the twentieth century we have seen scythes replaced by mowing machines and binders, then by combine harvesters and pick-up balers. Oats as a crop has been superseded by barley. New fertilisers have produced greater yields. How ironic it is that now, in this last decade of the century, farmers are being urged to produce less! At this moment, the most productive field at Hunshelf Hall is being 'set aside' for a year because it pays the farmer better to leave it idle!

Clothiers

There is much evidence to show that some families in Hunshelf were formerly involved in the home-weaving of cloth. The names of Tenter House and Cloth Hall, two farms at Snowdenhill, are indicative of this occupation. The hilly nature of the township did not lend itself to large farms generally and many of the small-holders saw weaving as a means of increasing their income from the land. This applied particularly to people on Hunshelf Bank where the ground was steep and rough. Some of the old houses in that area had the kind of windows typical of eighteenth century weavers' cottages, windows which would admit enough light for the weavers to see to operate.

George and Thomas Roebuck had a house and small acreage of land there in the early nineteenth century but were described as clothiers in parish records. It would seem their business was flourishing because in 1800 they took on an apprentice. He was named in the Indenture as Joseph Pool, a poor boy being placed in work by the Hunshelf Overseer who dealt with such cases.

Another clothier whose name occurs frequently in old records was Jonas Ramsden. He had a few acres of land on the Bank and a cottage called Gin House. This dwelling has since undergone alteration and is now known as Well House. Jonas Ramsden had a daughter Ann who married Charles Askham, a weaver, and their daughter Elizabeth who later became Mrs Cuttil lived to be more than ninety years old. Before

Below: Apprenticeship indenture of Ephram Mitchell, 1743

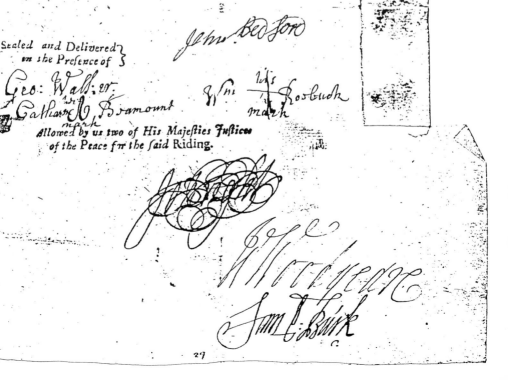

Riding of the County of York (To wit,) Pleneea Quire

This Indenture made the *Twenty third* day of *September* in the Year of our Lord 1743 Between *William Roobuck and John Bedford* the —— Church-Warden and Overseers of the Poor of *the Township of Hunshelfm* And *Ephraim Mitchell* —— a poor Child of the said Town on the one Part, And *Joseph Rhodes* of the same Town on the other Part: Witnesseth, That the said Church-Wardens and Overseers of the Poor Do, f, by and with the Consent, Allowance and Approbation of two of His Majesty's Justices of the Peace for the said Riding, (Quorum unus) put, placed and bound, the said *Ephraim Mitchell* —— as an Apprentice to and with the said *Joseph Rhodes* —— with him to dwell and remain from the Day of the Date hereof, until the said Apprentice shall attain his Age of *Twenty four years* —— according to the Form of the Statute in that Case made and provided. During all which Term the said Apprentice his said Master —— well and truly shall serve, his Secrets shall keep, his Commands (being lawful and honest) at all times willingly shall perform, and in all Things as a good and faithful Servant shall demean himself towards his said Master and all his Family. And the said *Joseph Rhodes* —— for himself, his Executors, Administrators and Assigns, doth Covenant, promise and agree to and with the said Church-Wardens Overseers and his said Apprentice, That he will educate and bring up in some honest and lawful Calling, and in the Fear of God; and that he will find provide for, and allow unto his said Apprentice sufficient, wholesome and competent Meat, Drink, Washing, Lodging, Apparel, and other Necessaries meet for such an Apprentice, during all the said Term; and at the End of the said Term shall find, provide for, and deliver unto his said Apprentice double Apparel of all sorts; (that is to say) one good and new Suit for the Lord's-Days, and another for the Working Days, of Linnen, Woollen, Hose, Shoes, and all other Necessaries meet for such an Apprentice to have and wear.

In Witness whereof, the said Parties to these Presents have hereunto Interchangably set their Hands and Seals the Day and Year above written.

John Bedford

Sealed and Delivered in the Presence of }

Geo: Walker
Catharine O Bramount mark

Wm his mark Roobuck

Allowed by us two of His Majesties Justices of the Peace for the said Riding.

27

she died in 1916 she told how the late Stocksbridge historian, Joseph Kenworthy, (1852-1929) how, as a child, she had often assisted her father and his brother in one of the tenements at Over House where her parents resided.[17] Her job was to help them tread pieces of cloth that had been treated with 'weetings'. She explained to Joseph Kenworthy how a piece of cloth, when taken off the loom, was spread out on the floor and sprinkled with old urine and swine's dung strained through straw. As one piece was 'lecked' another piece was laid on it and more 'weetings' sprinkled on top until several layers were formed, whereupon all members of the family would trample on it. The cloth was then taken to the fulling mill to be scoured. When Elizabeth Cuttil related the practice to Joseph Kenworthy she told him: '. . . . and a nice stink ther wor i' th' hoil aw con tell ye, but we noan bother'd abaht that i' them days.'

Another old homestead on the Bank where large quantities of cloth were made was Birken-under-Edge. The name has since been changed to Burton-under-Edge and the premises are currently undergoing extensive alterations. In the nineteenth century, however, the place was supposed to be haunted by Nancy who had fallen into a large vat of boiling liquid used for dyeing wool. She was said to be related to Jonas Ramsden of Well House. Martha Newton, who died in 1910, aged 88, said three loud raps could sometimes be heard at the back of the set-pot in Birken-under-Edge, whereupon folks would say, 'Listen, there's owd Nancy; she's at it again.'

For a short period at the end of the eighteenth century a cotton mill was in operation at the bottom of Hunshelf Bank. One of its young employess was Hannah, a girl of eight who lived near Greenmoor. In later life, as Hannah Pickford, she told me how she wore a leather apron when working because of the damp. The mill was erected in 1794 and sold in 1807, later becoming used as a blacking mill. Eventually the steelworks of Samuel Fox were founded on the site, and Census Returns of the mid-nineteenth century show that many Hunshelf inhabitants, including children as young as nine, had become 'wire-workers' engaged in the manufacture of crinoline frames to support the current fashion.

Stone-Quarrying

Hunshelf's population today is mainly concentrated in and around the villagbe of Greenmoor at the eastern end of the parish. This is primarily due to the stone-quarrying which prevailed on a large scale in that area throughout the nineteenth century and into the twentieth. The group of houses now known as Office Fold were originally offices connected with the quarrying. Lower down Well Hill the dwellings which are now

Above: Newbiggin Quarry, Well Hill c.1921

Pond Cottages were then The Travellers Rest, an inn for the benefit of thirsty quarrymen. Other houses were built to accommodate men who naturally wanted to be near their work. It can be seen from Census Returns that men came from outside the parish to work in the quarries. Some families took in lodgers whose homes were some distance away, while at Trunce Farm in 1871 the occupants were not farmers but two stone-masons and their families.

Stone had been got from Greenmoor on a small scale for local needs since the seventeenth century. When Ralph Parkin gave his deposition in the Commons Dispute of 1707 he said: *'whenever they had occasion . . gott Stone and Slate on all or any the Moores belonging to the said Mannor as They thought fit and did also burne Bracken and Gott Peates and Turfs on the said Moores from time to time . . .* '[18] Greenmoor was obviously part of the common land at that time.

The situation changed in 1813 when, from the Inclosure Award, the Hon. J.A.S. Wortley was allotted Greenmoor and Trunce Commons. He was quick to realise their potential and leased part of the land for quarrying to Reuben Marsh of Penistone. The exact date when this occurred is not certain. We do know that some time later a family of Browns, also of Penistone, purchased part of the lease from Reuben Marsh. Whilst in the hands of these two owners, many thousands of tons of the finest stone were got and sent to all parts of the country. We are told that in 1835 Joseph Brown had wagons conveying stone to London.[19] Some stone was sent to Goole by boat from Worsbrough, then to Hull and finally by sea to London. When railways were built it was transported by rail from Wortley station.

The first two quarries, known as Isle o' Skye and the Delph, were on Greenmoor. When a third quarry came into operation on land adjoining Trunce Farm it was called the 'California' or 'Cali'. This might suggest it was started around 1849 and named after the American state where mining and quarrying were being done, albeit for gold and not for stone. From the Cali a stone roadway was laid down across the grassy field between the quarry and Greenmoor road to enable the carts to get out with their heavy loads. Most of this cartway is now overgrown but in places the huge stone slabs can still be seen, the grooves which were chiselled out to accommodate the cart wheels being much in evidence. In a survey of 'Lands in Hunshelf 1875' the 'Quarry in Trunce Farm' is owned by Brown and Booth.[20]

Mr Benjamin Brodie Booth had come to Yorkshire from Suffolk. He was the last owner of the Well Hill quarry known as New Biggin. This was a very deep cavity by the roadside near the hill bottom. The quarrymen made their descent to the working levels by 'monkey-pole',

Above: 'Old Vic' Quarry, Greenmoor: Mr Swift (wearing bowler hat) was foreman.

Below: Newbiggin Quarry. Left to right: Johnny Wright, George Bramall, J. T. Walton, Percy Illingworth and Harvey G. Thompson.

Above: 'Old Vic' Quarry, Greenmoor c.1890s.

a type of ladder which consisted of one long pole with iron rods driven through until of equal length on each side. The men went up and down the poles, hands and feet on the iron rods. To reach the very bottom they went down one monkey-pole, walked along a ledge, down another monkey-pole, along another ledge, and finally down a third ledge. Water often seeped into the bottom and had to be pumped away.

It was said that the quality of stone from New Biggin was probably the best in the whole Hunshelf area. It was blue in colour and made very fine gravestones. Some slabs were used for County Hall steps and sets were sent to towns to be used on the streets as cobble-stones. Some of the paving-stones in the yard outside the Houses of Parliament were reputed to be of Greenmoor Stone. Stone from the Delph, Skye, and Cali workings was also of fine quality. It had a sheen and was pale green in colour. Some of the last stone to be used locally may be seen at Stocksbridge, where the Clock Tower War Memorial was built from it after the first World War. The stone flags around Sheffield City Hall also came from Greenmoor.

On the opposite side of the road from New Biggin was the smaller Victoria site. Here were workmen's cabins, stables, blacksmith's shop and joiner's shop. The sawmill was moved to this site after first being in operation at Wortley station. Some quarrying was also done in Rocher Wood, but this did not last long as the stone was not of the best.

The wagons which transported the stone were known as 'drugs'. Their four heavy wheels had iron tyres 4½″ wide and 5/8″ thick. A team of powerful horses was needed to haul the loads and shires were usually employed. A wagon could hold 18 tons of stone. From the Cali it was uphill work to get the loads onto the road, and several horses were used. For the steep downhill journey to the sawmill the horseman had to reshuffle his team, tethering some at the back to steady the load. A kind of iron shoe was placed under one of the back wheels and locked in position by chains put round the spokes, so preventing the wheel from turning. It just skid downhill but things did not get out of hand because the horses at the rear were trained to hold back.

Quarrying could be dangerous work and many accidents were recorded. In 1859 William Illingworth died after falling in Greenmoor quarry. He was thirty-three years old.[21] His small son Samuel became a quarryman too when he grew up and he too lost his life when a horse and cart backed into him and knocked him over the edge. He was thirty-nine and, like his father, left behind a young family.

On a day towards the end of the nineteenth century George Bramall was killed at the Victoria site. It happened just before the men stopped work for dinner. His workmates lifted his body into a cart and proceeded to take it to his home at Woodman Row on Old Mill Lane. On the way they met his wife. One of the men in the cart asked where she was going. "I'm taking George his dinner", she replied. The man said, "Well, I shouldn't bother lass, he'll not be wanting it today." Then between them the workmates broke to her the sad news. Another accident happened at the same site when Bill Brooke, sone of George Brooke the shot-firer was killed.[22] A man named Wright died when a stone fell on him. It was the men's first day back at work after a long period of severe frost. As the thaw started the stone had loosened. A man called Jennings was killed at Rocher quarry when a dray horse bolted. These are just a few of the many fatalities which occurred.

From about 1912 when cement became plentiful and the mixing of concrete was introduced the demand for stone lessened. Workers were gradually laid off until 1936 when quarrying finally came to an end with the closure of New Biggin. All the quarries have since been filled in. The Cali at Trunce Farm was last to be done. It was completed and grassed over in the 1970s.

Education and Religion

The first school in Hunshelf was opened about 1811 in the cottage at Burton-under-Edge occupied by William Newton. The Overseers of the township appointed Benjamin Micklethwaite as school-master and provided him with fuel free of charge. The school was fitted with a range and table, and eleven forms were obtained in 1812. A few years later the cottage needed repair and the school was moved for a time to Well House close by.

In 1836 Mr Micklethwaite moved again, this time to the Town House at Greenmoor to which a schoolroom had been attached by public subscription. He opened a shop in the Town House to sell groceries and provisions, and his wife Sarah baked bread. The property belonged to the township. Mr Micklethwaite was followed in 1844 by Mr Thomas Roebuck. It is said that this master had to break stones for road-making to augment his school pay. He died in 1865 and was succeeded by Mr Stacey, Mr Fletcher and Mr Whittle.

In 1877 the first School Board was formed. Its members were:- John Armitage, Sheffield, a fire-brick manufacturer, George Couldwell, Dean Head, Hunshelf, a farmer, John Dyson of Penistone, an iron master, Francis Hill of Stocksbridge, a manager, and John Milnes, also of Stocksbridge, a draper.

It was then decided to build a new school at Greenmoor, close to the existing one. Work was under way during 1879 and the school was opened in 1880. The first schoolmaster appointed was Mr Hardcastle, whose salary was £80 per annum with free house and coals. At the start there were 82 children on register, 42 boys and 40 girls, but the number soon increased to 100. At this time copybooks were 1/6d a dozen, slates were 3/6d a dozen, and geography and grammar books 1d each. In 1881 the school fees were 4d per week for a child over seven years and 3d for one under seven. Mr Hardcastle's wife helped with the teaching and in 1883 additional help was given by a pupil teacher, Ada Thompson, who was about fifteen years old. Children were promoted by ability rather than age in those days and could leave school at thirteen if they had reached the required standard.

During the nineteenth century children were often kept off school to help with farmwork at busy times. An entry in the log book for July 1882 says 'Haymaking has interfered with attendance.'[23] This is but one example of many similar entries. In 1893 several parents received warnings for the non-attendance of their children. Some of these were William Rusby, Pat Sullivan, David Watts of Tin Mill, Joseph Couldwell of Hunshelf Hall, Ben Watts of Dean Head and Mary Walton of Dean Head. After 1891 education at the school was free but children had to pay for their books until 1896, after which these were free too. Members of the School Board were elected every three years, some of them serving more than one term.

In 1902 the Balfour Act was passed in Parliament. This ordered the abolition of School Boards and placed education under the management of County Councils. At a meeting of the Hunshelf School Board in 1904, administration was handed over to the West Riding County Council. The headmaster at that time was Mr Edward Prew.

During the early years of the twentieth century there were over a hundred children on roll. Besides the headmaster there would be two, or sometimes three assistants. Numbers decreased after 1930 when children over eleven had to leave Hunshelf school and travel to Stocksbridge, that is unless they gained a County Minor Scholarship to Penistone Grammar School. By 1953 the number was as low as sixteen so the teacher, Mrs Birkhead, managed on her own for four years. In 1979 there were twenty-nine children in attendance and Mrs Jones was allowed a full-time assistant and a non-teaching one.

Barnsley Metropolitan Borough Council took over Hunshelf school from the West Riding in 1974 but decided after a while that to keep it open was no longer viable. Education finished there in 1982 and the building has since been converted into three dwelling houses. Hunshelf children under eleven now attend Oxspring school and the over elevens Penistone Grammar School.

Greenmoor's first chapel was built in 1812, but several years later before then there was a Methodist cause in the area started by Mr George Jubb who was associated with wire manufacture in the Don valley. For some years services were held in the mill warehouse and in people's homes. These Methodists joined a Sheffield circuit in 1802 and a few years later it was decided to build a chapel at Greenmoor. It is said that on New Year's Day 1812 the building was brought up to the square, ready for the roof being put on. On that day a small flag was seen fluttering in the breeze to mark this important stage in the building. Before the roof was put on a tablet was placed in the wall over the door, showing the date 1812 and the name 'Providence'. It is thought that Couldwells, then living at Hunshelf Hall and Waltons and Crosslands of Hill Top were all workers in the 'new' chapel during the early part of the nineteenth century. There is a record of Thomas Walton of Hill Top helping to measure out land as a boy of thirteen.[24] Nathaniel Crossland of Don Hill carted the first load of stone for the building and, in his capacity as a carpenter, helped with the woodwork. He was my husband's great-great-grandfather. The chapel was later extended to provide Sunday school and caretaker accommodation.

A new chapel was built in 1906 because it was considered the first one was no longer suitable for services. Some renovations were carried out, however and the old chapel continued to be used for concerts and other social events until fairly recently. Last year the building was sold and its interior extensively altered to fit it for its present use – a recreational centre for the Boys' Brigade. Besides the new Methodist chapel at Green Moor, there is a 'mission room' at Snowdenhill where monthly services are held. The room is actually part of Chapel Farm and clergy come from Penistone to officiate.

Overseers' Accounts

Before 1686 the townships of Hunshelf and Oxspring had only one Overseer of the Poor between them but in that year two were appointed. Unfortunately, we cannot know what their early records told us about Hunshelf people because these no longer exist. It is thought they were kept at Hunshelf Hall and were accidentally destroyed when the house was burnt down. The fact that the Hall was rebuilt in 1746 and the existing records date from 1747 seems to bear this out.[25] Throughout the eighteenth century and the first half of the nineteenth the township had to support its own poor. The overseers were appointed yearly to ensure this was properly done and to keep a written account of expenditure. They had to be men of integrity who could read, write and reckon. Some of their names, along with those of the parish constables at the time, are still familiar. They include Pearson, Mitchell,

Greaves, Couldwell, Wainwright, Bramall, Hague, Ramsden, Grayson, Roebuck, Walton, Crawshaw, Steel, Senior, and Helliwell.

Much of the township's expenditure went on to dole money, clothing, coals, and other requisites for the folk who were unable to support themselves. For example:

> *'John Pools a pair of blankets 10s, a bed 7s 6d, a pair of stockings 2s, a pair of Breeches 5s 6d, a Coat 7s6d, 3 yards of cotton 3s. Going to buy them 5s.*
> *To Mary Pool for Looking to Mother 9 weeks at 2s — 18s*
> *Two loads of coals from Sheephouse Wood to Barracks and leading, 16s.*
> *Thomas Earnshaw for new smock frock 8s*
> *Paid Captain Wood for setting Edward Elliotts Shoulder 2s 6d*
> *Hannah Pool new Shifts 6s 6d*
> *Doctor Booth Phisicking Paupers £8 17s 5d*
> *Abigail Wood — Moos for the House 2s 6d Moosing 4s 6d*
> *School mossing ards and lime 6s 0d.'*[26]

It was common practice during the early years of the nineteenth to use moss for blocking up cracks and draught holes in houses.

In 1828 are some interesting items relating to the illness and death of John Otter, evidently one of the poor:

> *'Feb. 16 Paid Thos. Roebuck for Attending John Otter 3½ days 6s 0d*
> *" 23 "   "   "   "   "   "   "   4½ days 7s 6d*
> *" 25 "Edward Whisom   "   "   "   "4 days 7s 0d*
> *" 25 Paid towards John Otter funeral —*
> *   Correns and eggs 1/3. Meat 12½ lb 7s 3d*
> *   Tobacco pipe and letters for Coffin 2/8, pound of shuger 9d*
> *   Coffin 20/—*
> *   Paid George Roebuck for finding meat for the attenders*
> *   and burying dress of John Otter £1 10s*
> *   Paid Mary Eyre for making Burying Dress of John Otter 1s 2d*
> *   Earsh fetching and taking 3s 0d*
> *   Paid for Leeches Setting on 6s 0d '*[27]

We may wonder what kind of man John Otter was to warrant 12½lb of meat being consumed at his funeral. Incidentally, leeches were still being used to give 'relief' to people in 1836 and 1837

When poor children were apprenticed to local farmers or clothiers the overseer had to ensure they were provided with adequate clothing. In 1835 Hannah Poole was apprenticed to Thomas Couldwell and was given: '2 Pare Stays, 4 Petticoates, 3 Pare Stockings, 4 aprons, 3 shifts, 1 night cap, 1 shole, 1 bedgown, 2 frocks, 3 bonnits, 2 pare shoos (one pare new) at Rotherham 1 frock, 1 shole, 1 apron, 1 night cap.'[28]

The overseers had responsibility to see that single mothers received 'bastard pay', which appeared to be1/6 a week in 1811. It is evident though from accounts of 'bastard money received' that some money at least was recovered from the children's fathers.

In 1813 an agreement was made for mole-catching throughout the township. This was to be for a duration of twenty-one years, whereby 14 gns. were to be paid for the first three years and 12 gns. for the remainder of the term. The moles must still have been a problem at the end of the period because we then see the following:- 'March 15, 1834 This is an agreement on the other part that the said Joseph Pool shall catch the Moulds in the said Township for the sum of Six Guineas for one year.' Joseph Pool made his mark with a cross to confirm the agreement.[29]

Above: Hunshelf Hall (rear view). The gabled, west part, survived the fire.

Hunshelf Hall

This is officially classed as 'a house of architectural and historic interest'. Mainly Georgian in style, it was built into the surviving part of an earlier Hall which was destroyed by fire in the 1740s. This older part has mullioned windows, some of which retain iron bars. The two cellars, one large and one small, belonged to the former house. The steps leading down into the cellars had obviously been much trodden over a long period of years because newer slabs of stone have been fixed, at some more recent stage, into their centres to level them again.

Until 1757 Hunshelf Hall was the residence of several generations of the Walker family but after George died in that year his son leased the property for twenty-one years to Mr William Pearson at a rent of £90 per annum.[30] The next tenant was Mr John Greaves who farmed there until 1816, paying his rent on a yearly basis. During this time the acreage was increased by the addition of town fields and commons. His rent doubled accordingly to £240.[31] Perhaps this caused him hardship as, in 1807 he was paying £29 8s for arrears left on his previous Michaelmas rent. John's tenancy agreement included certain rules. He had not to plough more than 60 acres at a time. He had not to sow potatoes except for use of his own family. He must do all repairs to house, buildings, gates, doors, fences, etc. All hay, straw and manure was to be consumed on the premises. When he left the Hall he received payment for fixtures named:

> *'In Pantrey 2 stone tables and supporters*
> *In Best Kitchen Trenchercase and Drawers and Sinkstone*
> > *Set Pot Stone and Cover ---- Racken and Chimney Pipe*
> *In Small Sellor 3 stone tables and Pillors*
> *In Large Sellor large Beef Stone and Stone Table*
> > *Total Sum £5 0s 6d '*

Mr Joseph Cauldwell took over the tenancy in 1816 and members of his family occupied the house and farmed the land until 1903. In 1817 a new barn was erected by the Walker landlords and expenses for this are shown in their accounts. Other interesting items of expenditure in 1818 are: 'To Benj. Marsh for making up windows at Hunshelf 19s 6d' and 'Bricks to Block Windows Hunshelf Hall 15s.'[32] The windows were blocked up so as to avoid paying tax on them; one remained blocked for the following 128 years.

The last of the Walkers to own Hunshelf Hall were two elderly spinster sisters, Misses Betty and Mary. After their deaths it passed to the Smiths. We are told the two families were friendly and that the Walker sisters acted as sponsors when a baby of the Smiths was christened. Because of this the child was given the names George Walker. The sisters, evidently pleased that their father's name should be continued, arranged for the boy to inherit their propery when he reached the age of twenty-four. This he did in 1826, but in 1838 he conveyed it to his father, William Smith. When he died in 1851 all the Smith property, which included possessions in places other than Hunshelf, was divided between his two sons. George Walker Smith regained Hunshelf Hall and the adjoining properties of Dean Head farm, Peck Pond and Dunhill House. On his death in 1879 the Hunshelf properties passed to his son Frederick Ridsdale who resided in

Nottinghamshire. Before he died in 1930 he sold them all.[33] Hunshelf Hall, Dean Head and Peck Pond were bought by Mrs Emily Maplebeck Crossland, wife of Mr Allan Crossland of Stocksbridge. The price she paid for Hunshelf Hall and Peck Pond was £2900. The property was afterwards in the possession of their two sons, Hugh and Charles, until the 1950s when Hunshelf Hall and Dean Head were bought by Messrs Samuel Fox and Co. Ltd. Peck Pond was bought by Mr Oswald Burton.

When the Couldwells left the farm in 1903 all the crops for that year were harvested by Mr Ben Watts and his men from the neighbouring farm at Dean Head. In 1904 the tenancy of Hunshelf Hall was taken over by Mr Arthur Taylor whose family stayed there until 1946. My husband Mr Charles Crossland became tenant in that year and I joined him two years later. We were there for the next thirty years, being followed by our daughter and son-in-law who now own the property. They are the first owners to live in the house since George Walker died there in 1757.

Our years at Hunshelf Hall were a time of tremendous change. We changed quite soon from well water to mainswater. The earth closets were then replaced by flush toilets, and instead of a tin bath, we revelled in the luxury of a modern bathroom. The biggest breakthrough came in 1956 when electricity was at last brought to us. No longer did we have to fill paraffin lamps to give us light. In due course we obtained the various modern conveniences such as electric cooker, vaccuum cleaner, and washer — luxuries which townsfolk had long enjoyed. On the farm horses were replaced by tractors, while the acquisition of more machinery meant that Charles could eventually manage with only one worker. Hand-milking on a three-legged stool soon gave way to machine-milking, which was later updated onto the modern system of pipe-line and bulk tank. We kept dairy cows, beef cattle, sheep, pigs and poultry. The crops we grew included hay, cereals, potatoes, turnips and kale.

Since Mr Fox has had the farm, more changes have taken place. He has greatly increased his number of cows, specialising in Friesians for better milk production. A beef-type bull is kept so that calves can be sold to the beef feeders. The cows are milked in a herring-bone parlour and housed in cubicle houses during the winter months. A silage barn and cubicle house were erected in what was formerly the stack-yard. Additional housing has since been provided in part of the 1817 barn. Most of the buildings have undergone a change of use, being adapted to present-day requirements.

When Mr Crossland went to the Hall in 1946 he saw that one of the bedroom windows was bricked up so, in order to let in more light, decided to unblock it. Having done so, he was interested to discover, scratched on the thick glass of one pane, the words 'Dear Miss Walker'. The writing was old-fashioned and had probably been done by a diamond of some kind.

One year we had visitors who appeared interested in the old building and expressed a wish to see the cellars. As we began to descend the stone steps the lady called to her dog to accompany us. She thought it very odd when he refused. He just stood on the top step, looking down and whining, his hair on end. "That's very strange," his owner remarked, "he usually follows us everywhere. That's the only time he hasn't wanted to." It was clear the dog was sensing something he didn't like, but of which we were unaware. No amount of coaxing could persuade the animal to go down those steps and our visitor was soon convinced we had a ghost in that cellar. While asking ourselves whether a historic house like Hunshelf Hall could harbour such beings, we can

Below: Date '1746' and initals 'G. A. W.' on arched lintel over doorway of Hunshelf Hall.
(B. Tryer, Farmers Weekly)

also ask about that fire of long ago. Why did it happen? Was anyone in the cellar while the rooms above were enveloped in smoke and flame? To these questions there are no answers. We can only wonder.

Notes and References

1. *Yorkshire Archaelogical Society* (YAS), Record Series, v.39 (1909)
2. YAS, Yorks Deeds, v.II.p.38 (1914)
3. YAS, Journal, v.5 (1879)
4. YAS, Record Series, v.39 (1909)
5. A souter was a shoemaker or leatherworker; a sclasterer was a slaterer; 'Mawker' may have been a transcription error for 'mawher' (mower).
6. YAS, Record Series, Yorks Fines I, p.366 (1887)
7. Sheffield Archives (SA), Wh.M.70
8. SA, Sp.St. 32/33 9. SA, Wh.M.76
10. West Yorkshire Archive Service (Wakefield Library HQ), West Riding Hearth Tax (1672), Y 942 509 896 D
11. SA, Sp.St. 32/1
12. SA, Sp.St. 32; Barnsley Local Studies Library (BLSL), Penistone Parish Register.
13. SA, Sp.St. 32/2
14. W. Crossland, *History in Hunshelf* (unpublished Penistone Grammar School project) 1980
15. Barnsley Archives (BA), Hunshelf Enclosure Award
16. SA, S.C. 517/17
17. Stocksbridge Library, J. Kenworthy Records
18. SA, Sp.St. 32
19. J. Branston, *History of Stocksbridge* (1983)
20. SA, Wh.M.664
21. BLSL, Penistone PR
22. Branston, *op cit*
23. Crossland, *op cit*
24. ibid
25. SA, S.C. 517/9
26. BA, Hunshelf Parish Records (HPR)
27. BA, HPR
28. BA, HPR
29. BA, HPR
30. SA, S.C. 517
31. SA, S.C. 537
32. SA, S.C. 439
33. SA, S.C. 569

THESE OLD STOCKS
ORIGINALLY NEAR BECK POND
WERE RE-ERECTED BY THE
PEOPLE OF THIS PARISH
TO COMMEMORATE
THE CROWNING OF
KING GEORGE VI
MAY 12TH 1937

Above: Greenmoor Stocks.   *(Pat James)*

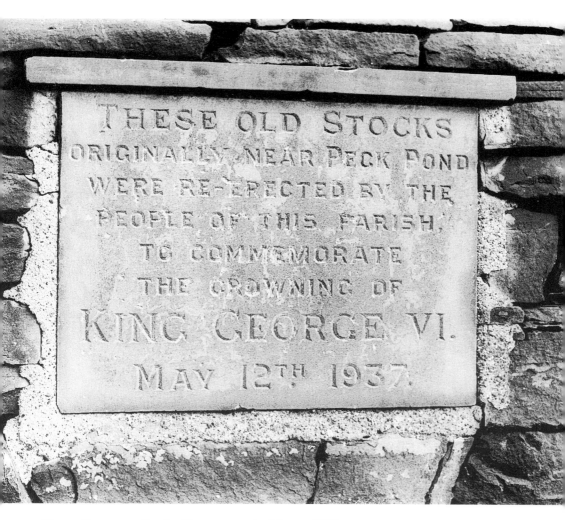

Above: Greenmoor Stocks: Commemorative Plaque, 1937   *(Pat James)*

Acknowledgements

I am grateful to the copyright owners for permission to quote from the documents referred to. I thank Dr George Redmonds for explanation of medieval occupations and Mr Maurice Hepworth of Barnsley Local Studies Library for supplying nineteenth century population figures, also Barnsley Archives for allowing access to the Hunshelf Parish Records. The datestone '1746' at Hunshelf Hall courtesy of Farmers Weekly library service.

10.   THE THORNCLIFFE RIOTS 1869-1870

by Melvyn Jones

TOWARDS THE END OF THE 1960s a small isolated settlement lying on the extreme southern edge of Tankersley Parish was demolished. Unlike many of the ancient villages in the surrounding countryside it had come and gone within a hundred years. The site was subsequently open-cast mined and then landscaped and seeded to form part of the proposed Westwood Country Park. Today no sign remains of the settlement that for most of its short existence housed more than 300 men, women and children.

The settlement in question was called the Westwood Rows or just Westwood Row. In some documents it is referred to simply as Newfoundland - a not inappropriate name for a new colony in what to its early inhabitants was alien and hostile territory. The location of the settlement is shown in Figure 1. Figure 2 is one of a series of photographs that are known to have survived showing the Rows towards the end of their lives.

The rows were built to accommodate non-union labour during the mining dispute involving employees in the collieries of Newton Chambers and Company at Tankersley and Thorncliffe that lasted for seventeen months from 26 March, 1869 to 17 August, 1870. There had been a dispute only three years earlier that had lasted for nine months and this was followed by an uneasy two years in which there were two more disputes, but all that had gone before paled into insignificance when compared to the bitterness, resentment and physical disturbance associated with the 1869-70 dispute, the worst violence taking place in and about Westwood Rows.

Periods of rapid economic development and related population growth and settlement expansion, punctuated by periods of stability, only to be followed by disputes often accompanied by structural change, have been characteristic features of the South Yorkshire Coalfield over the last two centuries. The Thorncliffe dispute was a microcosm - though more dramatic and violent than most - of the volatile events that have been such marked features of the coalfield's development and decline.

It is beyond the scope of this brief study to enter into a full discussion of the background of the strike and the tactics adopted by the Miners' Union, the striking miners and the employers during the strike. Inevitably, contemporary reports were partisan[1] and in subsequent

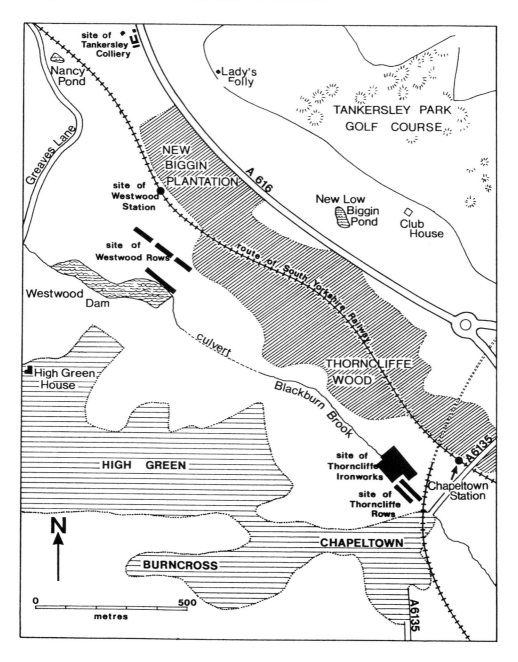

Above: Figure 1. Thorncliffe and the surrounding area today, showing the locations of the places mentioned in the text.

writing the dispute has also been seen either from the Union's or the employer's point of view.[2] Briefly the dispute stemmed from the decision of Newton Chambers and Company to reduce wages by 7.5 per cent and their refusal to negotiate with the Miners' Union. Workers were to continue to be employed provided they agreed to abide by the rules and by-laws of the Company's collieries which involved them in, among other things, negotiating individually over wages and working an eight hour day when required to do so. It was essentially then, an attempt to eliminate collective bargaining, and the workers at the Company's five collieries - Thorncliffe Drift, Tankersley, Norfolk, Newbiggin and Staindrop - were given a month's notice to cease work or to submit to the Company's demands. On 24 March, 1869, 850 men and boys were locked out, although several hundred remained at work.

This article aims to bring to the attention of the modern reader the main features of the dispute which in its day attained just as much notoriety as the more recent 1984 national miners' strike, occasioning coverage in the national as well as the local press. The sources for the study of the strike and the violent activity associated with it are unusually rich and varied. They include the records of the Miners' Union, Newton Chambers Company Records, personal diaries, newspaper reports, letters to local and national newspapers, court proceedings and the 1871 census returns. The diaries are particularly interesting. One surviving diary is that of George Dawson,[3] head of the ironworks, a figure seen by the striking miners as a major stumbling block in the way of a swift and fair settlement. Another is that of William Nesbitt,[4] a man from the North-East of England, who had been appointed foreman engineer in the fitting shops at Newton Chambers in December 1868, only a few months before the dispute began. The first diary records the sense of personal danger of someone very close to 'the action', the other of a 'fly on the wall' watching the action unfold.

The evidence reveals a situation in which there was constant tension, anxiety and foreboding. The employer stood firm and attempted to replace the striking miners with blackleg labour from other coalfields. The strikers, not surprisingly, tried to persuade the blacklegs to return home. They succeeded in this to some extent, but inevitably the supply of blackleg labour increased and this was combatted by outbreaks of violent behaviour aimed at intimidating the newcomers. This, in turn, led to police and military reinforcements being brought to the area, and inevitably the tension increased. The immediate surroundings of Thorncliffe Works must have taken on the appearance of a town under siege.

William Nesbitt recorded the beginning of the dispute in his diary in

Above: Figure 3. A large crowd of striking miners, some armed with staves waiting at Westwood Station for a train carrying blacklegs. *The Graphic, 29 January 1870*

a very matter of fact way:

> *March 24th Finished 3ft pulley for hay cutting machine for company's farm, being 5 days in the lathe.*
>
> *Mr Thomas Chambers youngest daughter was married today to Mr Hawett of Nottingham and the affair came off very quietly.*
>
> *All the coalminers of the Thorncliffe Coal Co'y came out on strike.*

By the beginning of April he noted that several policemen had arrived at Thorncliffe 'to protect property and the men that have started work at the pits, against the men that are out on strike.' The next day (2 April) he noted that two blacklegs who had started work at Thorncliffe Drift Pit 'were guarded to work by policemen.' A month into the strike and with no sign of a settlement, Nesbitt noted that orders had been given 'for all tenants to clear out of Thorncliffe Cottages as he (Mr John Chambers, the partner principally concerned with the collieries) wanted the houses for his blacksheep.' Despite the fact that some newcomers were being induced to return home before taking up residence and work at Thorncliffe (Nesbitt recorded blacklegs being met at Chapeltown station on 27 April and having their return passages paid for them) the eviction of the striking miners and their families

Above: Figure 2. Westwood Rows in the 1960s shortly before they were demolished.

from Thorncliffe Rows and the installation there of blackleg miners and their families led to the first major outbreak of violent behaviour.

William Nesbitt, who was living in Thorncliffe Rows at the time, recorded the event thus:

April 29th Last night at 10 o'clock strikers attacked the blacksheep in Thorncliffe Cottages in a body. Drove the policemen out and broke all the glass windows in five houses, but no-one was injured. They were about two hundred in number. The policemen ran in all directions, some hiding themselves in the water closets.

Subsequently 22 of the strikers received summonses to attend court for riotous behaviour, and the ringleaders were sent to prison.

Throughout the rest of 1869 there were outbreaks of violence of various degrees of severity and periods of mounting tension when it was believed a major disturbance was about to occur, these being accompanied by reports of 'many strangers' being in the district. Potential blackleg miners were also met at the local railway stations by angry crowds of strikers.

As the conflict raged John Chambers died and for a moment the conflict was forgotten as the local community mourned one of its leading members. William Nesbitt noted in his diary on 11 June:

Morning fine but rather dull. Temp 62 F. At 10.30am a large number of miners and the workmen of Thorncliffe Iron Works, mustered at the residence of the late Mr J Chambers to pay their last respects to their departed friend, which will be interred at Tankersley Church Yard at 12.30pm. On the procession leaving Chapeltown it would muster about four-hundred people besides 12 carriages.

George Dawson, in his diary for the same day, specifically refers to the strikers:

June 11th, 1869. Mr John Chambers buried at Tankersley. The colliers on strike followed in procession and behaved very well.

But a settlement to the dispute was as far away as ever and as the year wore on positions became entrenched, tensions became unbearable and violence was increasingly expected. William Nesbitt recorded in his diary on 21 October that

at 6pm. The alarm whistle commenced to blow at Tankersley Colliery. About 100 miners made their appearance in the neighbourhood armed with sticks in a threatening attitude, but all passed off quietly. Three troops of policemen were brought from Sheffield on a wild goose chase.

By 23 October it was reported in the *Sheffield and Rotherham Independent* that representatives of Newton Chambers were seeking the assistance of the army in the form of a permanent garrison because the neighbourhood was 'in a state of constant terror' and an attack was expected on the homes of the working miners. In November, 1869 the union admitted that as many as 100 blacksheep were working in the collieries and in the face of what must have been a steady stream of new recruits, as winter approached and then set in, large-scale violence erupted again. On 7 January, 1870 a crowd attacked Tankersley Pit and broke windows, smashed lamps and pushed several corves (coal wagons) down the shaft.

The senior partners were also worried because of threats on their lives. George Dawson noted that on 11 December, 1869 that he had been warned that the colliers contemplated doing him an injury 'in consequence of their belief that the dispute would be settled if I was not in the way'. On 20 December he noted that 'we had a dreadful threatening letter at Thorncliffe this morning. I do not know what the end of it will be'.

By the beginning of 1870 matters were coming to a head. George Dawson recorded in his diary on 10 January:

Today we have been advised to be never out after dark as the unionists intend to try the effect of powder and shot. I trust to the loving hand of Providence to deliver me from their cruel assassination, but it is very miserable to think that at any hour my dear children may be fatherless.

Threatening letters continued to be received by leading members of the company, a copy of one of which is shown in Figure 4. This is what it threatens:

Mr Chambers 1870 Sir. Prepare to meet thy God. as I insist on thee been a dead man. before long. if thou means to keep us this winter We are determined not to let you see the end of it. if thou means to let us clam & starve. we mean to have it out of you you bugger as thy Days are numbered. so prepare to meet thy God.
your truly one who wishes you in hell fire.

Then on Friday 21 January at seven o'clock in the morning a crowd, variously estimated at between 300 and 1500 men, some "armed with pistols, some with bludgeons, the heads of which bristled with spikes, some with picks" according to the *Sheffield and Rotherham Independent*,[5] simultaneously attacked the backs and fronts of the cottages in the Westwood Rows. The cottages were defended by a force of ten policemen who were overwhelmed, though not before despatching a messenger to Barnsley for reinforcements. In the ensuing mayhem windows were smashed, doors and furniture demolished, houses looted and an unsuccessful attempt was made to set fire to the houses by burning clothing, bedclothes and broken furniture.

Eventually the alarm was raised by blowing the buzzer at Tankersley Colliery which apparently caused the attackers to begin to disperse but

Above: Figure 4. Threatening letter received by Arthur Marshall Chambers in early 1870.
Thorncliffe Records, Sheffield Record Office

before this was complete, police reinforcements from Barnsley arrived on the scene and reportedly set about the crowd with cutlasses to which the miners replied with their bludgeons. No one was killed though at least one policeman and one miner received serious injuries. Twenty-three men were eventually sent for trial at York assizes, eleven receiving sentences of imprisonment, three of them for five years.

William Nesbitt recorded the riot in his diary in graphic detail:

January 21 Morning very dull with heavy fog. Men variously employed in the shops. At 7am the alarm was given that the union miners locked out of the Thorncliffe Colliery had commenced an attack on the houses of the Black or non-unionist miners at work in the pits, and in a few minutes it proved to be too correct, as the shouts and yells of the mob were heard for a mile distant from the scene of action. The mob numbered about 1,000 men and the destruction amounted to about 400. Every door and window in 30 houses were broken to pieces besides both men and women and children most brutally assaulted by the lawless mob. The police attacked them in different quarters, but being overpowered by numbers they were obliged to retreat for a time. They again advanced with drawn cutlass, and beat them off, but not before several were wounded, and one taken prisoner. On examining the houses at Westwood Row, it was found that all the furniture, bedding, clothing and other valuables in the houses were burned by fire or otherwise destroyed. Many of the inmates were left without any clothes, other than those they had been sleeping in during the night. The last attack was on the Tankersley Pit, but the police succeeded in driving them off, before damage was done. 8pm. All quiet, police reinforced to 100 men.

At this point it is interesting to turn to Figure 5. This drawing was one of four that accompanied a short report of the dispute in *The Graphic* on 29 January, 1870. It is of the 'artist's impression' school

Below: Figure 5. The Westwood Riot, 21 January 1870, as depicted in *The Graphic, 29 January 1870*

of visual reporting, arrived at probably by visiting the site and adding the action after reading other reports and possibly interviewing eye-witnesses. The dispute had been going on for 10 months when the 'riot' occurred so it may be that the newspaper already had on its files a drawing of the Westwood Rows which, together with the Thorncliffe Rows and the working pits, must have been obvious subjects for the illustrator's pen. Did he then add the action to an already existing drawing? It must be remembered that the illustration in question must have had to be completed within seven days. The reason for this rather protracted discussion of the possible life history of the illustration is that it appears to contain a number of errors. The location and siting of the two rows is sound, but the bottom row, although accurate in terms of house type with the outshots at the back and the two larger cottages at each end is not much more than half of its real length. Additionally the large cottage at the near end is shown as a one-storey building; it had three storeys.

Turning to the violent scene depicted in the foreground of the illustration, some doubt has to be cast on the action and the title. It will be remembered that the miners attacked the **cottages,** in the process of which they came to blows with the small detachment of **police**; a **police** reinforcement attacked the miners; the 'military' were not involved at any point. So what is shown in the illustration is either the original attack on the cottages or the subsequent confrontation between the dispersing attackers and the police reinforcements. The figures running down the slopes between the two rows suggest flight and the amount of skirmishing is not consistent with the facts surrounding the original attack when only eight policemen were left to face a crowd of at least 300 people. The assumption is that the menfolk living at the cottages were at their work at Tankersley and Thorncliffe Drift pits at the time of the attack. At this point another uncomfortable fact needs to be presented. Contemporary reports suggest that the crowd had begun to disperse before the reinforcements arrived and the historian of Newton Chambers writing in the 1950s[6] stated that the attackers, "for the most part 'strangers' "were intercepted on their way back over Tankersley Park", the edge of which is at least a quarter of a mile from the cottages.

A week after the riot twenty-five of the rioters were brought before the magistrates at Barnsley (Figure 6-7) and this induced a further disturbance. William Nesbitt again recorded the details in his diary:

January 28th The Thorncliffe rioters were brought before the magistrates at Barnsley and remanded to Wakefield for a week....On removing the prisoners to the Railway Station they were guarded by the police, and 50 of

Above: Figure 6. Men accused of being involved in the Westwood Riot on 21 January 1870, being accompanied to the Courthouse in Barnsley, 28 January 1870.

The Illustrated London News, 19 February 1870

Below: Figure 7. Inside Barnsley Courthouse the accused men are 'examined'.

The Illustrated London News, 19 February 1870

the 22 Regiment to keep order. All were safely removed, but as the witnesses were leaving for their homes, they were stoned by the mob and several of the soldiers were hit with stones, and one woman had her head cut with a stone. The famous 'Nellie' of Westwood Row.

Following the January disturbances, soldiers, about 100 in all, were quartered at the Workman's Hall at Mortomley Lane End and at Tankersley Farm for six months and an uneasy peace returned to the area. The dispute lasted another seven months, ending on 17 August, 1870. Wages were reduced, former workmen had to apply on an individual basis and there were no vacancies at Thorncliffe Drift Pit, presumably all places being already filled by non-union men, local and migrant. The concessions made by the employers were relatively minor: subscriptions to the accident fund were to be optional rather than compulsory, all Saturday working was reduced to a half day (it had previously been one half day Saturday per fortnight) and, although fortnightly pay days remained, money could be advanced on a weekly basis if earned.

One question that naturally arises is, who exactly were the blacklegs? It is known that the company employed an agent to recruit miners in coalfield areas and that the miners' union tried to combat this by distributing leaflets in the same areas putting their side of the argument and asking miners from those areas to stay away from Thorncliffe.

Some light can be thrown on the origins of the non-union miners by analysing the enumerators' returns of the 1871 census for the Westwood Rows, the census having taken place some seven months after the end of the dispute. The returns show that forty-seven of the fifty cottages were occupied with a total population of 327 people. Altogether there were 125 males in employment whose ages ranged from ten to sixty-nine years of age. Ninety per-cent of these were employed at collieries, overwhelmingly described as coal miner, miner, collier or pit labourer, but also including three trappers, two pony drivers, two engine drivers, two engine tenters, two deputies, a carpenter, a blacksmith, an assistant underground steward and an underground viewer. The evidence provided by the birthplaces of the residents suggests that the majority were families or single men from other areas who had been recruited during the dispute. The remainder appear to have been locally born blacksheep. Of the 125 employed males, thirty-five were born in South Yorkshire, mostly in Tankersley and Ecclesfield parishes; the next biggest group (22) were born in Derbyshire and seem to have been recruited in the Chesterfield and Ilkeston areas; there were eighteen from Leicestershire, all born in and around the mining settlements of Moira and Donisthorpe in the north of the county

Name and Surname	Relation	Condition	Age	Occupation	Where born
Michael Grealy	Head	Mar	33	Miner	Ireland
Ann Do	Wife	Mar	31		Do
Martin Do	Son		7		Derbys. Chesterfield
Patrick Do	Son		5		Do Do
Michael Do	Son		3		Durham, Houton
Mary Do	Daur		1		Yorks. Tankersley
Ann Fannon	Lodger	Wid	41		Ireland
James Do	Do Son		19		Derbys. Chesterfield
William Do	Do Son		16		Do Do
James Corrigan	Head	Mar	45	Miner & beerhousekeeper	Ireland
Alice Do	Wife	Mar			Lancashire
John Do	Son		18	Pit Labourer	Lancashire
Mary Do	Dau		16		Do
Joseph Do	Son		15	Pit Labourer	Do
Isabella Do	Dau		12		Do
James Do	Son		10		Do
Alice Do	Dau		7	Scholar	Do
Richard Do	Son		2 days		Tankersley
Ann Corrigan	Mother	Wid	68		Ireland
Edwin Crompton	Boarder		15	Mng Labourer	Lancashire
James Christy	Boarder		16	Do	Lancashire

Above: Figure 8. Extracts from the 1871 Census Enumerators' Returns for Westwood Rows.

and from Overseal just across the county boundary in Derbyshire; and there was another substantial group (14) who had been born in Ireland though the birthplaces of their wives and families show that they had been resident in south Lancashire, north Derbyshire, Durham and the Black Country before coming to the Westwood Rows (see Figure 8). The remainder of the migrants originated from mining areas throughout the country including Lancashire, Staffordshire, Durham, Northumberland, Shropshire, South Wales and Scotland.

Notes and References

1. These were in the form either of reports in newspapers or letters to the editor, for example, **The Graphic**, 29 January, 1870; *The Illustrated London News*, 19 February, 1870; *Sheffield and Rotherham Independent*, regularly throughout the dispute; *The Times*, 20 January, 1870.

2. See Frank Machin, *The Yorkshire Miners*, Vol.1, NUM, 1958 ch.VII and *Thorncliffe: A Short History of Newton Chambers and Company Limited and its People*, Chapter X, 'Strife', published with Thorncliffe News during the 1950s.

3. A transcript of George Dawson's diary is in the Newton Chambers Archive (Thorncliffe Records) in Sheffield Record Office.

4. William Nesbitt's diary is unpublished. Copies are in the possession of his descendants. The 1869-70 extracts used here were provided by Mrs C M Smith of Chapeltown.

5. *Sheffield and Rotherham Independent*, 22 January, 1870.

6. In *A Short History of Newton Chambers*, n.d.

11. EBENEZER ELLIOTT, CORN LAW RHYMER: (1781-1849)

by Ray Hearne

THE PEOPLE'S ANTHEM (1847)

When wilt thou save the people?
Oh, God of mercy! when?
Not kings and lords, but nations!
Not thrones and crowns, but men!
Flowers of thy heart, oh God, are they!
Let them not pass, like weeds, away!
Their heritage a sunless day!
God, save the people!

Shall crime bring crime for ever,
Strength aiding still the strong?
Is it thy will, oh Father,
That man shall toil for wrong?
"No!" say thy mountains; "No!" thy skies:
"Man's clouded sun shall brightly rise
And songs be heard instead of sighs."
God, save the people!

When wilt thou save the people?
Oh God of Mercy! when?
The people, Lord, the people!
Not thrones and crowns but men!
God! save the people! thine they are,
Thy children, as thy angels fair;
Save them from bondage and despair!
God! save the people![1]

For the greater part of two decades, from 1831 to his death in 1849, long before the mass media rendered such things commonplace, Ebenezer Elliott C.L.R. as he was wont to sign himself, was as near to being a household name as it was possible to be, certainly for a poet from provincial South Yorkshire. Hymns such as the above were declaimed and sung far and wide, and indeed even to this day *The People's Anthem* can be found in the hymn-books of certain Christian denominations! Nor was his reputation restricted to his native environs;

he was well-known amongst poets, "radicals" and "reformers" in many parts of continental Europe; throughout the still-expanding English-speaking colonies, and across North America, most particularly the pre-Civil War northern states. He was, in the words of his Barnsley contemporary Thomas Lister,

> *"a fearless, out-spoken man, not caring whether his words of terrivle earnestness accord[ed] with the canonical rules of poetic taste, or conventional propriety. . ."*[2]

This blunt outspokenness made him enemies too, usually the wealthy, landed and powerful, principal targets of his frequently bludgeoning invective, so much so that attempts were made on at least one occasion to the the Attorney General prosecute his for "promoting revolution",[3] though these came to nothing it is ironic to find him denounced vehemently as traitor and turncoat by Chartists after his break with them in 1839 on account of their flirtations with "physical force." Elliott was nothing if not his own man; his one-word motto"Right" gives perhaps some insight into the forcefulness with which he pursued his mission as he came to define it — nothing less than "saving the people;" bringing about, through spiritual and material means, their wholesale liberation from hunger, want and oppression; from tyranny and "law-created pain;" though his language was often vituperative, if not violent, his methods were avowedly peaceful always; he believed profoundly, and professed loudly from public platforms and through poem, ballad, hymn and newspaper-column that the world could indeed be changed for the better without bloodshed; through education, hard work, good habits, dialogue between the classes, love of Nature, the spirit of Christianity and the harnessing of steam! "Poetry," he declared "is impassioned truth,"[4] and Elliott at his ranting best had the fire of conviction in his eyes and in his belly!

> *"Our weapon is the whip of words*
> *And truth's all-teaching ire"*[5]

However it might sound to world-weary ears in our own age, Elliott's commitment was sincere and brave; he ranks amongst the greatest South Yorkshiremen, both for the quality of his aspirations and for the magnanimity of his achievements; he was thus described by the renowned victorian seer Carlyle:

> *"a genuine man, with something of the eye and speech and bearing that becomes a man. . .an earnest, truth-speaking man; no theoriser but a practical man of work and endeavour, full of sufferance and endurance. . .he says in volcanic dialect, his feelings have been hammered till they are cold-shot, so they will no longer bend: they*

Above: Ebenezer Elliott, from a painting by John Birch (in *Two Sheffield Poets*, Rev. W. Odem, 1929)

snap and fly off in the face of the hammerer. Nevertheless, under all
the guises of the Radical, the poet is still recognisable: a certain music
breathes through all his dissonances as the prophecy and ground tone
of returning harmony."[6]

Wordsworth too thought him "an extraordinary man" and while
unable to approve of his apparent "hatred of existing things" adjudged;
"None of us have done better than he has in his best."[7] The critic
Dowden in 1877 went so far as to declare that Elliott's poetry had
actually "helped to fill the mouths of the hungry with food,"[8] and
indeed the tributes and eulogies, popular and literary, that followed
his death were formidably wide-ranging; most significant of all perhaps
was the still hugely impressive statue commissioned and paid for via
subscription by "the working men of Sheffield" which stands today
just inside the entrance to Weston Park, inscribed simply ELLIOTT.

So who was this self-ordained Corn Law Rhymer? What kind of
things did he say to elicit such splendid testimonials? How can he have
been almost wholly forgotten? Whoever he became ultimately, he
certainly remained the archetypal South Yorkshireman; Rotherham,
Sheffield and Barnsley all have claimed him at one time or another!
Born in his father's small foundry in Masborough, Rotherham, he
made his name in Sheffield, retired and died in Hargate Hill, Great
Houghton, and lies to this day in Darfield churchyard. Whatever else
they might seek to do, Elliott's poems return time after time for
comfort, solace and inspiration to the local landscapes familiar to him,
whether as memories from childhood, before the onset of the encroaching
industrial revolution, or from his wide-ranging walks through the
surrounding countryside as an adult;

> *"New streets invade the country; and he strays*
> *Lost in strange paths, still seeking, and in vain,*
> *For ancient landmarks, or the lonely lane*
> *Where oft he play'd at Crusoe, when a boy.*
> *Fire vomits darkness, where his lime-trees grew;*
> *Harsh grates the saw, where coo'd the wood-dove coy;"*[9]

"Don and Rother", "Ribbledin," "The Maltby Yews;" addresses to
"Winco," "Osgathorpe," "Kinder" and "Mam Tor;" meditations upon
"Dalton," "Thrybergh," "Conisborough," "Wentworth," "Hargate-
rill." It is frequently hard, in the smugness of hindsight to repress a
smile, when in our collective wisdom we know what history had made
of some of these places!

> *"Roch Abbey! Canklow! Aldwark! if I crave,*
> *Now, a boy's joy, from some lone flower's deep blue,*

Will your loved flowers assume a pensive hue?
Or smile as once they smiled, still growing where they grew?"[10]

Though never as mystically-inclined as his fellow Northerner Wordsworth, ("A primose to me is a primrose and nothing more: I love it because it is nothing more."[11]) he was no less passionate in his own evocations of native flora and fauna, and of the outstanding natural beauty of the whole of his South Yorkshire (and at times North Derbyshire) provenance. Nature to Elliott and to many of the characters in his verses represented simply a world unpolluted and unsoiled, a haven of pure fresh air, cleansing and enlivening wind and rain utterly antithetical to the soot, grime and squalor of town and workshop that claimed so much of their lives. To Enoch Wray "The Village Patriarch" and Miles Gordon "The Ranter" removed momentarily from their ritual denunctiations of "titled scoundrels" and legalised "locustry," "Nature" becomes no more than an elemental meeting-place where sober communication with the Almighty can occur as a matter of course;

"God blames not him who toils six days in seven,
Where smoke and dust bedim the golden day,
If he delight beneath the dome of Heaven,
To hear the wind and see the clouds at play,
Or climb the hills among the flowers to pray."[12]

Elliott's own relationship to the "smoke and dust" of the workshop is complex and contradictory but it holds the key to understanding his writings, poetical and political; growing up in and around "The New Foundry," he remembered it as a "beautiful thoroughfare of light" and learned to love its sounds, smells, acoutrements and processes, as much of his later imagery reveals;

"my thoughts are passions that rush burning from my
mind like white-hot bolts of steel. . ."[13]

Much of this thunderous passion he seems to have inherited, along ultimately with the foundry itself, from his father, "a man who knew no fear. . .except of poverty," and who espoused both his religious and political views so fiercely that he was well-known locally as "Devil Elliott." Also something of a versifier, he published in 1792 a *Rhymed Paraphrase on The Book Of Job*. The walls of the family's living-quarters bore portraits of Cromwell and Washington, and the children's bed-time stories were stirring tales of victories by American and French revolutionaries overcoming the monstrous forces of Old Corruption, kings and Bastille-builders. Devil Elliott had come to Rotherham as clerk to Walker Brothers of Masborough, where Tom Paine himself had worked on his iron bridge in the late 1870s. Needless to say, if we are to accept Ebenezer's self-assessment, he seems to have been a solitary, even somewhat gormless child; he tells the tale of how his formal association with the Barnsley area began somewhat unexpectedly at the age of nine, when he stowed away in a large pan that his father had cast for his wife's brother in Thurlstone;

> *"I have not forgotten how much I was excited by the*
> *solemnity of the night and its shooting stars."*[14]

Then he describes how he was unable to find his way back again, and how for whatever reasons he had to stay in Thurlstone for year and a half! This may have been where he derived his life-long affinity with Robinson Crusoe! at any rate, he was placed at school in Penistone, and his evenings were spent

> *"looking from the back of my uncle's house to Hoyland*
> *Swaine, for I had discovered that Masbro' lay beyond*
> *that village: and ever, when the sun went down, I felt as*
> *if some great wrong had been done me."*[15]

On his return from "the land of the great pan," though sent back to school in Dalton he seems to have spent much of his time playing truant, until in an effort to discipline him his father finally set him to work at the foundry; later on in his teens, in an effort to wean him away from his mates in the Yorkshire Keelman, his anxious aunt lent him a copy of Sowerby's *English Botany* and *Dried Plants*; these texts and others like them catalysed his inarticulate ardour for things natural and catapulted him into the world of words and books; reminiscent of Keat's discovery of Chapman's Homer,

> *"Columbus when he discovered the new world was*
> *not a greater man than I at that moment. . .I was lifted*
> *at once above the inmates of the alehouse*
> *at least a foot in mental stature"*[16]

and sought intoxication from that point on solely through reading, principally the English poets, gothic novels, romances and travel books, a heady mixture which was to form the basis for most of his early work; extravagantly long ballads of deserted maids, wandering seducers, cruel misfortune and premature death-beds. As in another context he had encapsulated the life of his own mother; "a tale of pain terminated by death − one long sigh."[17] Though encouraged throughout these years by no less a personage than the future poet laureate Southey. It is as if, while possessing the creative energy and developing the linguistic power, he lacked a meaningful theme appropriate to his capabilities. This was to present itself quite traumatically in 1818 when he found himself bankrupt and penniless. In the slump that followed the

Above: Elliott's monument, Weston Park, Sheffield.

Napoleonic wars the bottom had fallen out of the market for iron and even huge established firms like Walkers collapsed. Elliott however, convinced himself that the causes were simpler and closer to home; in 1815 the government made up predominantly of land-owners, had passed the corn-laws, a set of measures designed to restrict imports, thereby keeping the price of grain artifically high and guaranteeing for themselves continuing healthy profits. This of course had several other effects; it drove up the price of bread, and to Elliott's mind it reduced the demand for manufactured goods; ie, it increased the possibility of famine and it interfered with the mechanisms of "Freetrade" as he would characteristically spell it. The poet had his theme; all his accumulated bile had found its target; the devil himself acting through his agents; the idle, parasitic rich; "Lord Pauper" and "Squire Leech" along with their "drones" "palaced worms" and "satraps" had framed the corn laws in his own image to lay waste the land and destroy its people!

"Whoever does not oppose the Corn Law is a patron
of want, national immorality, bankruptcy, child-murder,
incendiary fires, midnight assassination and anarchy."[18]

And elsewhere, with an accompanying swipe at literary critics in certain august journals who had raised their eyebrows at the iron-founder's presumption;

*"If my compositions smell of the workshop and the dingy warehouse,
I cannot help it; soot is soot, and he who lives in a chimney will doe
well to take the air when he can, and ruralise now and then, even in
imagination. But we are cursed with evils infinitely worse than a sooty
atmosphere — we are bread-taxed. Our Labour, our skill, our profits,
our hopes, our lives, our childrens' souls, are bread-taxed."*[19]

Elliott had read Shakespeare, Milton, Pope, Crabbe, Burns,
Wordsworth, Coleridge, Southey, Byron and probably Shelley too; he
knew that,

*"all genuine poets are fervid politicians. . .and any subject
whatever in which a man takes interest, however humble
and commonplace it may be, is capable of inspiring high
and true poetry."*[20]

For reasons of trade and "profit" certainly, but also out of genuine
empathy for the hard-driven working classes he campaigned throughout
the 1820s against what he termed the "bread tax," letters to the press
buttressed his poems, the most successful of which pitched into the
fray perhaps his best-drawn creations, the aforementioned Old
Testament prophet-like pair, *The Village Patriarch* and *The Ranter*,

*"Where draymen bawl, while rogues kick up a row;
And fishwives grin, while fopling fopling meets;
And milk-lad his rebellious donkey beats;
While dwarfish cripple shuffles to the wall;
And hopeless tradesman sneaks to alehouse mean;
And imps of beggary curse their dad, and squall
For mammy's gin; and matron, poor and clean,
With tearful eye, begs crust for lodger lean;
And famish'd weaver, with his children three,
Sings hymns for bread; and legless soldier, borne
In dog-drawn car, imploreth charity;
And theif with steak from butcher runs forlorn;
And debtor bows, while banker smiles in scorn;
And landed pauper, in his coach and four,
Bound to far countries from a realm betray'd
Scowls on the crowd, who curse the scoundrel's power,
While coachee grins, and lofty lady's maid
Turns up her nose at bread-tax paying trade. . ."*[21]

Elliott was a key figure in the formation in 1830 of the Sheffield
Mechanics' Anti-Bread-Tax Society, the organisation that in 1831
published his most popular attack, the Corn-Law Rhymes. Drawing
on popular ballad and sentimental song as well as the satirical pamphlets

of Colonel Perronet Thompson, the jacobinism of his father as well as his own vision of redemption through "Freetrade," these forty-odd pieces represent the culmination of Elliott's sustained and savage righteous indignation in verse. Littered with famished children, clammed fathers and broken-hearted mothers at the mercy of "robbers," "wolves" and "reptiles" those "bulwarks of Tory dictation," who devour the bread-taxed, body and soul; "Honest Hare and Burke," we are reminded, took only bodies that were already dead! In pieces such as, *Child is thy father dead?*, *The Taxed Cake*, *The Death Feast*, *Caged Rats*, and *The Black Hole of Calcutta*, the issues as Elliott sees them are graphically outlined; in *The Jacobin's Prayer* he calls curses down upon the heads of the oppressors;

> *"Avenge the plunder'd poor, oh Lord!*
> *But not with fire, but not with sword,*
> *Not as at Peterloo they died,*
> *Beneath the hoofs of coward pride.*
> *Avenge our rags, our chains, our sighs,*
> *The famine in our children's eyes!*
> *But not with sword-no, not with fire*
> *Chastise thou Britain's locustry!*
> *Lord, let them feel thy heavier ire;*
> *Whip them, oh Lord! with poverty!*

The rhymes are also full of dire warnings of what might happen if changes of heart and policy are not immediately effected;

> *"A whisper cometh, which shall rend*
> *What thunder hath not riven."*[22]

Roger Dataller records the views of one South Yorkshire artisan to whom the book meant much:

> *"I read the poems over one after another, first to myself*
> *and then to my wife and children. As the subjects were*
> *chiefly suffering poverty, of which we had been and still*
> *were, large partakers, they suited us amazingly. . .An*
> *honest-hearted old collier, worn out with a life of hard work*
> *and who was then a pauper, and frequented my little shop*
> *as a place for pastime, wept again and again as I read*
> *the passages to him."*[23]

Elliott, despite his jeremiad of prognostications did not want the inevitable blood-letting of revolution; he did want reform and an extension of the franchise, but only to Property-holders, though that should include, he believed, all who lived and worked "honestly" and were able to save a proportion of their earnings. The landed locustry should move aside and follow into parliament the new men; manufacturers and men of business, whose "Freetrade" principles and whose burgeoning revolution in the spheres of industry and commerce represented the force which would redeem the old world and remake it anew; "Capital has a right to rule the land," indeed "Competition is the great social law of God." The poem which for me best explores Elliott's vision of what might be is his *Verses on the Opening of the Sheffield and Rotherham Railway."* It must also represent one of the earliest celebrations of new technology; to the watcher standing on top of Wincobank, the steam-engine enacts a breathless "triumph for mankind;" the imminent "funeral/Of law-created pain;" "Another victory of mind/O'er man's worst enemies."

> *"For Mind shall conquer time and space;*
> *Bid East and West shake hands!*
> *Bring, over Ocean, face to face,*
> *Earth's ocean-sever'd strands;*
> *And, on his path of iron, bear*
> *Words that shall wither in despair,*
> *The tyrants of all lands."*

A hundred and fifty years on, we might be pardoned a momentary "if only!" And indeed, Elliott himself saw little further progress in his own lifetime. All the Reform Act of 1832 gave to the working classes was an even more draconian Poor Law, and the Corn Laws remained firmly in place. Elliott continued to join and to form radical and progressive organisations dedicated to the betterment of the people's lot; in 1831, the Sheffield Political Union; in 1834 the Sheffield Anti-Corn law Society; in 1837 the Sheffield Working Men's Association till their fall-out the following year; he was also a corner-stone of the Mechanics' Institute and a tireless advocate of education for working-class people. Eventually in 1841, after losing a third of his fortune following the "crash"of 1837, "the bitter foe of the squires found himself a landed proprietor"[24] having purchased ten acres of land at Hargate Hill, Great Houghton, and having built an eight-room cottage;

> " 'Great Houghton is the road to Nowhere,' said the Lawyer when I purchased; 'just so,' said I, 'therefore I buy.' But it is only two and three-quarter miles each from two North Midland station. There is a weekly carrier from Pontefract and Rotherham, a post three times a week, and a village two miles off, where anything can be had but fish."[25]

Many of his Sheffield friends, and indeed neighbouring farmers, laughed at the idea of this town-bred ranter-poet making anything either comfortable or productive out of what was deemed to be no more that a mere "fox-cover." As Thomas Lister describes, all these scoffers

". . .*were mistaken. In his new home the old iron-*
founder began to enjoy life as he had never time to enjoy
it before. Under his supervision the "fox-cover" was made
a beautiful and prosperous estate. He had his books,
friends came to visit him, and his time was spent happily
in laying out his garden, planting trees, walking, driving,
reading and writing."[26]

In a letter to Tait, his publisher, Elliott confided that he had also "set up a grindstone,"[27] presumably to keep his hand in, even in retirement! Indeed he was still sharpening and honing poems and letters, as well as other writings throughout this latter period; he was able to reflect on his turbulent times and upon his own voluble role at their centre, particularly after the Corn Laws were finally repealed in 1846; (as much to do with Peel's conversion to policies of "Freetrade" and the genocidal potato-famine in Ireland as anything else!)

"*I claim to have been a pioneer of the greatest, the most*
beneficial, the only crimeless revolution which man has
yet seen. . .I also claim to be the poet of that Revolution —
the Bard of Freedtrade. . .and ultimately the Bard of Universal
Peace."[28]

And on another occasion:

"*I have won my name as 'Rhymer of the Revolution' and*
am prouder of that distinction than I should be if I were made Poet
Laureate of England."[29]

Possibly it was statements like these which ensured Elliott's ultimate exclusion from the mainstream canon of English poetry; possibly, having lashed himself so tightly to his demon bread-tax he was doomed to follow it into oblivion, even though he is still a better read than several "laureates" I can think of! Perhaps at the end of his life, as he composed the preface to his *Miscellaneous Poems* he had already anticipated the likely judgements of posterity; the tone is distinctly quieter!

"*I am sufficiently rewarded if my poetry has led one poor*
despairing victim of misrule from the alehouse to the fields;
If I have been chosen of God to show his desolated heart
that, though his wrongs have been heavy and his fall deep,
and though the spoiler is yet abroad, still in the green lanes

*of England the primrose is blowing, and on the mountain-top
the lonely fir, with her many fingers pointing to our Father
in Heaven."*

Notes and References

1. All poems or parts thereof, from *The Poetical Works of Ebenezer Elliott*, Two
   volumes, Ed. Edwin Elliott, King and Co., London 1876, unless otherwise
   specified.

2. "Remarks upon Elliott's Poetry and Memoranda of the Poet" in *Ebenezer
   Elliott, Life, Character and Genius*. George Searle Philips, London 1850, Local
   Studies section, Rotherham Library.

3. *Ebenezer Elliott*, John Watkins, 1850. p.126. (Rotherham Library)

4. Preface to *Corn Law Rhymes*, 1831, p.49

5. OH LORD, HOW LONG? *Corn Law Rhymes* p.85

6. *Two Sheffield Poets, Elliott and Montgomery*, Rev W Odom, 1929, pp.99-100
   (Rotherham Library)

7. *Ibid* p.97.

8. E R Seary; PhD thesis *Ebenezer Elliott* 1929, University of Sheffield, p.168

9. THE VILLAGE PATRIARCH, section X11

10. RETROSPECTION

11. Autobiographical fragment in Watkins *op cit*, p.25

12. THE RANTER, section 1V

13. Watkins *op cit*, pp.89-90

14. *Ibid* p.13

15. *Ibid* p.13

16. *Ibid* p.18

17. *Ibid* p.3

18. Odom, *op cit* p.88

19. Watkins, *op cit* p.86

20. Preface to *Corn Law Rhymes* p.86

21. THE VILLAGE PATRIARCH, Section X111

22. THE TREE OF RIVELIN

23. *Ebenezer Elliott: The Corn-Law Rhymer*, Roger Dataller, (A.A. Eaglestone)
    Centenary Commemoration Paper, 1949 (Rotherham Library)

24. Letter to Watkins; in *"A Reinvestigation into the Sources of the Biographical
    Materials of Ebenezer Elliott"* E R Seary, M.A. Thesis 1926 (Rotherham
    Library)

25. *Ibid*

26. *Ibid*

27. *Ibid*

28. More Prose and Verse Introduction

29. *Ibid*

Acknowledgements

1. Keith Chandler's M.Phil. thesis; *Ebenezer Elliott: A Study of his Poetry 1781-1849*. Sheffield Polytechnic, 1984. (Rotherham Library)

2. The staff of Rotherham Library Local Studies Section, in particular Freda Casson and Pat Hobson, for their kind assistance.

3. Brian Elliott for supplying photographs and illustrations.

Below: Elliott's resting place enclosed by a wrought-iron fence in Darfield churchyard.

Above: Roundhead enters the Great Barn: from *By the Sword Divided* (1992)

12. GUNTHWAITE AND THE BOSVILLES

by Vera Nicholson

COMING FROM NORMANDY WITH William the Conqueror were people like the Bosvilles and the Rich Families who achieved good positions and were given lands as rewards. The name Bosville is familiar to many being associated with Gunthwaite near Penistone for many centuries. It comes from the place Bosville in Normandy 'Bos' meaning ox and 'ville' town in Latin. Other versions occur such as the Boesaville, Boswell or Boswall. The English of the North may have refused the suffix 'ville' and substituted 'well' or 'wall' to give the latter.

Sir Martin Bosville became Treasurer to William the Conqueror's Army and later Treasurer to William Rufus. He died in 1092 and was buried at Missindry Abbey, now Faversham. Sir Martin had three sons, William, John and Elias and the latter settled in South Yorkshire but it was John who provided the line of descent which led eventually to Gunthwaite.

Around 1086 to 1120 was the period when the colonisation of Gunthwaite took place. Gunthwaite took its name from the Saxon, 'thwaite' or plot of ground of Gunnil or Gunnold. The earliest deeds are undated but a family named Gunthwaite are mentioned as tenants of Byrtons, then Darcys. By 1359 John, son of Roger, and his wife Christina in a grant from Darcys received the deed for the Manor of Gunthwaite with watermill and suit of tenants for life. On their deaths it passed to Thomas Bosville of Ardsley and his heirs. It is believed that Alice, wife of Thomas Bosville, was the daughter of John and Alicia Gunthwaite. In the battle of Poitiers (1356) Bosville was awarded three black bear heads in chief for his shield or coat of arms 'argent five fusils in fesse gules'.

At that time the people in the area would be expected to take their corn to grind at the Lord's mill and pay for the service. The dam, still well known as a local beauty spot, was of great importance to feed the small one by the mill via a goit alongside the lane. The small dam took about four hours to fill and drove an overshot wheel to work the four grindstones. Drying kiln tiles were perforated to allow heat from the fire to reach the upper chamber for corn drying. In 1731 a new house was built for the miller costing £15.7s.0d. Although disused since 1956 many interesting tools of by-gone days remain.

Around 1342 lands of the Le Hunts at Cawthorne passed into the

Above: The Mill House (1731) in 1987.

hands of Thomas Bosville of Ardsley. Later, in 1381, he was granted free warren giving him the right to kill game previously only the privilege of the king. This estate, named Cannon, was in the possession of John Boswell on his death, in 1443, and a quit claim was made by Richard his son. Since John had two wives Richard the son of the second marriage with Isabel Cresacre received the settlement. These lands later passed through the Hartleys to the Spencers and Stanhopes. Isabel Cresacre married Henry Langton after John Bosville's death and they founded a chantry of St Mary in Cawthorne Church in 1455 which was dissolved in 1547. In later years there is evidence of rents being paid for pews at Cawthorne Church so some of them must have worshipped there with their tenants. Consequently Richard became the real founder of the Gunthwaite branch including several hundred acres in the north-west part of Cawthorne Parish until this century. The first wife's son, William Bosville, took as his portion Newhall, Ardsley.

 Richard Bosville married Jane Neville of Liversedge, residing at Gunthwaite and had six children. His eldest son, John, who married Ann Redman of Clapham, succeeded him on his death in 1501. The eldest son of John, also named John married Muriel Barnby and lived at Gunthwaite while his brother Thomas resided at Tickhill.

Following John, his eldest son, the first Godfrey Bosville came into possession of Gunthwaite being born in 1519 and he died in 1580. He married Jane Hardwick sister to the famous Elizabeth, Countess of Shrewsbury. He spent much of his time at Gunthwaite and was noted for his disputes concerning rights of way with which he did not comply till brought to court. The flagged pack horse route from Penistone to Denby with a branch from Thurlstone, as a well known highway for travellers.

At Broad Oak, probably called 'The Royds' at that time, lived the Hawksworth family, the richest freeholders of the locality where the centre of activity took place around a one time green. They were in contention with Godfrey Bosville over rights to pasture near the hall on common land. Having denied them their rights by turning their cattle back and wishing to enclose the land he decided to build great barn about 1550. We are extremely lucky to have his magnificent aisled structure (a listed building) with us today to show the type of craftsmanship which then existed. This immense structure, with fold, covers nearly half-an-acre and has eleven bays. The three threshing floors were so big a large wain with a team of six oxen could turn in it.

The building is of timber framework filled up with stonework to the height of eight feet nine inches, the remainder being timber and plaster, black and white. It is one hundred and sixty five feet long, forty three feet broad and thirty feet high with a floor area of seven thousand one hundred square feet. It consists of a nave and two aisles. Two rows of

Below: Gunthwaite Hall.

Above: Gunthwaite Barn.

wooden pillars are standing on stone pedestals with twenty eight feet between the tie beams. Six tall barn doors, three on each side, give access and all was put together with wooden pegs. All corners were chamferred for the safety of the animals. Produce from the estate was stored there, the larger division for rye and the smaller for wheat.

The Hawksworths made a case against Godfrey but he died in 1580 before it was heard in court, and so did the oldest Hawksworth. Eventually their descendants settled out of court.

Oxspring was held in coparcency by the Eyres for three generations till 1517, when Richard, son of Ralph, sold his part to Sir Thomas Rockley whose descendants sold to Godfrey Bosville for £113.6s.8d to be paid in Silkstone Church. The other part came from Richard, son of George, in 1547. It was extensive, comprising Oxspring, Roughbirchworth, Thurlstone, Penistone, Cudworth, Brierley and Darton with rents and services at Hunshelf and Thurgoland.

In Oxspring was a hunting lodge, sometimes called a manor house, frequently let to tenant farmers. Thick stone walls masked a timber framed building in the post and truss style about thirty-eight feet long and twenty-five feet wide and three storeys high. One room had oak panelling, but elsewhere the timbers were exposed and gaps filled with clay. The staircase wound round a newel post with solid oak steps. Courts were held there in 1549. An inventory of John Pashley, 1727, refers to rooms in the building as house, parlour, near chamber, far chamber and milk house. There was a fire place in each storey, the attic being used for servants. It was derelict by 1900 but some remains were visible like the covered well, footings and tree when I visited the site in the 1950s.

Oxspring manor included the corn mill site by the River Don while Roughbirchworth Manor, later known as Dawson's Mill, combined to form the village of Oxspring. Hornthwaite in Thurlstone was the site of another corn mill higher up the Don where a new building was erected in 1580 by Bosville. Oxspring Lodge was bequeathed in his will to son Francis, with bed and bedsteads also tables and forms with harness, crossbows, rack and artillery. In addition, to his eldest son he left the manor of Gunthwaite with lease of the manor at Beighton where he asked to be buried. Amongst other heirlooms at Gunthwaite were two carved bedsteads and a goblet of silver gilt with cover. To executors, brother Henry and son Francis, he left his manors of Oxspring, Penistone, Cawthorne and Keresforth for seven years to pay debts and raise portions for his three daughters Mary, Dorothy and Elizabeth supervised by his brother Ralph and cousin Thomas Barnby.

The advowson of Penistone Church was purchased by Ralph Bosville, brother of Godfrey before 1580 and from that time until 1915 Bosvilles retained the right of presenting the vicars, when the right was given to the Bishop of Wakefield. Ralph Bosville married Ann Clement of Ightham, Kent, where they settled and he was buried at Sevenoaks, Kent in 1580.

Francis, born 1563, did not have a long life, dying before 1593. He married Dorothy Copley who survived him and then Lionel Rolston, continuing to reside at Gunthwaite. A daughter, Grace, was born but no son so Gunthwaite passed through Godfrey's brother Ralph to his third son Ralph who was a captain in the Army. He died in Ireland leaving Gunthwaite to his son who was the second Godfrey Bosville. Born in 1596 this Godfrey married Margaret Greville.

Around 1627 a Church at Denby was inaugurated, Penistone being considered too remote for regular visits, particularly in winter. It remained a Chapelry of Penistone until 1857, although a new Church was built in 1842.

Above: Gunthwaite Spa Well.

Godfrey, baptised in Sprotborough, 12 April 1596, spent most time in Wroxall, Warwick where he became a Member of Parliament in 1640 and Deputy Lieutenant of Warwick in 1642; and in 1648 named as one of the Justices of the High Court. He was in the Long Parliament and became a Colonel of the Regiment of Foot in the Parliamentary Army. Being a large landowner he raised a band of a thousand strong to fight on the side of Cromwell. The story told, is that not one of the troopers was under six feet in height, a forbidding sight, maybe the Yorkshire Regiment known as the 'Havercake lads'. He took to praying and became not only colonel but chaplain to his men.

At this time a platoon of Roundhead officers and nurses were stationed at Gunthwaite and while there succumbed to an epidemic of typhoid fever. Many died and it is believed were buried in a mass grave by the giant oak near the hall. Penistone Church was garrisoned at this time by Adam Eyre, Rich, Shirt and Wordsworth. *By the Sword Divided* was a television programme relating to this period whilst in 1993 a school's programme called *As We Used to Live* portrayed scenes in costume at the barn of Gunthwaite. After being pardoned by the King, Godfrey returned to live quietly at Gunthwaite until his death in 1658.

During the period 1646-1647 Captain Adam Eyre kept a diary in which he recorded paying money to the Bosville's and sending letters to Godfrey in London. He mentions meeting Godfrey and his son William and being present at a baptism when Godfrey was a sponsor. At this time of unrest Godfrey Bosville had a steward called John Shirt of Cawthorne to manage in his absence.

During the Middle Ages communal celebrations were held on feast days and holidays. Such an occasion took place at the 'Spa' or 'Spaw' in the valley of Gunthwaite. This was the Blessing of the Well, believed to have medicinal properties, especially on the first Sunday in May. Many people gathered from the surrounding districts to see the procession led by a young man with a banner on which were displayed a silver cross, chalice and host. Wearing a black tunic with a bugle over his shoulder, he had a chain around his neck to which was attached a silver plate with the insignia of the Abbot of Pontefract. Behind him came two Benedictine monks in black gowns and hoods. On the back of a pony in riding habit and black mantle followed the Abbot of Pontefract holding his pastoral staff, attended by the vicar of Silkstone, Church officials and more monks. Walking alongside the dam they would reach the Well where the Abbot would dismount and take his stand before the other dignitaries. Assembled in positions of vantage were the gentry, Bosvilles, Burdetts, Micklethwaites, among others, while the farmers, woodmen and labourers with their wives and families took up places where they could best see the ceremony. With solemnity the Abbot would bless the water in Latin "Deus Aqua Sanctus" before the hushed congregation.

To complete the occasion there would be feasting as the narrow road was flanked with pedlars and food and drinks stalls. Dancing may also have taken place since it was the 'Merry month of May'. Cathill, built around 1584, would have many guests to entertain before their return home, some even staying overnight.

Although many partook of the water, some with distaste, only few praised its value. It took its unusual colouration from the silver content of the rocks in that area and smelled of sulphur, which put people off. To this day it is collected by some who suffer from arthritis — it is also claimed that the water makes a good cup of tea.

Returning to the Bosvilles, the only son of Godfrey was William, born about 1620, who later became an officer in the army. He married

Above: Hounds at Cathill Hall c1937.

Mary Wilkinson who died in 1661 and he died the following year — both are buried at Penistone.

We now come to the third Godfrey, eldest son of William, born in 1655 and who married Bridget Hotham of Scarborough. To commemorate the occasion the coat-of-arms of both families were depicted on a stained glass window at Penistone Church. Dwelling at Gunthwaite he built stables on the property in 1688 and another block to match in 1690, as date stones show, while he built a summer house in the garden in 1688. The park was enlarged by the purchase of lands in Ingbirchworth and Micklethwaite Fields. At the age of fifty he was Justice of the Peace and High Sheriff of the County.

In 1690 Godfrey bought the Manor of Midhope, with free warren for Midhope, Langside, Ewden Hordoon, Waldershaigh, Mickleden and Barnside for £2,256 from Henry Hall. In 1705 he restored the chapel, building a porch on which he put his shield and date stone with 'G.B.B.' It was partially rebuilt and a gallery was made with box pews, replacing the forms. On the North side seven pews remaining were for freeholders and on the South side five pews for Godfrey and his tenants.

A market which had been granted to Elias de Midhope by Edward I at Penisale, a hamlet which had disappeared, had lapsed. Godfrey Bosville wished to revive this custom so petitions were made which other towns contested. Finally permission was granted on 28th October, 1699 to Godfrey Bosville and his heirs to hold a market at Penistone each Thursday and a fair on June 10th, 11th and 12th yearly in the Manor of Penistone. A copy of this charter is now in possession of the Penistone Urban District Council. This market was held in the streets until 1910 and drainage runnels down the west side are still visible.

Rights of way were jealously guarded and often led to disputes in the manor court. The Spencer family in 1698 were giving the tenants of the Bosville family at Rawrogd, Cawthorne leave to take carts, carriages and packhorses up Bridsley Lane to Cannon Hall, only as far as Jowett House Mill and back again.

Another petition in 1707 was made for the inhabitants of Denby, Silkstone, Hoylandswaine and the neighbourhood regarding the condition of the wooden bridge at Denby, used daily by pack horses. It was destroyed by floods in 1706 which now hindered trade to other parts of Yorkshire, Lancashire and Cheshire. Rebuilding in stone was more practical so the sum of £7.10s was paid to Godfrey Bosville but

Below: Penistone Market c1900.

a further £40 was needed from the local people to finish the bridge.

In 1713 Godfrey Bosville bought the manor of Newhall, in their possession previously having been left to William Bosville about 1443. He paid William Marsden £2,400 to regain it.

Monuments to commemorate both Bridget (nee Hotham) who died in 1708 and Godfrey who died in 1714 are to be found in Penistone Church. Below them are the shields of arms divided in eight divisions depicting 1) Bosville, 2) Darfield, 3) Unknown, 4) Dransfield, 5) Stainton, 6) Gunthwaite, 7) Oxspring, 8) Wilkinson.

Godfrey made his brother William's second son William, his heir since the eldest son Henry had died previously. He married Bridget Wheatley of Woolley but died in 1724. An interesting note in the Cawthorne Church Register records Bridget Bosville marrying Hugh Bosville second son of Thomas of Braithwell in Midhope Church 1729. Thomas Cockshutt officiated.

In the estate book for 1722 it is interesting to discover the copyhold rents payable on St Thomas' Day for Penistone Manor, and other rents due at Martinmas. The following paid rent at Gunthwaite: Francis Ellison, John Horn, Thomas Walshaw, Timothy France, John Lockwood, John Rich, William Gaunt, John Kilber, Joseph Archer and widow Micklethwaite. Details of others listed in Dransfield's *History of Penistone* are from the following places, Oxspring, Roughbirchworth, Midhope, Gunthwaite Cottage, Denby, Penistone, Cottage Rents and Langsett.

Again we have a Godfrey Bosville, the second son of William as the first one died at an early age. He became an orphan at the age of seven and John Hobson in his diary states that Garforth, the Minister at Midhope, was Bosville's tutor in 1725/6. Incidentally, Garforth won the plate at Penistone races September 23rd, 1726 at Racecommon. Hobson also says it was Bosville's birthday on St Marks Day, April 25th.

Godfrey married Diana, eldest daughter of William Wentworth of West Bretton. He wrote his memoirs and from these have come much of the family history. About 1740 he composed a poem called 'The Moors' which expresses his deep feelings for the countryside.

At last the opportunity came to purchase Broad Oak to add to the estate due to the improvident and dissolute ways of the younger Hawksworths who were obliged to sell for £1,200 in 1726. In 1748 he bought Shepherd's Castle and to avoid disputes over boundaries, marker stones were placed with the initials 'G.B.' on one side and 'E.W.' (for Edward Wortley) on the reverse. Another boundary stone was placed at the junction of his land with Hoylandswaine.   About this time a grant was given to search for silver on Gadding Moor near the waterside.

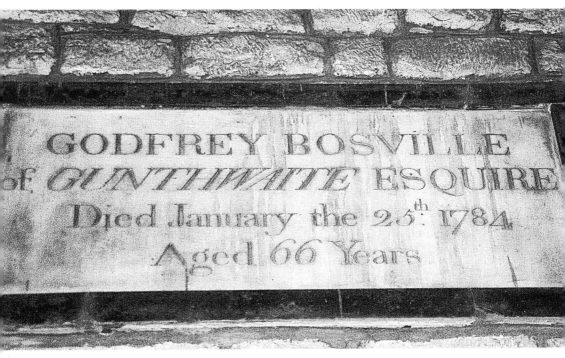

Above: Memorial plaque to Godfrey Bosville, 1784.

A pound of silver ore was said to produce eight ounces of silver and some was found in the building of a house in 1731. Great expectations came to nothing, though Butterworth of Cawthorne made a pair of silver buckles from it.

Thorpe Hall, Rudston, near Bridlington was bequeathed to Godfrey by Thomas Hassell in 1773 and became his chief residence, being a more fashionable house, so Gunthwaite was left to tenants. There is a plaque in Penistone Church to commemorate the death of Godfrey, aged 66, in 1784. The fourth Godfrey was succeeded by his eldest son, William, who became heir to both Gunthwaite and Thorpe Hall. He was unmarried and his other brother Thomas died before him so the direct line of descent was passed to the second son of his sister, Diana Bosville, who married Sir Alexander Macdonald in 1768.

Godfrey Macdonald assumed the name of Bosville by royal sign manual in 1814. When his elder brother Sir Alexander Macdonald died in 1824 he became third Lord Macdonald and eleventh baronet Macdonald. He married Louisa Maria daughter of the Duke of Gloucester. It appears that money must have been needed for improvements and extensions at Thorpe Hall so in 1830 estates were offered for sale in thirty lots.

Of particular interest at the sale were the following :

Lot 1.   Copyhold Manor of Penistone and Spread Eagle.
 " 2.   Shepherds Castle — R.G. Ramsden?
 "10.   Kirkwood Farm — Henry & William Bray.
 "17-20. Roughbirchworth — to Michael Camm, £3810.
 "23.   Watercornmill Oxspring — to John Rolling, £7,000.
 "24.   Manor of Langsett — to Benjamin Harrop, £1,600.
 "27.   Raw royd, Cawthorne — to Mr Beaumont, £16,000.

About this decade the agent Earnshaw at Gunthwaite, perhaps beset by problems saw fit to demolish the original timber-framed building which matched the barn all those years ago and built the house which exists today.

Hunting with the Penistone hounds was a common pastime for the gentry and their followers from 1260 when Elias de Midhope was master in the reign of Edward I the first under a charter which granted permission for free warren in Penisale, Midhope, Langside, Ewden, Hordron, Waldershaigh, Mickleden and Barnside. No one could chase game without his permission under forfeit of £10 fine an extortionate sum in those days. Mainly they hunted hares in early times then later foxes. Though the Bosvilles were never known as Masters of the Hunt they were interested and sometimes took part especially when their estates were the venue. Gamekeepers were their tenants no doubt and in 1797 John Crossley was gamekeeper for Midhope and Langsett, later William Ellis, Michael Fox at New Hall, Darfield, James Hargrave at Gunthwaite followed by his son in 1819.

Game was decreasing and in need of preservation by 1777 so keepers were required to give information to Peter Auriel Drummond Esq., Gunthwaite or Mr Marsden in Wakefield so offenders could be prosecuted. Consequently gamekeepers must have a certificate which was registered. Abraham and John Crossley supplied game to the Bosville and were paid 1s each for grouse, 6d for partridge, 1s hares, 6d woodcock and snipe 9d to 1/2 for a couple of ducks, 7d and 8d for a couple of chickens, butter 6d a lb, beef 3d a lb, mutton 4d a lb.

The Bosvilles encouraged their tenants to lease a hound and feed it . At the time when Captain Ellis, farmer and corn miller, who died in 1807 was Master of the Hunt there were about twenty hounds on lease at Midhope and he kept three or four himself. He was granted permission by Bosville to hunt the pack three or four times a week. Sometimes wagers were taken on the ability to chase so competitions were held

Above: "Duffers Day" in 1883.
Back L to R: Thos Stanley, John Kilner, John Hy. Turner, George Stones, Dr Sanderson, Thos Stones.
Next Row: John Hague, Edwin W. Wilcock, Jas Durrans, Sutcliffe Oldroyd, Geo. R. Dransfield, John Wm. Day.
Next Row: Wm Peace, Jackson, John N. Dransfield, Ben Silverwood, Jas S. Noakes, John Greaves.
Front Line: John Mate, Joseph Taylor, John Siddons, John Hague (Snr), Boy, Wm Mate, Henry Kaye, Joe Hill.

with other packs. During Mr Hague's time as Master (1829-43) Bosville visited Midhope and asked to have the Hounds assembled so he could inspect them.

Nathaniel Priest of Burncote, Gunthwaite owed his life to the hound called 'Leader' that he had on lease. Having been to the hunt and imbibed too much liquor, on the way home he stumbled on to a lime heap and fell asleep. In the early morning the dog awakened his son Richard who, failing to discover his father at home, followed the dog. Finding his father he quickly roused him and pulled him upright or he would soon have been overcome by the fumes emanating from the lime.

The moors were leased and sporting rights much sought after gradually increased in rent through the nineteenth century. An interesting event was 'Duffers Day' when the game keepers were allowed to invite their friends to join the sport. Much fun would be had and many tales told when they adjourned to the Club Inn, Midhope, to partake of the meal provided by Mr and Mrs Siddons after tramping the moors. Once a year a hunt ball was held in Penistone.

Alexander William Robert Bosville Macdonald became heir on Godfrey's death in 1832. He married Matilda Moffat Bayard, living at Thorpe Hall.

Continuing the line we have Godfrey number six following in 1847. He married Harriet Cassandra Willoughby. At this period we get the construction of the Penistone to Huddersfield Railway cutting through the Gunthwaite estate. In Whites directory of 1852 the following people resided at Gunthwaite :- farmers George Brown, John Burgin (miller), Rachel Fisher, Benjamin Holmes, James Holmes, Hall; Miles Ingham, Joseph and Richard Mills, Broad Oak; Nathaniel Priest, Burncote; and George and John Wood. Seventy-seven inhabitants and 1080 acres of land comprise this township of scattered farms.

Godfrey Wentworth Bayard Bosville Macdonald, to give him his full title, died in 1865 and was followed by Alexander Wentworth his son who married Alice Edith Middleton in 1886.

Festivities around the Spa on the first Sunday in May had reached such proportions with many brass bands in attendance and crowds invading fields, rowdyism developed, so these ceased about 1870.

Two unsold estates in the earliest sale were now sold:- Oxspring estate to Thomas Edward Taylor of Dodworth Hall and the Denby Estate to Walter Norton of Rockwood House, Denby Dale.

As a boy Alexander played the organ at All Saints Church, Rudston and became choir master so after fifty years as such a window was designed showing him surrounded by choir boys. Music was his chief interest and in 1894 he became Musical Society conductor and continued for eleven years. In 1900 he became High Sheriff of the county. His wife Alice was very industrious reshaping the garden and planning the lakes. Besides this she studied the records of the Bosvilles and wrote book *Fortunes of a Family* and *House of the Isles*, published in 1927.

On 19 April, 1908 Mrs A.W.M. Bosville Macdonald came to Penistone with her husband to open the three day bazaar at St John the Baptist School to raise money for the Church Restoration Fund.

July 13th, 1909 was a day of festivities for the coming of age of Godfrey Middleton Bosville Macdonald who was present with his parents and sister at Gunthwaite when guests were the West Riding tenants and ladies and gentlemen of the district.

Next in line was Godfrey Middleton Bosville Macdonald, the seventh Godfrey, who inherited on the death of his father in 1933. He married

Above: Gunthwaite Dam (1992)

Rachel Audrey Campbell and still made Thorpe Hall their residence. He became Clerk of Peace and County Clerk of the East Riding. On his death in 1951 it was decided to sell the Gunthwaite Estate having been held for 600 years. Messrs. Lockwood, Elliot of Woodsome Sanitary Pipe Works, Ferry Bridge, near Huddersfield bought it for £45,000 for the use of the clay on the land in 1953. The estate had fifteen farms and some tied cottages, with 1,150 acres and a rental of £1,407.

The Midhope Grouse Moor, owned since Elizabeth I, with 2,109 acres, shooting lodge and outbuildings in Midhope village, fishing rights for Midhope reservoir and all hunting, shooting, coursing and sporting rights was sold for £8,000 to Mr L.G. Glugston of Scawby, Lincs.

After ten years the Gunthwaite Estate was put up for auction in 1963 after repairs and improvements had been made. This was purchased privately by Major and Mrs N.C. Macdonald another member of the clan. Unfortunately they were unlucky with investments and had to sell in 1982 so a farmers consortium purchased and resold to individual tenants who wished to own their own farms.

Personally I have many happy memories of outings from Thurlstone over the fields from Long Lane, before Scout Dyke Reservoir was made, to Gunthwaite. Those excursions were the highlights of the holidays, taken at different seasons to enjoy the flora and fauna in its infinite variety. What a vista, to see the woods carpeted with bluebells and enjoy the scent, then stop to watch the fish in the stream leading to

the dam where the stately swan swam, while making our way to have a picnic and cup of tea at Mrs Holmes' in Gunthwaite Gardens.

Sometimes we took the route past Crabtree Farm and down Cathill where Mr Fisher kept exotic birds and sometimes a fox. Then we travelled the flagged causey to reach our destination. In late summer we would gather blackberries en route to see what fruit was available for sale in the redbrick walled garden. Mr Holmes loaded his cart with fruit and set out for Thurlstone shouting "Apples to eat or bake". We bought apples and pears each time storing them in the attic if they were keepers or making jam with soft fruits if available.

During the 1939-45 War, although living then at Stocksbridge, I spent a week in summer on two occasions with friends in the caravans at Gunthwaite. We traversed the tracks of earlier disputed rights of way to enjoy the peace and tranquility of the countryside enjoying the birdsong and nature in general. I recall my cousin losing the apple pie filling donated by an Aunt in Penistone, as she cycled up the causey. A sad loss in times of rationing. Wandering around the coach road we called to visit a friend living at Broad Oak and noted the tree which gave its name to the farm. After the war we often drove round that way to revive nostalgic dreams of early pleasures which can still be invoked today.

Notes and References

History of Penistone — J.N. Dransfield (1906)

Fortunes of a Family — Lady Macdonald of the Isles (1927)

The House of the Isles — Lady Macdonald of the Isles (1927)

Parish of Silkstone — Rev. J.F. Prince (1922)

Kenworthy — (1927)

John Woods Almanacks

Historic Homes of Yorkshire — G.B. Wood (1957)

Yorkshire Diaries — Surtees Society (1877)

Yorkshire Notes and Queries (1907)

South Yorkshire Volume II — Rev. J. Hunter (1831)

Thanks to Barnsley and Penistone Libraries for their help.

Left: Causeway, 'Gunthwaite Lane' (Old Packhorse route)

The descent of 'Gunthwaite'

John Bosville m. Isabel Cresacre

Richard Bosville m. Jane Nevile
   -1501

John Bosville m. Ann Clapham

John Bosville m. Muriel Barnby
        -1542

I   Godfrey Bosville m. Jane Hardwick   Ralph Bosville m. Ann Clement
        1518-1580   -1580

    Francis Bosville m. Dorothy   Henry   Ralph m. Mary Copley
        1563-1596   Bosville

II Grace Bosville   Godfrey Bosville m. Margaret Greville
        1585- died young   1596-1658

                                             William Bosville m. Mary Wilkinson
                                                 1620-1662   -1661

III Godfrey Bosville m. Bridget Hotham   William Bosville m. Benedicta
        -1714 no issue   -1708   died before 1714   Fisher -1719

                         William Bosville m. Bridget Wheatley
                             1683-1724

IV William Bosville   Godfrey Bosville m. Diana Wentworth
        died young   1717-1784

    William Bosville   Elizabeth Diana Bosville m. Sir Alexander
        1745-1813   1748-1789   Macdonald
    Line extinct

V   Alexander   Sir Godfrey Macdonald m. Louisa Maria
        -1824   heir to uncle, became
    no issue   Bosville in 1814
                                                 1775-1832

    Alexander William Robert Macdonald m. Matilda Moffat Bayard
        became Bosville
        1800-1847

VI Godfrey Wentworth Bayard Bosville m. Harriet Cassandra Willoughby
        1826-1865   -1903

    Alexander Wentworth Macdonald Bosville m. Alice Edith Middleton
        1865-1933

VII Godfrey Middleton Bosville m. Rachel Audrey Campbell
        1887-1951

    ┌──────────────────────────────────────┐
    │ 1953 Gunthwaite Estate sold   │
    └──────────────────────────────────────┘

13.   THE PATCHWORK QUILT – DODWORTH'S MEDIEVAL LANDSCAPE[1]

by Sam Sykes

EVERY VILLAGE WILL REVEAL A STORY and all of them have their own special aspects. Sometimes however we find one that is remarkable not for what is different, but for what is typical, standard and ordinary. Dodworth is one such village. By analysing its changes and developments we can draw general rules by which to judge other places. It is a true 'model' village and ironically, it is in the survival of these ordinary patterns that we see the true uniqueness of this village.

Dodworth is now a typical dormitory suburb, but until a few years ago it was a typical mining village and a century and a half before that it was a good example of the kind of small settlement where domestic industries flourished, in this case primarily linen weaving. However throughout all of these economic and industrial changes the majority of its 1915 acres have been given over to agriculture. The most remarkable aspect of all is that this agricultural pattern has been so slow

Below: Dodworth Green today, the buildings on the right are the only remains of the former tanyard, an industry vital to Dodworth's medieval prosperity.

in changing that not only does it still reveal the earliest settlement features, but it also allows us to peel back the layers of history and observe the changes as they have occurred over more than a thousand years. In the following pages I wish to tell this story. The information has been gleaned from many sources, much of it directly from the surviving landscape, but also by many references to archive sources.

To interpret this story we need some signposts, one of the best of which is the nineteenth century Tithe Map of Dodworth which was drawn before large scale industrial and urbanisation affected the township. It is therefore a reasonable representation of the pre-industrial agricultural pattern of the village. As I shall demonstrate, numerous other references suggest that this pattern had evolved slowly over several centuries. There was no single dramatic act that altered the Dodworth landscape in one fell swoop. For example, the Act of Parliamentary Enclosure in 1806 applied only to a few acres of commons, Dodworth's 'open' fields having been slowly enclosed in a piecemeal fashion over the previous four or five hundred years. Furthermore since 1540 Dodworth had not been under the control of any single all powerful Lord of the Manor who could create hunting parks (as at Wortley,

Below: Dodworth's former open fields have been mostly built over or ploughed up, but part of the "Cliffe Field" has been fossilised as permanent grasslands on what is now the golf course. The corrugated "ridge and furrow" pattern is a typical remnant of medieval farming methods.

Tankersley and Stainborough) or other wholesale changes. In fact since the dissolution of the monasteries Dodworth's land had been subdivided amongst about twenty freeholders. This division ensured that unless the majority of freeholders could agree, any changes could only be piecemeal, restricted to the portion of land that each individual owner controlled. There is no evidence that such communal agreements were reached at any time other than immediately after the dissolution, when the monastics spoils were being divided up. We can therefore say with some certainty that the landscape of Dodworth in the mid-nineteenth century must have grown directly out of the medieval landscape that was controlled by the monks of Pontefract. We should expect it therefore to give some clear signposts as to the kind of landscape that existed in medieval times. It may even reveal some aspects of an even earlier era, the settlement that already existed when the monks were granted ownership of Dodworth around 1090.

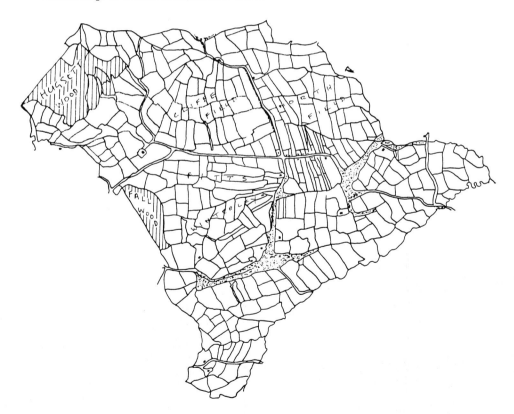

Map 1; Field Pattern as shown by Tithe Map

The Tithe Map clearly shows that housing in the village was concentrated along both sides of Town Street (the modern High Street), from the present crossroads to the sharp bend by the modern 'pop' factory. Each home or farmstead had behind it a long thin croft that stretched down to one of the streams. Indeed this pattern has only finally disappeared in the post war years, until then the High Street still contained several farms whose courtyards were arranged at right angles to the street. At the time of writing only one such set-up remains, and this is due for redevelopment. The crofting system has left its trace however in the names of 'Jermyn Croft' (formerly Jeremy after the owner) and 'Salter's Croft', both of which are still extant alongside the High Street. A very similar pattern to what Dodworth must have looked like can still be observed at Hooton Pagnell, where almost every farm retains its right-angled courtyard arrangement and the crofts beyond lead to the old open fields. Hooton still has a market cross in situ in the main street, indicating its former prominence on a trading route. This is a typical medieval layout, the like of which can be seen in many villages and small towns. Wentworth is another good local example. We can therefore presume that the High Street is a direct relict of the early medieval landscape and we shall begin our investigations there.

Until about a hundred years ago, High Street was known as the Town Street. This street runs east-west along a broad ridge, to either side are small valleys each carrying a stream. This ridge probably carried an ancient trackway long before Dodworth was ever settled, and innumerous generations of foot travellers and packhorses must have made this crossing. Certainly by the middle ages it had become a major trade route linking the market town of Barnsley to the Cheshire salt producing areas. 'Salter's Croft', a house standing near the crossroads, still bears evidence of this ancient trade. Until last century it continued to be used as part of the main cross-Pennine track between South West Yorkshire, Cheshire and South Lancashire. The modern A628 takes a slightly less arduous line to the north of the old village centre. Place-name evidence suggests that Dodworth was established sometime between the sixth and eighth centuries when a group of the growing population of Anglo-Saxons cleared a bit of the wastes hereabouts and established a small farming community. There were already other settlements in the area. Just to the south, for example, Stainborough was an ancient site already, Silkstone was already settled and likely Keresforth too.

Dodworth's first farmstead was probably enclosed in a semi-defensive position on the eastern edge of the ridge, from where it could overlook considerable distances and also had easy access to essential water

Above: These three-storey houses date from the early C19 when Dodworth was becoming an important linen weaving centre. They stand at the head of "Jermyn Croft", one of the old medieval crofts that ran at right angles from the Town Street.

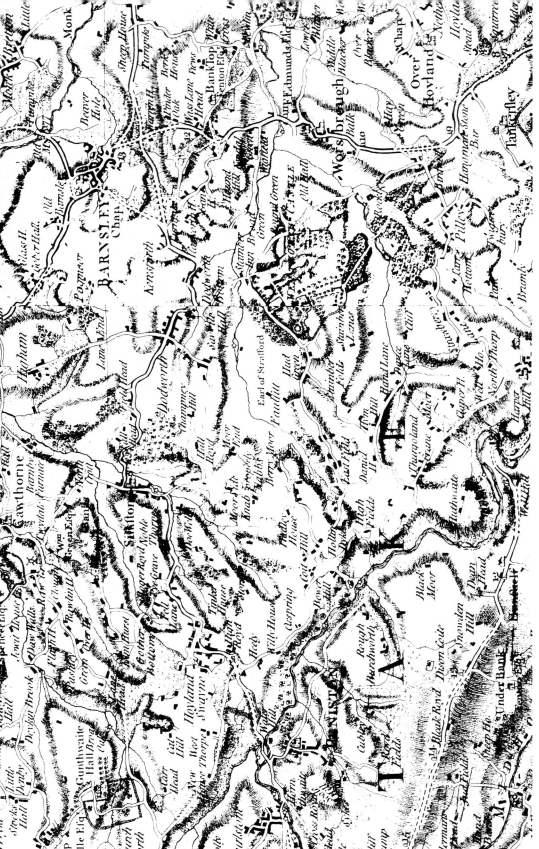

Map 2: Extract from Jeffries Yorkshire map of C1770.

Above: Nestling in the sharp bend of High Street is this grand seventeenth century house. The site however is much older and was probably where Dodworth's first lords established their enclosure.

supplies from the small streams to either side. This site is in fact still preserved. Travellers approaching Dodworth from the Keresforth (Western) side have to negotiate two severe right angle bends before reaching the High Street. Such an arrangement is a typical feature where the road is going around an important site, like a hall, church or market. Nearby villages of Wortley and Tankersley both retain similar road alignments around their churches. Dodworth however was not to get a church until 1846, prior to this it remained ecclesiastically subservient to Silkstone. The bends at Dodworth almost certainly circumvented the hall or dominant house/farmstead in the village. Not only is the geographical position perfect, but place name evidence, architecture and other archive references help to confirm this picture. In the arc of the bend still stands a substantial house of

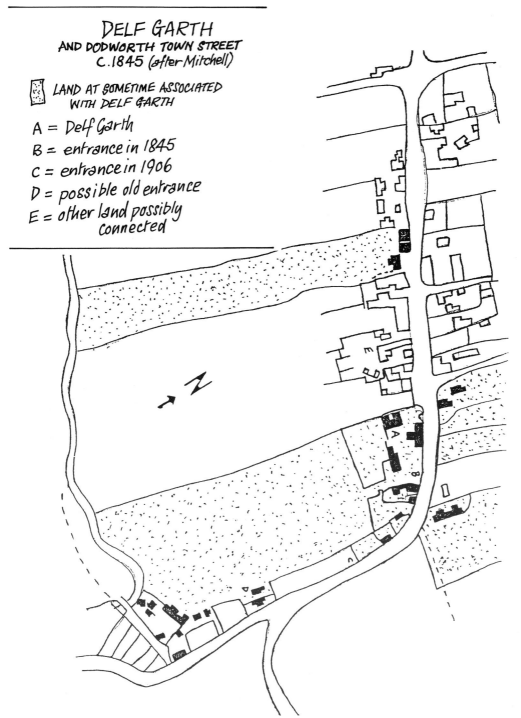

DELF GARTH
AND DODWORTH TOWN STREET
C.1845 (after Mitchell)

LAND AT SOMETIME ASSOCIATED
    WITH DELF GARTH

A = Delf Garth
B = entrance in 1845
C = entrance in 1906
D = possible old entrance
E = other land possibly
        connected

Map 3: Town Street & Delf Garth

sixteenth/seventeenth century date. According to the Hearth Tax returns of 1672 it was then the second largest house in the village and owned by a family called Senior. They were prominent yeoman farmers whose influence and standing spread over the surrounding villages as far as Penistone, where they were influential in the parish church. This house has been known variously as 'The Grove', 'Dodworth Old Hall' and 'Delf Garth'. The latter name is the earliest recorded and suggests a quarried enclosure. This would be entirely consistent with the layout of the earliest hall site that gave it's name to 'Dod's-worth' for 'worth' is a Saxon term for an enclosed farm. Unfortunatley we are unlikely ever to know who Dod was. The one house in the Hearth Tax return that was larger than Delf Garth belonged to the Brooke family, relative newcomers to the village who were developing a site at the opposite end of the Town Street. It seems likely therefore that until the early seventeenth century 'Delf Garth', was the most prestigious house and farmstead in the village.

Behind Delf Garth the Town Street stretches westwards up the ridge towards Silkstone. Visitors are often surprised at the width of this street and yet this dimension is typical of the market towns of the East and North Ridings. It might well indicate that the main street served as a trading area. This again is consistent with Dodworth's situation on the old salt way and invites comparison to Wentworth and Hooton Pagnell as mentioned earlier. However there is no record of any formal markets ever being held here. The answer may therefore lie elsewhere, in the second stage of Dodworth's development.

Most of the Dodworth crofts were of set proportions, the narrowest being approximately the same width as the Town Street, others being twice or three times as wide. This organised pattern is remarkably consistent and suggests that the street was either planned or controlled by someone with the power to allocate set plots to desiring applicants. Recent archaeological work has suggested that such a pattern is typical of some villages developed by Norse settlers in the tenth century or thereabouts. Once again however Dodworth shows no place-name evidence of Norse settlement. It is possible that this has simply not survived, but the more probable reason is that the planning was done later, by another all powerful unitary authority, the Monks of Pontefract.

The township had been granted to the Monastery of St John by its Norman owner, Ilbert de Lacy, in around 1090 A.D. They would have had both the organisational skill and political power to exercise this design, but to what end? What did the monks want of Dodworth?

There are several likely reasons. Dodworth was a day's horse ride away from Pontefract, so a convenient place to have a resting and horse changing station. It was close to the ironstone mines that began to be worked here in the twelfth century and it was at the centre of a heavily wooded region that could provide the monastery with the vital resource of timber. Indeed this last reason is specifically highlighted in a Pontefract charter leasing out some of the lands of Dodworth but stipulating that the farmer "shall save to us our oaks". These oaks would have been used for more than just the raw timber. They would have yielded charcoal used in the iron smelting furnaces at Stainborough and the oak bark was an essential ingredient in the tanning process. By the sixteenth century Dodworth had four tanyards and, along with Cawthorne, was one of the centres of the South Yorkshire tanning industry. It is quite probable that this trade had began under the management of the monks. These would have been reasons enough for the monks to establish a stable community at Dodworth and it seems highly likely therefore that the layout of Town Street was a direct consequence of monastic ownership.

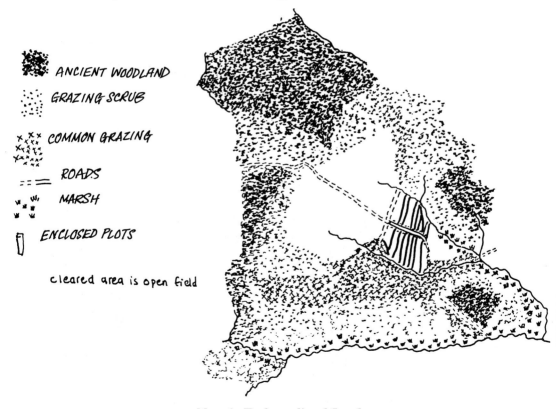

ANCIENT WOODLAND

GRAZING SCRUB

COMMON GRAZING

ROADS

MARSH

ENCLOSED PLOTS

cleared area is open field

Map 4: Early medieval Landscape

Above: Until recent years this lone cruck stood prominent on Dodworth's High Street, sole survivor of a medieval timber framed building. Standing at right-angles to the street it shows the typical alignment of Dodworth's early farms, each had their long thin crofts running down to the stream behind. *(Photo courtesy of Brian Elliott)*

If little else seems left of the monastic regime today it is not surprising, but look a little closer. Close to the present crossroads is still a row of very low shops. At least one of these has internal timber work of a fourteenth or fifteenth century date and until very recently a free standing cruck remained visible in the garden of a neighbouring shop. These were undoubtedly remnants of Dodworth's medieval community.

The Fields

The medieval settlers could not rely upon producing all their food needs from the small crofts attached to the farmsteads. Indeed, with a farming system that was much less intensive than that practised today it was necessary for them to bring a considerably larger area under cultivation just to support a small population. There are many charters survivng detailing the monks letting and farming activities and from these we can ascertain that the population of Dodworth in the fourteenth century would be around 150 people, yet almost the same area of land was needed to feed these as was still under cultivation in the middle of the twentieth century! To understand the agricultural pattern however it is once again necessary to work backwards from the nineteenth century documents which provide very detailed pictures of land ownership.

In 1806 each of the Town Street farms had a further set of fields scattered around the village, seemingly in haphazard fashion. In fact this apparently random distribution is evidence of the old 'open fields' where each farm held a number of strips distributed around the good and bad lands of the township. It is a remnant of feudal farming, where individuals were forced to work collectively, sharing resources like the number of oxen required to make up a plough team and the human muscle power needed to harvest the crops. Of necessity therefore both the timing of various tasks and the nature of crops planted had to be co-ordinated. Such a system demanded the kind of planning and obedience that could only be enforced by a dominant power such as a Lord of the Manor or, as in this case, the monastic landlords and their stewards.

Much of the old field pattern has now disappeared under colliery muckstacks or housing estates, a lovely patch of 'ridge and furrow' having recently been lost to the Keresforth Park estate. However older maps, a few surviving hedgerows and some place-names bear witness to the old open fields and their method of ploughing by ox team. Cliff Field (under the pit-stack) was the largest and is commemorated in Cliffe Crescent, North Field (under South Road ironically) remains as a house name. Butterleys and Cramlands have recently been rejuvenated as estate roads, but both record the productive pastures north and west

Above: This timber framed building dates from the late C16 of early C17, a time when Fall head was an active Tanyard in the occupation of the powerful Hobson family.

of Town Street. Old maps clearly show that these fields had the kind of curving boundaries we associate with the old cumbersome ox plough teams.

Under monastic management some of these fields were partly enclosed, with parcels of strips being let off to individual farmers. The most part however remained open, unfenced until after the dissolution of the monastery in 1540. At this time the Crown raised revenue by selling off monastic lands. Dodworth's were bought by a syndicate of people who had already been gaining prestige and power under the monks, some of whom had probably already begun to enclose their own parcels. Principal amongst these were the tanning families, two of whom, Hobsons and Brooks, were to dominate village life for the next two centuries. The sixteenth and seventeenth centuries record numerous examples of piecemeal enclosure, either by agreement with the tenants or because the tenants had insufficient power to obstruct their landlords but Delf Garth was still rationalising, swapping and enclosing its lands in the mid-eighteenth century. The effect of all of this enclosure was to make the ownership map look like a patchwork quilt and the actual landscape came to sport a host of new hedgerows.

Documents survive to demonstrate this process in several different farm holdings. One of the most distinctive of these is the 'Dickensty'. This small farm unit undoubtedly takes its name from an early tenant whose identity is now lost, although the earliest records show it to have belonged to the family who took the name of De Dodsworth when they moved to Gawber Hall. In 1341

> *Thomas, son of John de Dodworth and heir of Agnes de Galbergh . . . acknowledges that he held of the lord of the Manor the moiety of one tenement called Dickerode at twelve pence per annum.*

Later documents show that the Dickerode (Richard's clearing) descended to the Brook family who knew it as Dickensty. It comprised of a house and barn on the High Street (where the Thornley Arms now stands) with a croft beyond this leading down to the stream, a portion of the open field beyond the stream in Cramblands, a further portion in the North Field and two old clearings in the Middlewood, towards Keresforth. The holding retained its identity until 1702 when John Brook absorbed it into his Pond farm estate, even then he continued to rent it out as a seperate parcel until at least 1724. The shape of this holding had not changed therefore for at least four hundred years.

Map 5: Dickinsty, example of a dispersed holding.

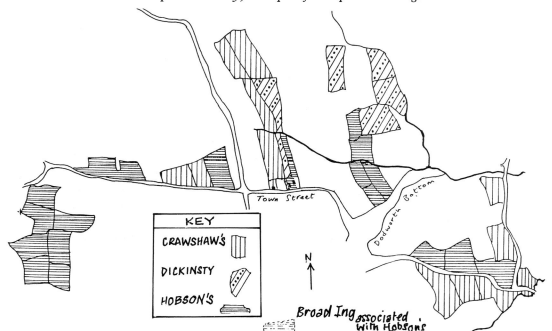

The Commons and the Assarts

When the monks first gained control in the late eleventh century Dodworth's boundaries were accurately described in a charter of ownership. They have remained remarkably consistent up to the present day, nine hundred years later. At the time most of the boundary area was scrub, woodland or marsh. It was amongst these marginal lands that villagers exercised their 'rights of common'. These were a vital part of peasant agriculture, the commons allowed smaller farmers access for grazing their animals, for the gathering of fuel and to a limited extent the quarrying of stones. So important were these rights that they were enshrined in several of the monastic charters, for example in a lease of the Moor Ends farm of 1184 the Prior of Pontefract decreed that:

> *John and his heirs shall have common of pasture and easement of water from Dodworth, after our men have reaped their wheat and carried their hay.*

No substantial manorial court records have survived for Dodworth but those for neighbouring Stainborough clearly demonstrate the importance of the commons, people are variously fined for collecting too much wood, grazing too many swine out of season and digging stones without the lord's permission.

By the late eighteenth century only about ninety acres of commons survived, these were mainly around Ben Bank, Dodworth Bottom and The Green. The latter two had in fact become the site of quite extensive squatting with a variety of both residential and industrial properties springing up around them. The semi-public nature of the Green (its name implies an open public space) was later consolidated when, in the nineteenth century, its last remaining spaces were devoted to public use with the erection upon them of schools, church, chapel and the conversion of a private house into a licensed, public one.

These commons were not the only encroachments into the wastes however. Almost from the start of their ownership the monks had been raising revenue by selling or leasing plots of land around the edges of the village. These 'assarts' were uncultivated pieces of waste upon which the new owners were allowed to build a farmstead and bring the newly won land under cultivation. Many field names are testament to this, names like royd and stubbing both signify cleared land, so obviously does the term 'wood' when applied to a field. Such names abound around the edges of the township. The farms created by assarting show a very different pattern to those that spread out amongst the open fields from the Town Street crofts. Whereas the latter have fields dispersed around the village in a seemingly random pattern, the assarts have all

Above: The "Land of Hawkhirst" was confirmed as belonging to Dodworth by 1194 and the family called Hawkhirst lived at this farm until the C17. They were responsible for building this cruck barn, which originally supported a thatched roof.

their fields grouped tightly around the farmhouse inside a ring fence. These ring fenced plots surround the village, their boundaries often being co-terminus with the village boundary. They became the seats of the yeomanry who were to syndicate together and buy Dodworth from the Crown after dissolution. Saville Hall, The Green (Home Farm), Ben Bank, Hawkhirst (Moor Ends), Champney, Field Head, Fall Head, Lane Head and Lane Side all owe their origins to the assarters. The number of times that 'head' occurs in their names is sufficient to indicate that they were developed beyond the existing limits of settlement.

We can presume therefore that all of these assarted farms date from a later stage of development than do the Town Street farms. They were all created between the twelfth and fourteenth centuries and interestingly they all retain examples of building work completed before the end of the seventeenth century. Field Head and Hawkhirst have cruck barns,

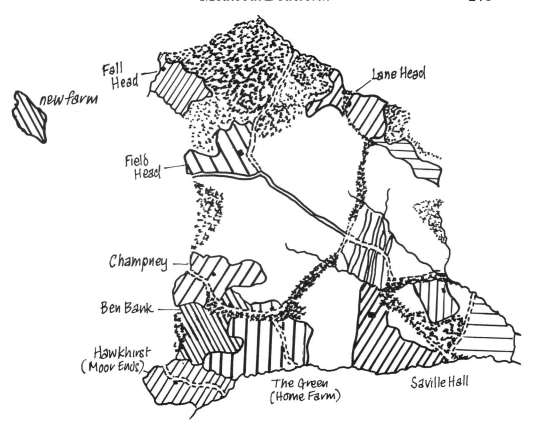

Map 6: The Late medieval Landscape

whilst The Green, Fall Head Lane Head and Lane Side have timber framed post and truss buildings. Saville Hall has suggestions of a medieval 'hall house' as well as a seventeenth century stone house and barn. This latter place seems to have been a stopping off point for the Saville family who were later to own much property and exercise considerable power throughout West Yorkshire. They are not however to be found in Dodworth after the thirteenth century although their potent name continues to be used for the farmstead seven hundred years later.

Another, less influential, family gave their name to the assart at Champney, but they did not arrive until 1575 and had departed by the middle of the following century. Although Champney's were not the first farmers in this location (they obtained the farm from William Hedelay) they may well have been the first to have the farm wholly considered as in Dodworth. Its fields straddle the border with Silkstone

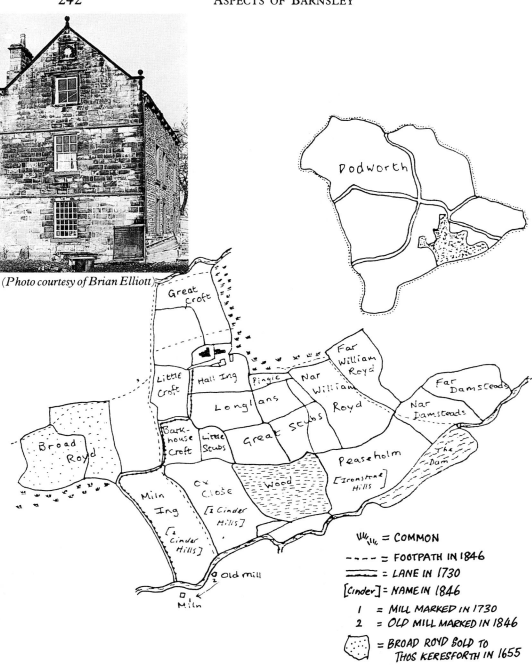

(Photo courtesy of Brian Elliott)

Dodworth

Great Croft

Little Croft

Hall Ing

Pingle

Nar William Royd

Far William Royd

Far Damsteads

Nar Damsteads

Longlans

Broad Royd

Barkhouse Croft

Little Stubs

Great Stubs

Peaseholm

[Ironstone Hills]

The Dam

Miln Ing

Ox Close

Wood

[2 Cinder Hills]

[2 Cinder Hills]

Old mill

Miln

〜〜〜 = COMMON
- - - - = FOOTPATH IN 1846
━━━ = LANE IN 1730
[Cinder] = NAME IN 1846
1 = MILL MARKED IN 1730
2 = OLD MILL MARKED IN 1846
⬡ = BROAD ROYD SOLD TO
     THOS KERESFORTH IN 1655

Map 7: Saville Hall, A Typical Assart

and there are several references to both townships claiming their possession. The modern surveyors boundary includes them in Dodworth, but the actual landscape still bears a substantial hedgerow that includes diverse species of shrub, amongst them being hazel and maple which are often associated with ancient hedgerows. This hedgerow may be around seven hundred years old and it seems likely that it was the old boundary between the townships, in which case part of Champney ought to belong to Silkstone!

As a general rule the fields associated with these assarted farms tend to support the best, most diversified and therefore probably the oldest hedgerows. This is a good indicator that they were enclosed and seperated well before the open field farms, in most cases perhaps around six to seven hundred years ago.

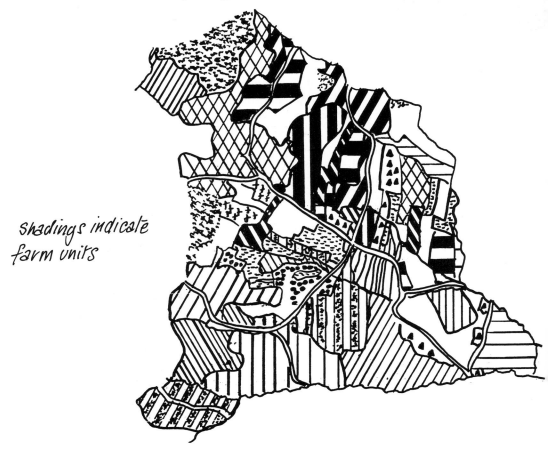

shadings indicate
farm units

Map 8: C19 Landscape; The Patchwork Quilt

Conclusion

Dodworth began as a tiny enclosed farmstead at the eastern end of High Street. Its occupants slowly began to clear and cultivate the surrounding landscape but from the twelfth century with the coming of the monastic ownership a more planned approach was adopted. Large areas of open fields were farmed collectively with grazing taking place on the common wastes beyond. These areas were also plundered for their building stone, ironstone and occasionally coal. The woodland timbers were utilised for both building and tanning purposes. The latter industry creating an incipient yeomanry which would later assume economic dominance in the village. By the early middle ages the woods were already being conserved but the wastes were being continually tamed as new farms were cut out of them for occupation by a new class of freeholders.

After the dissolution the new yeoman freeholders, lead by the tanners, replaced the monks as the economic and political power within the village. They gradually enclosed the open fields and subdivided these strips amongst themselves. However their organisation was never sufficiently strong or united enough to obliterate the old dispersed pattern of ownership. For another three centuries Dodworth's landscape changed slowly. Towards the end of the eighteenth century however the former commons at The Green and Dodworth Bottom became sites of new housing, usually low quality and often associated with domestic industry. The new owners were not bound by any overall plan and gradually began to sell off or develop their plots individually. Some, like the Taylors of Dodworth Green, concentrated upon building replica country estates, complete with parklands. Others like the Brookes of Fieldhead, became absentee landlords, leasing to tenant farmers whilst still others were more than happy to capitalise upon the new boom in domestic industry. Linen weaving came to town, houses complete with weaving cellars were built along the Town Street and at Dodworth Green, but whenever this industry was concentrated in these ares there were no substantial changes to the wider landscape. All of that was to change however in the mid-nineteenth century when the Charlesworth brothers of Wakefield bought out the Brooke's estates. The former field of Cliffe was chosen as the site for a massive colliery development. Within a few years this succesful development had completely transformed the landscape. The Cliffe field was now submerged under the pit yard and stack. Other smaller pits were sunk around the village. The Town Street became High Street and its courtyards became the sites of multiple housing and small workshops. Dodworth Bottom and the Green were inundated with low cost, low quality housing. From

Above: Standing high on the hill overlooking the boundaries of Dodworth and Silkstone, the isolated Champany farm is a classic medieval assart. It takes its name from a C16 owner, William Champney.

this change Dodworth could never look back. Although its pre-industrial pattern remains discernable to this day, the continuing effects of urbanisation make that an increasingly difficult task.

I said at the beginning that Dodworth could be taken as a model village. The process described above is indeed almost textbook stuff and similar patterns can be found up and down England, particularly on the midland plain. What makes Dodworth unique however is the fact that its past is (or was) so traceable. This is even more surprising when one considers Dodworth's geographical location. Situated in the Pennine foothills it is one of the last of the lowland villages, yet its pattern is more typically lowland than many of neighbours.

Notes and References

1. This study has been gleaned from many sources, much of it directly from the surviving landscape, but also by many references to archive sources. Should the reader wish, these can be followed up on more detail by reference to my thesis *In The Shadow of The Hill: A Comparative Study of the Growth and Development of Dodworth and Stainborough.* Copies are deposited in Barnsley Local Studies Library, Dodworth Library, Northern College Library and Sheffield University Library. The footnotes are extensive and detailed.

Acknowledgements

Archive sources include:

Sheffield City Archives (principally papers from the Vernon-Wentworth Muniments, Spencer Stanhope Papers, Elmhirst and N.C.B. Collections)

Barnsley Library (Maps and Printed Materials, Wilkinson's Notes)

West Riding Registry of Deeds, West Yorkshire Archive Service Wakefield, (Numerous Land Deeds)

Borthwick Institute of Historical Research, York (Original Wills and Probate Inventories)

Kirklees Archives (Whitlet-Beaumont Deeds)

LANE HEAD FARM
DODWORTH

THE CONTRIBUTORS

1.   BARNSLEY BOYS CLUB, 1933-93

Ian Harley classes himself as a true native of Barnsley having been born at Monk Bretton, raised in Worsbrough and now living at Dodworth with his wife Pat, daughter Adele and son James. Educated at Ward Green Primary School, Barnsley Holgate Grammar School and Bradford College of Technology, he left the textile industry to join the reporting staff of the Barnsley Chronicle in 1969. He was appointed Chief Reporter in 1976 and News Editor in 1986. The author of *Black Barnsley*, Ian is a member of Barnsley Crime Prevention Panel, Barnsley Canal Group, Barnsley Schwabisch-Gmund Society and a delegate to Barnsley Trades Union Council. When not chasing stories for the Chronicle, he enjoys chess, motorcycling and real ale.

2.   THE BLEACHWORKS OF THE BARNSLEY AREA IN THE NINETEENTH CENTURY AND THEIR INDUSTRIAL ARCHAEOLOGY

Harold Taylor was born in Staincross. After attending Barnsley Grammar School, he studied Geography at Cambridge University before entering a career in schoolteaching. Since retiring he has followed his interest in local history. Tracing his own family history in Staincross- Mapplewell led him to make a study of the hand-made nail industry of the village, and he has followed this with research into the influence of the Non-Conformist chapels on the musical, social and educational activities there in the 19th century. Membership of the Sheffield Trades Historical Society, whose interests cover the whole of South Yorkshire, led to study of the former linen industry of Barnsley and district, in particular the handloom weavers' cottages and the bleachworks which feature in this book.

3. THE PAPER MILLS OF BARNSLEY AND DISTRICT

Tanya Schmoller is a recent immigrant to the area who blesses the day she decided to make this move north. She was born in Uruguay, and came to England just after the last war to work at Penguin Books, who at the time intended to produce books in Spanish in South America. This scheme never fully took off, but she married Hans Schmoller, the firm's typographer, and thus became familiar with matters of book design and production. Apart from sporadic book-collecting Tanya's main interest is in decorated papers of the type used for the end-pages of books. An exhibition of some of these papers was held at the Ruskin Gallery in Sheffield in 1990. She and Hans were always interested in hand papermaking, particularly as practised in Japan. The research into papermaking in the Sheffield area came about quite accidentally when a lecturer in an adult education course on 'Practical Research' asked students what area they wished to research. Unprepared for the question, Tanya could only think of 'Papermaking', not really knowing whether there had been any papermaking in the vicinity, and these notes on mills around Barnsley are the result. They are taken from a book published in 1992.

4. BARNSLEY IN THE TURNPIKE ERA

John Goodchild is a native of Wakefield and was educated at the Grammar School there. He is the author of some 130 printed books and studies of aspects of the history of the West Riding, and was awarded an honorary Master's degree "for academic and scholarly distinction, and for public services." Each year he gives some one hundred one-off and specially-prepared talks, gratuitously, to a wide range of organisations, and he is constantly engaged in historical research to enable him to write, lecture and advise further. He regards his principal activity as being the assiduous collection over several decades of what is now a vast body of manuscript, printed and pictorial material relating to the central parts of the West Riding − a collection which in size and quality has never hitherto been approached. He is currently the Chairman of the Local History Study Section of the Yorkshire Archaeological Society and active also in the affairs of the Wakefield Historical Society and the Unitarian Historical Society. He is a past President of the Yorkshire Unitarian Union.

5. DAN RYLANDS: TRAGIC GENIUS OF THE BARNSLEY GLASS INDUSTRY

Denis Ashurst taught for many years as Head of Science and as Deputy Headmaster of a Comprehensive School before a period as Analyst for the Yorkshire and Lincolnshire Examinations Board. During this time he built up a national reputation as an Archaeologist concentrating mainly on the archaeology of the early iron and glass industries. He carried on his academic researches after retirement and in 1990 was awarded the Degree of Master of Arts (with Distinction) in History and English Literature at Sheffield University. He has recently been awarded the Degree of Doctor of Philosophy by Sheffield University following his researches into the history of South Yorkshire.

6. & 9. "OWD WATTER JOE", BARNSLEY'S ORIGINAL WATER VENDOR AND MARROW HOUSE AND ITS FAMILIES

Brian Elliott was born in Royston but spent his childhood in the mining community of Carlton. After an undistinguished spell as an apprentice professional footballer he obtained a proper job as a clerk with Barnsley Corporation and studied part-time at 'The Tech'. He subsequently completed a teacher training course, matriculating with a B. Ed(Hons) via the University of Nottingham. Brian taught Geography at Royston Comprehensive School, also lectured for the Workers' Education Association and University of Sheffield Divsion of Continuing Education before moving to a full-time post in adult education at Rother Valley College where he is now responsible for general education. His popular book *The Making of Barnsley* was described in a recent review as "a gloriously rich and varied compendium of material for Barnsley, a town which we underestimate at our peril" (*Family Tree Magazine*. 8.93). In 1991 he was awarded a Master of Philosophy degree by the University of Sheffield for his research on Barnsley and its hinterland. He lives at Warmsworth, with wife Angela and daughters Natalie and Hannah.

7. A KINGSTONE CHILDHOOD REMEMBERED

Annie Storey (nee Barrett) spent her childhood in Kingstone until the age of twelve, and then moved to New Lodge Estate. Educated at Longcar and Barnsley Girls' High School, she joined the John Tiller Girls, touring London, Leeds and Oldham. Her professional dancing career ended due to illness and a strong desire to return home. Annie has three children from her marriage (to Tony Wilson). She subsequently married Clive Storey and now has eleven grandchildren. Apart from her interest in writing, Annie enjoys art, with birds and flowers her favourite subjects, usually captured on wood. Annie, who lived 'down South' for many years, has been a carer and warden for the elderly but now looks after her mother who has Alzheimer's disease.

9. HISTORIC HUNSHELF

Phyllis Crossland (nee Bramall) was born at Oxspring. She received her early education in the village school and from there gained a County Minor Scholarship to Penistone Grammar School. Later on she successfully completed a two-year course at Darlington Training College and entered the teaching profession. Her last place of work prior to retirement was at Oxspring, the school she had first attended as a five-year old. Coming from a farming background and married to a farmer, she has also, over the years, helped with various kinds of farmwork. Mrs Crossland has always enjoyed reading, music and travels abroad. Her main interest in recent years has been research and study of family and local history. In this connection she has written articles for the national magazine *Farmers Weekly* and three books which are being widely read. Two of these were published by Penistone's 'Bridge Publications'. During her time as secretary of Penistone Local History Group she produced and contributed to *Times Remembered*, a book of short articles by members of the group. After living for more than thirty years at Hunshelf Hall, Mrs Crossland and her husband Charles are now at nearby Trunce Farm, Greenmoor. They have three married daughters, Angela, Julia, and Wendy, and four grandchildren.

10.   THE THORNCLIFFE RIOTS 1869-1870

Melvyn Jones was born in Smithies and educated at the Holgate Grammar School and Nottingham and Leeds Universities. He is now a Principal Lecturer at Sheffield Hallam University. He is a geographer by training but a landscape historian by inclination. He has written extensively on the economic and social history of South Yorkshire. Recent publications include *A Most Enterprising Thing* — an illustrated history of Newton Chambers, *Tankersley Parish Walks* a copiously illustrated guide to walks through the historic landscapes in the parish, a revised edition of the widely acclaimed *Sheffield's Woodland Heritage*, and a research report on the historic landscapes in the South Yorkshire Community Forest area.

11.   EBENEZER ELLIOTT, CORN LAW RHYMER

Ray Hearne lives in Wath Upon Dearne, with wife Jayne and daughters Rebecca and Emily. After working as a labourer on building-sites and in the steel industry he studied Literature at the University of Essex. He has worked since 1981 for the Workers' Educational Association organising and teaching programmes of adult education throughout the working-class communities of South Yorkshire, most notably Writers' Workshops, which can now be found dotted across the whole area. He is a writer and performer of poems and songs in the broad-sheet ballad tradition, and a one-time co-presenter of Radio Sheffield's Poetry Workshop. He has reviewed for various literary magazines and journals including most recently *Iron* and *The Wide Skirt*. Publications include *Anglo-Rotherham Rhymes* and *No Mean Response*, a history of Rotherham Trades Council. He is presently chairperson of *No Masters Voice* song-writing co-operative, and his forthcoming album of songs on that label will be available in early 1994.

12.   GUNTHWAITE AND THE BOSVILLES

Vera Nicholson was born at Thurlstone and attended the Infant School there at the age of three. She continued her education at Millhouse Mixed and Infant School followed by Penistone Grammar School. Having attained Matriculation she went to the City of Leeds Training College and followed a career in teaching, ending as Head Teacher of Oxspring Primary School. Taking a course at the College of Arts and Crafts, Sheffield, she was successful in obtaining a City and Guilds first class certificate in Embroidery and Design so taught in evening classes. Consequently, when St Aidan's Church was built at Oxspring, she helped to organise the altar embroideries, designing and executing a pair of panels. Interested in nature all her life, on moving to Penistone she created a new garden which is still one of her hobbies today. Since retiring, much time has been spent in writing the family history which is still proceeding. On joining the Local History Society research into the area has become another interest. She has written some articles for their booklet, *Times Remembered*, published in 1990.

13.   THE PATCHWORK QUILT – DODWORTH'S MEDIEVAL LANDSCAPE

Sam Sykes is now a lecturer in Adult Education at Sheffield College but began his working career as an apprentice at Dodworth Colliery. He left to take a BAHons in Fine Art and Art History, followed by a MA in Local History, Literature and Cultural Studies. His specialist interest is in landscape and rural history and he puts this into practice by breeding rare and ancient types of sheep and goats on the Pennine smallholding where he now lives with his wife Sue.

INDEX OF PEOPLE

INDEX OF PLACES